The Pilgrim Jubilees

The Pilgrim Jubilees

Alan Young

University Press of Mississippi
Jackson

www.upress.state.ms.us

Manufactured in the United States of America

09 08 07 06 05 04 03 02 01 4 3 2 1
∞
Library of Congress Cataloging-in-Publication Data

Young, Alan.
The Pilgrim Jubilees / Alan Young.
p. cm. — (American made music series)
Includes bibliographical references and index.
Discography: p.
ISBN 1-57806-415-5 (cloth : alk. paper) — ISBN 1-57806-416-3 (pbk. : alk. paper)
1. Pilgrim Jubilees (Musical group) 2. Gospel musicians—United States—Biography. 3. African American musicians—Biography. I. Title. II. Series.

ML421.P58 Y68 2001
782.25'4'0922—dc21
[B] 2001026369

British Library Cataloging-in-Publication Data available

To my wife, Beverley,
my mother, Jean,
and to the
Pilgrim Jubilee Singers
(and the other Jubes
will understand when I single out
for special mention
Cleave Graham, Clay Graham,
and Major Roberson)

Contents

Acknowledgments

When Houston, Mississippi, radio station owner Robin Mathis introduced me to the audience at the Pilgrim Jubilees' annual homecoming concert on June 5, 1999, he said: "He's come all the way from New Zealand . . . which is just about as far as you can go from here and still be in the world." The quip came during a ritual common at gospel music and church events in which out-of-town visitors are singled out for special mention; Auckland, New Zealand, was a hands-down winner in the distance-traveled-from stakes. It's also at least a contender in any writing-at-a-distance-from-the-subject contest. But despite my geographical remoteness, this book was not written in a vacuum. I have been enormously assisted by friends from around the world, to all of whom I am greatly indebted.

As with my last book, the list is led by my wife, Beverley, who now knows the Pilgrim Jubilees better than anyone else who has never met them. It was her idea that I should write another book, and she demurred not at all when the proposed new furniture turned into another expedition to the United States or when for the next year my time, the record player, and, to a probably excessive degree, my conversation were dominated by the Pilgrim Jubilees.

Should I, as biographer, thank my subjects? Why ever not? The Pilgrim

Jubilees were, I think, somewhat bemused when someone from the other side of the world arrived in Chicago to write a book on them. But Clay, Cleave, Major, Bobby, Ben, Michael, Eddie, and Fred received me graciously and cordially, set aside hours to talk with me, and accepted willingly the constant presence of me, my tape recorder, and my cameras. From them I learned a great deal, not only about their own lives and the life of their group but also about the world of gospel music—insights and information I could never have hoped to acquire otherwise. The test of their patience did not end when I left the United States. Over the following months, a number of information gaps appeared, virtually all of which were filled through long-distance telephone calls. The vagaries of time zones meant many of these calls arrived in the United States around breakfast time; anyone willing to discuss in detail what they were doing in 1966 while cooking grits is really trying to help.

The Pilgrim Jubilees made their first record in 1952 and have since recorded hundreds more songs. That I have managed to gather records or tapes of every one of them is to a large degree testimony to the generosity of other gospel music collectors. From England, Bob Laughton sent me recordings and information from his extensive collection and knowledge; from Belgium, Robert Sacré did likewise, also supplying many of the writer credits shown on the labels of the original issues. Although various electronic marvels make it easy for us to communicate, I have never met Bob or Robert, but I regard them as friends; certainly their responses to my requests came with the openhandedness and alacrity of friendship. The same applies to Chris Smith in the Shetland Islands, who gave me useful discographical and Internet pointers. From Oakland, California, Opal Nations—whom I have met—sent photographs and also gave me invaluable access to all takes of all the songs the Pilgrim Jubilees recorded for Specialty in 1955.

In Houston, Mississippi, Robin Mathis extracted for me the Pilgrim Jubilees recordings in the extensive collection of his WCPC radio station and immediately copied to tape those I didn't have—including "Stretch Out," the Jubes' biggest hit, which until then had eluded me. In Jackson, Mississippi, the Malaco recording company's director of gospel, Jerry Mannery, was extremely generous with time, information, photographs, and recordings; label owner Tommy Couch also made time in his busy schedule to provide valuable information. In Memphis, Tennessee, my friend (and series editor) David Evans produced two more missing singles—and an enjoyable break from the rigors of the road as he and Marice once again showed their southern hospitality and once again indulged my passion for barbecue.

Back in Jackson, the University Press of Mississippi has for the second time found my gospel explorations worthy of publication, and I very much appreciate its support and efforts. Senior editor Craig Gill was enthusiastic about this project before a word had been written; writing a book becomes very much easier when one knows it has a likelihood of seeing the light of day. I also had the pleasure of working once again with editor Anne Stascavage and, for the first time, with copyeditor Robert Burchfield, whose painstaking scrutiny and eye for detail were of invaluable assistance.

To all these people, I can offer only an inadequate but extremely heartfelt "thank you" for your help.

The Pilgrim Jubilees

1. Houlka, Mississippi

Standing in the shade doesn't help when it gets hot in Mississippi. As the temperature climbs through the nineties, the air grows heavy and the summer heat attacks from all sides, radiating from every surface and exerting a physical pressure that slows movement, thought, and speech. But the man who has engaged me in conversation seems immune to the temperature. His name is Willie Harris. He looks to be in his fifties, stocky and muscular in a blue suit and with a necktie pulled up to a powerful neck barely contained by his tightly buttoned collar. He is a church deacon and a gospel singer, a member of the Sensational Traveling Stars of Houston, Mississippi. "I always wanted to be a professional singer," he says. "But I never had the chance. Maybe it's because of where I was born. If I was in Jackson or Memphis, maybe I would've had a chance." The Sensational Traveling Stars are long established. "You've heard of my group?" says Willie in a mixture of statement and question. "I'm sure you've heard of my group." Back when records were made of vinyl and seven-inch 45-rpm discs ruled the airwaves, the Stars went to Nashville to make some singles and one album. "They're old now," says Willie, "but they still sound good." A puff of wind stirs the dust and flicks a furnace blast into our faces. We stand quietly for a moment, me trying to remember whether I've heard of the

Sensational Traveling Stars, Willie mulling on events of years ago. "You know, I was offered a contract to sing blues," he says, apropos of nothing that has gone before. "But I turned it down. It wouldn't have been right to go from singing the Lord's songs to singing blues." He pauses. "I can sing blues. Seems to me it's easier than gospel. All you got to do is get up there, holler a bit, do the step, and let the music take over. In gospel, every time you open your mouth you have to be saying something."

But isn't being a professional gospel singer a tough calling to follow? "No," Willie demurs. "Not if you keep your mind on the Lord. I could do it. You just have to want to do it." He's not singing today. He'll be in the audience. The stars today are the Pilgrim Jubilees, a group that forty years earlier also had the chance to become professional—and wanted to do it. They've been based in Chicago since 1952, but their roots are in Houston, Mississippi, and every year for the past eleven years they have returned on the first Saturday in June for a "homecoming." It's usually held at Houston's high school, but this year that venue is unavailable. The official reason is that the auditorium is being renovated, but it's also being suggested that school officials saw the masses of equipment brought in to record and film last year's homecoming and decided the Pilgrim Jubilees could afford to pay a bigger hire fee this year. "It seems like the Devil tried to block this homecoming," says its organizer, Joann Reel. "This is the closest I could find." "This" is the Houlka High School gymnasium, a hulking, dowdy, cavernous tin-roofed building that boasts it is the home of the male Houlka Wildcats and the female Houlka Wildcattes basketball teams. From the placards on the wall, it seems the Wildcats last appeared in a state final when they were beaten in 1991, and the Wildcattes' last taste of fame was in 1977. The gymnasium is not air-conditioned. And however hot it is outside, it's hotter inside. Two giant fans have been placed at each end of the room, but all they do is push the hot air around. So the audience waits outside until it's time for the music to start.

Houlka is the next town north from Houston, and many of those at the homecoming have driven the eleven miles up Highway 15. Although he is in a Houston-based group, Willie Harris has come quite a bit farther—he lives in West Point, about forty-five miles away. Two young women have come from Louisiana, a small group is here from Georgia, two women have driven from Nashville. Most of the Pilgrim Jubilees have come from Chicago. And I am from Auckland, New Zealand, at the farthest reaches of an eight thousand–mile journey that started nine months earlier when I met Pilgrim Jubilees manager and lead singer Clay Graham and suggested writing the group's story. Or maybe it was ten years earlier, when I was in the town of Clarksdale, in the heart of the Mississippi Delta and a mecca for blues fans seeking a glimpse of the gone-forever days when their music ruled and the Delta blues players were its royalty. Returning one evening from a day of blues sightseeing, I saw a sign outside the Clarksdale Civic Center advertising that the Pilgrim Jubilees would be there next Wednesday. Gospel was not then my main musical interest, but I knew enough to recognize the name and resolve that I, too, would be at the Civic Center next Wednesday.

The evening wasn't a great success. The Civic Center seated about six hundred; about five hundred of the seats were empty. But the Pilgrim Jubilees, led by Clay Graham and his elder brother, Cleave, performed to the hundred or so people present as though they were working a sell-out concert at Carnegie Hall. Ten years later, Cleave explained: "I don't sing according to how many people are there; I sing to the people that want to hear me that came. They're not responsible for the people that didn't come. So we sing. And I can't play at singing. If I'm gonna praise God, I'm gonna praise him." The concert was my first close-up exposure to the power and intensity of "hard" quartet gospel singing—the style, born in the late 1940s and developed through the 1950s and 1960s, that replaced the soft controlled harmonies of the earlier "jubilee" groups with one or two powerful lead singers able to whip any audience into a frenzy through the sheer power and intensity of their singing and stage technique. Clay and Cleave Graham are experts in the technique, and as Cleave left the stage and prowled into the audience, the cords in his neck standing out and sweat dripping from him as he sang, my blues archaeology didn't seem so important.

My subsequent efforts to find out more about the Pilgrim Jubilees had only limited success. This was not, it seemed, a group that appealed to the small number of academic and record-collecting gospel music researchers. Their attention was focused on the "golden age" of the 1940s and 1950s, when groups were singing a cappella or with only limited accompaniment. The Pilgrim Jubilees started their career in these glory days but achieved their gospel market fame in the 1960s as accompaniments expanded to include electric guitars and basses, drums, and keyboards. To the purists, this turned the golden age to brass and rendered groups working in that style all but invisible. But out on the "gospel highway"—the metaphorical network that links traveling singers and audiences across the United States—it was a different story. The unaccompanied performers were old-fashioned; today belonged to the new young groups with their four-and five-piece backing bands. And among the leaders in this style were the Pilgrim Jubilees.

The world of African American gospel music has never attracted "outsider" research and observation in the way the blues world has, and the closer one comes to the present, the more pronounced this neglect becomes. So the fact that the Pilgrim Jubilees are rarely mentioned in gospel studies is no indication of their status on the gospel highway, where they have been leaders for forty years. They didn't draw well that night in Clarksdale—it's always hard to get people out on midweek nights—but today they are still traveling all over the country, still heading the bill wherever they perform, and still producing recordings, blending gospel's past and present in a mixture that pleases African American religious audiences even if it doesn't appeal to the academics.

I returned to the United States in 1992. This time, my focus was on gospel music; the results were published in *Woke Me Up This Morning* (University Press of Mississippi, 1997). For some time after, I told myself and anybody who asked that *Woke Me Up* was two books in one—my first and my last. When that resolve weakened and I started looking for another topic, an early thought was to do a biography of the Pilgrim Jubilees. But I had no way of contacting the group, and so in 1998, I attended the annual Gospel Music Workshop of America convention in Philadelphia with vague thoughts of a study on gospel choirs. The GMWA is heavily choir-oriented, but it has a quartet division—and the Pilgrim Jubilees were on its main concert. I had my conversation with Clay Graham, and the choir project was shelved.

In May 1999 I went to the United States for five weeks with the Pilgrim Jubilees. The first two weeks were spent living in a South Side Chicago motel not far from Clay Graham's home, the rest in Mississippi following the group through a small part of the life of a gospel quartet on the road. It wasn't easy. Unexpectedly, most of the group members didn't know I was coming or were unsure of what I wanted, and very little progress was made until they held a meeting to discuss my project. Interview appointments could be difficult to make and weren't always kept, schedules were changed . . . one such change left me waiting in Meridian, Mississippi, for a group that was supposed to be there on Tuesday and arrived on Friday. This study is short of precise dates for many key events in the Pilgrim Jubilees' history because they can't remember them. But what they do know about is life as professional gospel singers. They know the pitfalls, the hardships, the days of arriving in a distant town so short of money they can't afford to refuel the car and discovering their concert has been canceled, of singing their hearts out and then finding that the promoter has absconded with the money, the days when racism meant that even a gospel singer could land in jail simply for being in the wrong place at the wrong time. And they know the joys—the elation of having a record at the top of the charts, the companionship within the group and with the people to whom they sing, and above all, the drive to keep spreading the Christian message that has sustained them through fifty-five years and hundreds of thousands of miles. So these were the things we talked about. And these are the things that, much more than dates and locations, define the gospel life. The Pilgrim Jubilees may not always be the most punctual of people, but they quickly accepted the presence of this strangely accented foreigner and not only answered all my questions but volunteered information I might not have thought to seek. The only exception came when the conversation turned to subjects that might reflect badly on people—such as the more unseemly side of competition among quartets. Group members would discuss such matters in broad terms but generally refused cite specific cases or people, deflecting questions with the stock phrase, "I don't want to call names."

In virtually every gospel quartet, one person—usually, but not always, the manager—is deputed to speak for the group; in some groups other members will refer interviewers to that person. This did not happen with the Pilgrim Jubilees—all members spoke freely and at length with me during the face-to-face interviews and in the many follow-up telephone calls. But by virtue of his position as manager and because he is the dominant personality in the group, Clay Graham is to a large degree the speaking voice of the Pilgrim Jubilees. For this reason, his name occurs most frequently in this book. More extensive interviews were also done with Cleave Graham and with baritone singer and songwriter Major Roberson because of the length of time they have been with the group. Where possible, I have used verbatim transcripts from the interviews. These taped conversations have been edited—speech does not always transfer easily to the printed page—and in some instances I have amalgamated more than one discussion on a topic into a single block. But the overall aim has been to keep the editing to the minimum needed to facilitate coherency. The opinions, viewpoints, and perspectives are also those of the group members. An overriding aim of this project was to let the Pilgrim Jubilees tell their story in their own words, as free as possible from editorial interpretation and qualification. Interpretation is generally limited to providing context and background, and the only area in which I have occasionally amended information provided by the group is in establishing the provenance of songs. Many parts of the narrative, of course, cannot be independently verified, neither do they need to be. This is the Pilgrim Jubilees' story, and if some areas, such as tales of rip-offs and bad deals, contain an element of hyperbole, this is the way they recall events—and it is their recollections that are the reason for this study.

Why the Pilgrim Jubilees? It was a question asked frequently while I was working on the book—not least by the Pilgrim Jubilees themselves. They know they are well established and popular in their field, but they're not the top-selling Canton Spirituals, or the globe-trotting Mighty Clouds of Joy, or the Blind Boys of Alabama with a string of international bookings keeping them so busy they now hardly ever perform to African American religious audiences. They are the Jubes. Their records sell a respectable but hardly chart-topping twenty thousand to fifty thousand copies each, they had to wait until 2000 to get a trip to Europe, and they seldom perform to any but black religious audiences. Why should someone from the other side of the world arrive in Chicago wanting to write about them? Part of the answer is easy. Clarksdale, Mississippi, 1989. Another part is almost as easy—the chance meeting with Clay Graham in Philadelphia. But many other quartets were also at that convention, including the Canton Spirituals and the Mighty Clouds of Joy. Again, why the Jubes? Mainly because they are not like the biggest of the big-name groups. They've had hit records (and some misses), they've played the big venues like the Apollo Theater in New York, New Jersey's Meadowlands, and even once at Disneyland. But they've never had that lucky break or the adroit management that would put them up there with the Cantons and the Clouds. They've been cheated and manipulated; they've made mistakes and wrong choices. And through it all, they've stayed out on the gospel highway, doing the only thing they've ever wanted to do. Their story is the story of gospel quartet singing; their lives echo those of hundreds of other gospel quartets. They're more successful than most. But after more than half a century, they're still grinding out the thousands of highway miles as they travel from town to town, city to city, singing their message in churches, auditoriums, civic centers—and the Houlka High School gymnasium.

It is now almost three o'clock, the time the program is supposed to start. It won't, of course. Nothing in gospel music ever starts on schedule. In the gymnasium, a crew is starting to erect the sound system. The room doesn't have a stage, so all the artists will perform on a cleared area of floor at one end of the room in front of a black cloth backdrop nowhere big enough for the job. At 3:30, the first musician strolls through the back door, places a guitar case on the ground, and saunters out again. By 3:50, about forty people are in the room, but many more are outside where a trailer-mounted stall is doing stand-in-line business selling drinks from tubs of ice, and another stall is doing a much slower business selling meat and fish sandwiches from a gas-fired barbecue. A little before four o'clock, the first Pilgrim Jubilee arrives. Clay Graham is an urbane and quietly spoken man, six feet tall with broad-featured movie-star good looks. He's wearing a dark red satin shirt, and the gray in his hair and the closely trimmed beard he's recently grown has magically vanished. He's sixty-two but looks ten years younger. He also looks unhappy. The change of venue and the heat have robbed the program of more than two hundred potential patrons, he says. "They know about this hall in the heat." Tickets are twelve dollars in advance, fourteen dollars at the door. All the groups on the program—including the Jubes—are being paid a percentage of the door takings, so the loss of up to three thousand dollars will have a serious effect on everyone's payday.

But there is work to be done. Clay speaks a quick "Check one, check one" into a microphone to test the sound system, then starts working the room, shaking hands with friends and fans, signing autographs, and taking requests for songs to be sung this afternoon. It's all part of his job, the reason he's here early, and he does it with the ease and skill of a veteran politician, smiling and listening attentively, then choosing the right moment to smoothly disengage from the conversation and move to the next. He doesn't perform this ritual before every program, but today is the Pilgrim Jubilees' day, so the walk-around adds a personal touch—and establishes him and his group as the main artists. Out front in the small foyer, his wife, Hazel, is helping Joann Reel keep track of the customers, taking tickets from those who have paid in advance and selling tickets to those paying at the door. Quiet and reserved, Hazel Graham is a senior manager in charge of two departments at one of Chicago's largest hospitals, the Rush-Presbyterian St. Luke's Medical Center. She's ten years younger than Clay; they have been married for thirty-four years. She doesn't usually travel with the Pilgrim Jubilees, but like Clay, she's from Houston, so the homecoming is a chance to visit family and friends.

Next to appear is tenor singer Ben Chandler, sixty years old and a Jube since 1969. Like the other senior group members, he was born in Mississippi and moved to Chicago. But ten years ago, he remarried and moved to his wife's hometown, Atlanta, Georgia. Of medium height with a light brown complexion and hair not as plentiful as it once was, he has a jovial expression and is quick to point out that he is "the joker" of the group. When the conversation turns serious, he sometimes distances himself slightly by referring to himself in the third person—of his shift from Chicago to Atlanta, he says, "I moved because it was better for Ben." Casually dressed in a tan short-sleeved shirt, he sits at the end of the ticket table, ostensibly helping Joann and Hazel but mainly greeting and chatting as the flow of people into the hall increases.

Outside, the group's second-generation Graham is leaning against the handrail of the ramp leading to the hall entrance, talking to friends. It's not a homecoming for second guitarist Eddie Graham. He lives in Houston. His father is second cousin to Clay and Cleave, and it seems youthful looks run wide in the Graham family, as Eddie looks much younger than his thirty-eight years. Short and of blocky build, he's been with the group since 1987, although he didn't become a full-time member until 1989. He looks relaxed and cool in laundry-powder-advertisement-white shirt and trousers, but he's a little nervous. The group's main guitarist, Bobby McDougle, is absent, so the burden of delivering the Jube guitar sound will fall much more on Eddie than usual. It's a sound Bobby McDougle has refined over thirty-five years. Bobby is fifty-four and has been a professional gospel guitarist since he was fourteen, although he backed his first group when he was "about eight or nine." Before joining the Jubes in 1964, he played with three other leading gospel acts, Tommy Ellison and the Five Singing Stars, Edna Gallmon Cooke, and Rev. Julius Cheeks. He's a short, ebullient man with broad spatulate fingers that belie his skill as a guitarist. He's not at Houlka today because his mother has died at the age of ninety, and he's gone home to Valdosta, Georgia.

But Eddie won't have to carry the guitar chores alone. Fred Rice, at twenty-six the youngest and newest Jube, is a skilled guitarist. He can also deputize for the bass player, the drummer, or any of the backing singers. "I'm like a spare," he says. Tall and powerfully built, he has the look of an athlete; before he joined the Jubes in 1993, he worked at a steel plant. He's the other group member who lives outside Chicago. He's from Starkville, Mississippi, but now lives in Meridian, in southeast Mississippi. Nobody's seen Fred today, but he'll be around. "He stays off by himself," says Clay Graham. "You hardly even know he's at a program unless you run into him."

Another who's keeping to himself today is drummer Greg "Bobo" Harris. His status with the group is ill-defined. He regards himself as a member; it's a view not shared by the senior Jubes, and today Bo's future with the Pilgrim Jubilees is far from certain. A lean, gangling, slow-spoken six-footer with a short beard shot through with undisguised gray, forty-one-year-old Bo has impeccable gospel credentials. His father is Rebert H. Harris, a doyen of quartet singers who made his name with the Soul Stirrers in the 1940s and 1950s; his mother, Jeanette Harris, sang with the all-female Golden Harps. Bo spent seventeen years with the Violinaires, a top Detroit gospel quartet, then joined the Jubes in 1987. He stayed four years, then returned to the Violinaires. Now he's quit the Violinaires again and is looking to return to the Jubes. But he's still on trial, and his last two outings have shown that he hasn't completely recaptured the style the Jubes demand from their drummer.

The "style" is very important. It's the sound that defines the Pilgrim Jubilees' music and defines them as a group. Instrumentally, it's the foundation, the support on which the singers rely. At the heart of it are Bobby McDougle and bass guitarist Michael Atkins. Bespectacled and burly with short-trimmed hair and beard, Michael was born and raised in Chicago and can tell hair-raising stories of the gangs on the South Side and the impact drugs have had on the area. In a suit, he looks like a prosperous business executive; in jeans and T-shirt, he looks a streetwise Chicagoan. In either guise he has the quiet self-assurance of a man who knows exactly what his role is and knows that he's good at it. He's forty-four years old and has been playing with the Jubes since 1970, when he was fifteen and going to school.

Outside the gymnasium, Cleave Graham's maroon Plymouth Grand Voyager is tucked into a parking spot handy to the door. The Pilgrim Jubilees' aged touring bus developed mechanical problems a while ago, and the Plymouth is now the main transport for the Chicago-based members. It has a bit more passenger room than a standard car, but its luggage space is limited, and it is not the ideal vehicle to take four or five men and their luggage on journeys that can cover hundreds of miles and several days. Clay Graham, in particular, is very keen to get another bus—for reasons of prestige as well as comfort. In the meantime, the Plymouth is performing another task as its air-conditioning unit hums at full blast, keeping the Mississippi summer away from Major Roberson. At seventy-four, he is the oldest Pilgrim Jubilee and, next to the Graham brothers, the longest serving. When the group first went on the road in the 1950s, Major was the manager and handled all the bookings. After Clay became manager, Major kept the bookings. Recently, Clay also took over this job when Major decided he needed a rest from it. His health has been troubling him—he has high blood pressure and a touch of emphysema—and often these days he doesn't sing a full program, performing on the first few numbers, then turning his baritone role over to Fred Rice and taking a seat at the back of the stage. But the years have not entirely vanquished the raffish good looks of his younger days. The once-sharp features have filled out, and the hooded eyes are now behind spectacles. But the pencil-line black mustache and the flashes of understated humor are still there, and he is still traveling with the group and writing songs for it, just as he has since 1952.

Cleave Graham's forename almost always appears in print spelled "Cleve." Usually, he doesn't worry too much about it, but for a book he wants it to be right—"C-L-E-A-V-E . . . I believe that makes me French," he says with a laugh. He is the senior Jube. Not the oldest, but the senior member, the patriarch of the group. Clay fronts the group, speaks for it, and is its manager. But Cleave is the powerful presence in the background, and it is extremely unlikely that anything of which he does not approve will come to pass in the Pilgrim Jubilees. He's seventy-one—or it might be seventy—slim and upright; on his right jaw he has a tuft of hair quite distinct from his mustache. Like other older group members, the amount of gray in his hair and mustache varies according to whether he's onstage or at home, but the tuft is always gray. He's had it "ever since I got old enough to grow hair," and it is there for no reason except that when he first grew facial hair, "I wanted to be different." Today, it's his trademark. He shaved it off once. "It was around 1970. And I got such kickback from people. They said, 'You don't look right without it.' So I let it grow back." It has also had an influence within the group—Eddie Graham wears one side of his mustache longer than the other and acknowledges that the idea came from Cleave. His extension is on the left side—"I said, 'I'm gonna do mine, but I'm gonna do it different.' "

Offstage, smoking his pipe and wearing his floppy white hat, Cleave Graham looks like somebody's grandfather, a man who would enjoy sitting quietly on a riverbank fishing. He has twenty-four grandchildren (and seven great-grandchildren), and his delight in fishing is such that other Jubes tell how if Cleave sees a likely-looking patch of water on his way to a program, he will stop there and then or, if time is tight, come back later. He's softspoken and chuckles expansively as he tells anecdotes from his youth and the group's early days. Onstage, he is a different figure. The skin around his eyes is dark, and under powerful stage lights this and the strong lines of his face give him an Old Testament look of veiled severity and purposefulness that is almost menacing. His singing does nothing to dispel this impression; he is a man with a message, and he delivers it with every fiber of his being. Any Jubes' audience confronted by Cleave telling them with incandescent intensity to "tell them that I told you . . . that I told you . . . that I told you" as he warms in to "Too Close" is unlikely to forget who it was that told them.

The Houlka High School gymnasium is filling slowly. The giant fans have made no progress in their battle against summer, and many seats are empty when at 4:30 Joann Reel opens the homecoming with an apology for the late start and the discomfort caused by "God's heat—there's nothing we can do about that." A local program, such as one held in a church, will almost always start with "devotions," a communal experience of prayer and audience singing before the featured artists appear. A fully commercial program held in an auditorium and featuring national acts will dispense with devotions, going straight to the performance. This program is somewhere between the two extremes, so it omits the prayer but starts with an audience sing-along, led by two women and what looks and sounds like a pickup band who take us through "Joy in the Land," "Pray," and the venerable long-meter hymn "I Love the Lord, He Heard My Cry." The response is muted, but the melancholy cadences of "I Love the Lord," with its slow, drawn-out syllables and elaborately ornamented melismatic singing style, are hard to resist, and after a hesitant start the lines resonate around the room—confirming that it not only has all the comforts of an oil drum but also the acoustics of one. Joint emcees and local gospel personalities Charles Anthony and Charles Golden take over and the heat gets another mention—"It might be hot here, but if we don't live for the Lord, we'll be going to a place much hotter."

The first half of the program is filled by local groups, each allocated two songs. First on is the Holy Visions of New Albany, three men and four women in matching lime green. One of the men takes the microphone and tells us that while it might be hot here today, if we don't live right we'll go to a much hotter place. Either he wasn't paying attention a few minutes ago or he figures a good line is worth repeating. The audience doesn't agree, and the quip falls flat, leaving an empty space where the applause and laughter were supposed to be. Being first act on the bill is a difficult job, and the group's staid "Stranger in the City" isn't perhaps the best choice as an opener, so the audience reaction as the song ends is subdued. But when the statuesque female bass player steps to the front and tears into a scorching up-tempo "Take It to Jesus," a rustle of animation flickers around the hall. Heads lift, feet begin to tap, hands begin to clap, and occasional calls of encouragement push the Holy Visions on. The Spirit is moving at the Pilgrim Jubilees' annual homecoming.

2. Got to Be for Real

It is late afternoon on the day before the homecoming program. Major Roberson sits at the small table in his motel room in Pontotoc, just north of Houlka. On the room's television set, a baseball game plays without sound; the curtains are pulled against the setting sun. Outside, people are splashing and laughing around the motel's swimming pool, but Major has spent the afternoon sleeping. The night before, he and Michael Atkins drove more than six hundred miles from Chicago, stopping only for a brief rest in Memphis, Tennessee, about a hundred miles away. Now in the self-contained world of his motel room, Major's voice grows quiet and his eyes gaze through the curtains into the past as he considers what makes a man dedicate his life to singing in a gospel quartet.

"First thing, you got to love it. You've got to love to do it. You see other groups doing it professionally, and you say, 'One day, my group's gonna be there.' So you set out and . . . every day, groups are doing this. They're struggling, striving to try to get to the point where they can come on the road and stay out here and get paid for it. And it looks like the opportunity never will come. But one day it does come. And hey! You're right there. So you say, like we did, 'Let's go out and try it for maybe three months. And if we don't like it, we'll come home.' We didn't make no money in three months. But we got a feeling out of it. And we said, 'Let's try a little bit more.' So we tried a little bit more. And you find out two years have passed. You're out there and meantime, your family thing is getting bad. And you're so carried away in this thing you don't even look at what you've done. And first thing you know you've lost your family. But once we got into it . . . like, you get old out here. Look round, and the years have passed on. You find yourself an old person. But you still find energy and a reason to keep going. So here I am. Seventy-four years old, still out here. I'm tough. Get a few hours sleep, I'm ready to go again. It's just a blessing. I don't think you get too old. If you just keep healthy and love gospel, you'll make it. But you've got to love gospel. You can't be a phony and stay here this long. Got to be for real."

"Your family thing getting bad" is a reference to the heavy toll life as a professional quartet singer can take on marriages and relationships. Marital strife is not usually acknowledged as a part of the gospel calling, but for the men in the quartets, it was—and still is—an ever-present risk. Theirs is a vocation that can require them to be away from home for weeks at a time but all too often pays poorly. The combined strains of separation and penury can overburden any but the strongest relationship. Yet, as Major also points out, even today groups are striving to join the professional ranks, to get on the road, to get a recording contract. And today it's tougher than ever, because quartets are no longer at the forefront of gospel music. That honor now belongs to the choirs and the big-name soloists-come-choir directors, such as Kirk Franklin, John P. Kee, and Hezekiah Walker. But at one time quartets were at the top. From the 1940s through the 1950s and into the 1960s, they were the rock stars of religious music, packing churches and auditoriums with the power of their message and the excitement of their delivery.

Quartets are one of the most fascinating aspects of gospel music.[1] They are among its best-known performers, rivaled only by the top soloists. Yet some church people, especially among the "sanctified" Pentecostal faiths, view them with suspicion because of their flamboyance and the worldly aspects of their craft. Quartets are usually not affiliated with a particular church and play no part in church services. They are "men only"—an ensemble with women in it is a "group," not a quartet, even if it performs in quartet style. Although their songs are religious and intended to convey a message, a substantial part of their performance is dedicated to entertainment. These factors contribute to the suspicion that comes even from some other branches of gospel music—the antipathy between choirs and quartets is deep-seated and, although not widely documented, often ill-disguised. The choir-based Gospel Music Workshop of America has for some years been trying to bridge the gap with its quartet division; while the quartets have their own events under this banner at the GMWA's annual convention, they remain generally quite separate from the choir events, with few signs of a genuine merging of interests.

The earliest written reference to African American quartets dates to 1851, when Frederika Bremer wrote of hearing Virginia slaves singing in "quartettes."[2] These were informal groups, without organized structure or musical arrangements. But in a study on the relationship between white "barbershop quartet" singing and black quartets, Lynn Abbott says that by the end of the nineteenth century quartet singing was so well established among African American males that it was the "black national pastime."[3] Formal organization and musical arrangement were definitely part of the African American university "jubilee" singing groups, pioneered by Nashville's Fisk University, which brought religious music into the previously secular quartet style. Fisk, founded in 1865 by the American Missionary Association, was short of money from the day it opened its doors in 1866 and by 1870 was facing bankruptcy. Its treasurer and choirmaster, George L. White, assembled a group of his best singers, who sang locally to raise money; in 1871 the university decided to send the singers "on the road," touring farther afield as traveling fund-raisers.[4]

Between 1871 and 1878, the singers raised $150,000 for Fisk University and provided the inspiration for similar groups from other African American learning centers. These troupes were usually large enough to be regarded as small choirs. However, by the 1890s, a separate tradition of university quartet singing was well established, and many larger jubilee singing groups included in their ranks male and mixed-sex foursomes. It appears the Fisk Jubilee Singers were using such groups as early as 1873.[5] The touring university groups also established the entertainment component of gospel music—they were singing sacred songs, but the songs were primarily performance pieces rather than religious instruction. This aspect was further developed by the minstrel shows, which reached their heyday in the later years of the nineteenth century. Minstrel shows were developed in the 1840s by white artists who caricatured southern black life, but by the 1870s, when the genre was most popular, black casts were as common as white. Initially the minstrels ignored religious music, but the success of groups such as the Fisk Jubilee Singers created a demand for it.

Informal singing within the community, of the type noted by Lynn Abbott, was the spawning ground for the predecessors of today's gospel quartets. Groups were started by people who had something in common—belonging to the same church, working at the same place, or living in the same area—and in the years following the turn of the twentieth century became an integral part of African American community life. As well as from their own hymn-and spiritual-singing tradition, influences for these groups came from the university groups and from minstrelsy. Says researcher Joyce Jackson: "The university quartets provided the model of close four-part harmony, a cappella singing style and sacred repertoire. The model for showmanship, humor and entertainment came from the minstrel tradition. The community-based quartets combined practices from both traditions, resulting in a set of aesthetic criteria which in many cases still applies to quartet singing today."[6]

This combination laid the path for generations of quartets. By the 1920s the concept of the gospel quartet was well established, and the advent of recording helped spread it. The earliest recordings, made on wax cylinders in the 1890s, were by minstrel-styled quartets that included some religious material in their repertoires.[7] The close-harmony singing on these early recordings is staid and formal, but it is clearly a quartet style. The market for these and other early recordings was probably white; certainly in the very early days of recording, African American buyers were not uppermost in the minds of record companies. But in the 1920s the burgeoning recording industry discovered black America. The earliest "race" recordings were of jazz and blues, but it was soon discovered that religious material would also sell.

The first quartet-style group recorded in this period was the Biddle University Quintet from Charlotte, North Carolina, which recorded four songs in April 1920.[8] In March 1921 the most prolific and popular of the early quartets made its first recordings. Initially the group was called the Norfolk

Jazz Quartet, and the first six tracks it made for the Okeh company were secular. Four months later it recorded another eight songs, including two religious pieces, "I Hope That I May Join the Band" and "Who Built the Ark?," issued as by the Norfolk Jubilee Quartet. In April 1923 the group joined the Paramount label. Its first session for Paramount was mainly secular but included two religious songs, "Father Prepare Me" and "My Lord's Gonna Move This Wicked Race." This latter song was so popular it stayed in Paramount's catalog until the company's demise in 1932. Quartet and record company took the hint, and virtually all the Norfolks' subsequent recordings—in a career that continued until 1940—were religious.[9]

The Norfolks were named for their hometown of Norfolk, Virginia, which was a recognized "quartet town."[10] Among other groups living there in the 1920s were the Silver Leaf Quartet of Norfolk and the Monarch Jazz/Jubilee Quartet, both popular recording groups. In Alabama, a strong a cappella gospel tradition developed in the industrial area of Jefferson County, which includes the cities of Birmingham and Bessemer, and continued into the 1990s.[11] The dominance of both areas is attributable to the rise of industry, which drew black workers in the first twenty years of the twentieth century. Later, northern cities—including New York, Chicago, Cleveland, and Detroit—would attract migrants seeking a better life and would become gospel centers.

Discussion on quartet repertoire and singing styles could fill several chapters on its own, but broadly, the groups sang unaccompanied, usually in three- or four-part harmonies. The standard quartet lineup was two tenors—often designated first and second—baritone, and bass; occasionally it was one tenor, two baritones, and bass. Some songs were sung in full harmony, with all the voices combining; the more usual style was for one voice, usually the first tenor, to lead the song, with the others providing a harmonized backing. This could be drawn from the lyrics, often in an antiphonal call-and-response style, or could be a simple repetitive phrase. One of the more effective such phrases was "clanka-lanka," sung as a rhythmic chant behind the lead voice. The phrase—and some variants using similar-sounding syllables—remained in use until the 1950s and almost certainly provide a link to the early minstrel quartets, which sometimes used banjo imitations as a backing vocal effect—one recorded rendition roughly transcribes as "ranki-plank, ranki-plank, rrrrankity-plank-plank." It is not a far leap from that to "clanka-lanka"—although it has to be said that most gospel groups who used the phrase probably weren't doing so in conscious imitation of the minstrel banjo.[12]

The repertoires of the early college-based groups and community quartets followed that of the Fisk Jubilee Singers, whose performances were consciously based on traditional songs going back to slavery. After a Fisk concert at the Lafayette Avenue Presbyterian Church of Brooklyn in late 1871, the minister, Dr. Cuyler, wrote to the *New York Tribune* describing the group as "living representatives of the only true native school of American music." And in a swipe at the minstrel troupes, he said: "We have long enough had its coarse caricatures in corked faces; our people can now listen to the genuine soul-music of the slave cabins. . . ."[13] This "soul-music" included such songs as "Steal Away," "Been In the Storm So Long," "Swing Low Sweet Chariot," and "Deep River"—all of which remain in quartet repertoire more than a century later.

By the 1920s the spiritual songs were being augmented by newer "gospel" songs, written as performance pieces and therefore tailor-made for the evolving quartet style. The earliest prominent writer in this style was Rev. Charles Albert Tindley (1851–1933), longtime pastor of the Tindley Temple United Methodist Church in Philadelphia. His songs include many that remain standards—"What Are They Doing In Heaven?" (1901), the classic "Stand By Me" (1905), "We'll Understand It Better By and By" (1905), and "Let Jesus Fix It for You (1923)."[14] In Chicago, Thomas A. Dorsey (1899–1993) turned from a career in jazz and blues to become known as the "father of gospel music." Dorsey's songwriting established gospel as a genre of African American religious music. A Georgia preacher's son, he had by the 1920s gained impressive credentials as a blues and jazz pianist, singer, composer, and arranger. He wrote his first religious song, "If I Don't Get There," in 1921; in that year, it was included in the National Baptist Convention's *Gospel Pearls* songbook.[15] But through the 1920s he was primarily active in secular music. In 1928, after a period of clinical depression, he underwent a religious conversion and started writing sacred songs again, employing a new technique of using blues-based tunes to accompany sacred words. The first songs he wrote in this vein were "If You See My Savior (Tell Him That You Saw Me)" and "How About You?," both of which he recorded in 1932 and which are still among his better-known pieces. Dorsey wrote more than five hundred songs and played a leading role in moving Chicago's mainstream African American churches away from copying white religious ceremony and music and back into a distinctively black style of worship. His name is attached to many of gospel's most popular songs—"Precious Lord" (1932), "Peace in the Valley" (1938), "Remember Me" (1939), "I'm Going to Live the Life I Sing About in My Song" (1941)—many so well known they are sometimes assumed to be traditional.[16]

The Great Depression had a devastating effect on America's recording industry. Recording for the African American market had almost completely halted by 1932, and gospel was one of the hardest-hit genres. A gradual recovery started in 1934, and when it did, the quartets' ascendancy in African American religious music began to make itself apparent. In the earlier years of the decade the leading groups were Mitchell's Christian Singers from Kinston, North Carolina, and the Heavenly Gospel Singers, founded in Detroit but based in North Carolina from 1936. Both groups recorded extensively. Mitchell's Christian Singers—originally called The New Four, but renamed in 1934 for manager Willie Mitchell—made more than eighty recordings between 1934 and 1940, including an early quartet version of a Thomas Dorsey song, "How About You?," recorded in 1934.[17] The Heavenly Gospel Singers recorded more than a hundred songs between 1935 and 1941. They were a professional group—one of the few at the time—and traveled extensively, mainly on the East Coast.[18] But the quartet that eclipsed all others in the 1930s and provided a bridge between the staid deliveries of the earlier groups and the overt entertainment that came to the fore in the 1950s was the Golden Gate Quartet. William Langford (first tenor), Henry Owens (second tenor), Willie Johnson (baritone), and Orlandus Wilson (bass) formed their close-harmony jubilee group in 1934. They borrowed heavily from the top-selling secular singing group The Mills Brothers and created a fast-moving, intricately arranged style that was recorded extensively. The Golden Gates' singing, their arrangements, and their repertoire introduced a new standard of professionalism to gospel music. Onstage, they wore matching tailored suits, and their harmonies were imaginative, tight, and crystal clear. They raised the tempo of their music, moving well away from the more measured tones of their contemporaries toward what Willie Johnson described in a 1980 interview with researcher Doug Seroff as "vocal percussion."[19]

Much of the Golden Gates' material, especially in the early years, was drawn from the traditional sources also mined by other groups. But the group also developed narrative songs about specific incidents in the Bible, often sung in a quick-paced semichant that modern gospel singers cite to support their claims that the rap singers of forty years later were doing nothing new. These stories were extremely popular and laid a trail that many other gospel quartets would follow. Another aspect of their repertoire that set a pattern was that group members wrote songs. Writer credits on their early recordings are usually not given or on reissues are attributed to the ubiquitous "trad" (traditional) or "PD" (public domain). But the Bible-based "Jezebel" and "God Told Nicodemus," recorded in 1941, are by Willie Johnson; Orlandus Wilson also wrote songs for the group.[20]

Through the 1940s the quartets' appeal widened rapidly, and the number of groups proliferated. The main factors contributing to this were recordings and radio broadcasts. After World War II, a number of small, independent record companies emerged to challenge the dominance of the major companies. As the majors had largely lost interest in anything but mainstream entertainment, gospel—and blues—recording became almost exclusively the preserve of these small companies. At the same time, gospel broadcasting was increasing, with stations selling airtime either directly to quartets or to sponsors who employed quartets to broadcast. The effect was to widen the groups' potential audience and establish them as a form of entertainment as well as part of religious life. This made it easier for singers to contemplate making a living from their talent. Before the early 1940s professional groups were rare. But through the 1940s an increasing number of singers went "on the road," working circuits that developed through the South, along the East Coast, into the Midwest, and across to California.

In the late 1940s quartet singing started its move toward the dynamic and spectacular "hard" style. This development is sometimes credited to one or two influential singers. Gospel researcher Anthony Heilbut cites Rebert H. Harris of the Soul Stirrers, crediting him with creating "the entire gospel tradition."[21] Doug Seroff says Silas Steele of the Famous Blue Jay Singers "fathered" a new era in quartet singing by being the "first emotional gospel singer."[22] Harris and Steele are important figures in quartet singing. But a style closely related to hard quartet singing—although not in a quartet structure—had existed at least since the 1920s in the "sanctified" or "holiness" Pentecostalist churches. One recorded example is the singing of Bessie Johnson, whose shouted back-of-the-throat rasp anticipated the power and passion of the hard groups by twenty-five years.[23] In an interview with researcher Ray Allen, Ralph Moragne of the New York–based Sunset Jubilees recalled his young days in Florida: "The holiness people, they actually made what you call gospel singing. We used to go . . . on Sunday night and look through the window—and they were actually singing gospel then. . . . See, we [*quartet singers*] rearranged it, but that type of hard gospel singing came out of the holiness churches."[24]

Rebert Harris can almost certainly take credit for devising the "twin lead" system that helped give the hard groups their power, creating arrangements in which one lead took the basic melody and the other provided an overlay of interpolation and ornamentation, often taking over the lead midsong at a higher pitch and with a higher energy level.[25] A side effect of this development was that the true quartet became a rarity, as groups took on more members to fill all the parts. The Five Blind Boys of Mississippi, for example, often had six singers (and not all of them blind); a 1953 photograph of the New Orleans Chosen Five shows six singers and a guitarist. Today, backing musicians are often ranked as full members, so a group can have eight, nine, or ten members. The word "quartet," therefore, seldom now appears in a group name, but the style is still known as "quartet." Having extra singers also enabled groups to extend the basic tenor/baritone/bass format. The most common addition was a "high fifth," a falsetto part above the tenor. The sound of an ultrahigh voice soaring over the others was not new to gospel music, but until the advent of the quartets' high fifth, it had belonged to the female singers. Willa Ward, a member of the Ward Singers with her more famous sister, Clara, claims to have invented what she calls "the high who" and to have been using it by 1943.[26] The "who"—named for the sound of the syllable usually sung—was a drawn-out high note either floated over the top of the melody line or used as a bridging device between verses. Male quartet fifth singers—most of whom can also sing a standard tenor part—adopted the same techniques but also take leads in their high range or sing a falsetto part embellishing the lead.

The 1950s were the great quartet days, when programs drew standing-room-only audiences in large auditoriums and the top singers were gospel-household names. The Soul Stirrers, from Houston, Texas, had the inventive Rebert Harris as their lead until 1950, when he quit, disturbed by what he saw as increasing immorality in the relationship between the traveling groups and their female fans. His replacement was twenty-year-old Sam Cooke, from the Highway QCs in Chicago. Although Cooke subsequently made an international name for himself as a pop-soul singer, it is easy to argue that he never sang a secular note as fine as the best work of his seven years with the Soul Stirrers. The Five Blind Boys of Mississippi, formed at the Piney Woods School for the Blind in Mississippi and professional since 1944, were led in their greatest years by Archie Brownlee, revered as one of the hardest-shouting singers of all. Rivaling him was Rev. Julius "June" Cheeks of the Sensational Nightingales, who sang with a power that eventually shattered his voice, leaving him with all the passion and all the technique but only a splintered rasp with which to deliver it. From Alabama came the "other" Five Blind Boys, formed at the Talladega Institute for the Deaf and Blind and led by Clarence Fountain. In Memphis, the Spirit of Memphis played an important role in the development of quartet style, both through its singing and through its early promotion of professional programs. The Dixie Hummingbirds, from Greenville, South Carolina, made their first recordings in 1939 and became a hard gospel powerhouse in the 1940s when they recruited lead singer Ira Tucker from his home in Spartanburg, South Carolina, and bass singer William Bobo from the Heavenly Gospel Singers. The Pilgrim Travelers, formed in Houston in the early 1930s, moved to Los Angeles in 1942 and, with Kylo Turner and Keith Barber as leads, recorded more than a hundred songs between 1947 and 1956.

Not all groups performed in the frenetic hard style. The Harmonizing Four, formed in Richmond, Virginia, in 1927 and still performing in the 1990s with some prewar members, retained a soft melodic approach, with the bass singer often as the lead voice. The Swan Silvertones featured the silken lead voice of founder Claude Jeter, whose main contribution to quartet singing was his astounding falsetto reach, which prompted many imitators and provided a powerful impetus for the use of the high fifth part. The Silvertones were founded in 1938 and initially performed in the jubilee style. But after World War II Jeter saw the changes coming and hired Solomon Womack (uncle of soul star Bobby Womack) to be a hard lead singer. When ill-health put Womack out of the group, he was followed by a number of other singers, including some of the leading names in quartet singing—Rev. Robert Crenshaw, Rev. Percell Perkins, Paul Owens, and Dewey Young among them.

To the gospel purist, the halcyon days of quartet singing ended around the mid-1950s as instrumental accompaniment became standard, moving gradually from one discreet guitar doing little more than stabilizing pitch and rhythm to fuller backings using electric guitars, organ and/or piano, bass, and drums. Fortunately, no one told the groups the best was behind them, so they kept singing. Several new and powerful groups emerged during the late 1950s and 1960s, building on the style that had gone before. A few overdid the histrionic side of the hard style, collapsing the structure beneath the weight of unconvincing artifice. But the best were worthy successors to the earlier masters. The Gospelaires of Dayton, Ohio, were formed in 1954 but did not become well known until the 1960s. Their featured attributes were the gravelly lead singing of Rev. Robert Washington, rendered even more distinctive by his ostentatiously guttural breathing—a technique more commonly used by preachers—and the stratospheric high fifth of Charles McLean. The Pilgrim Jubilees established their popularity in the early 1960s. The Supreme Angels, later renamed Slim and the Supreme Angels to give more prominence to leader Howard "Slim" Hunt—who now owns the group name and hires singers and musicians as employees—have attracted little critical attention, but the stream of recordings they produced through the 1960s and 1970s attests to their popularity. One of the most prominent quartets of the 1960s was the Mighty Clouds of Joy, formed in Los Angeles in the late 1950s and featuring the lead singing—heavily influenced by Rev. Julius Cheeks—of expatriate Alabaman Willie Joe Ligon. Most of the original Clouds have now gone, but Ligon is still leading his group, which has maintained its popularity and has toured England, Europe, and Japan.

The 1960s was also a time when secular music came calling. Quartet artists who also performed nonsacred popular music were nothing new—many of those who helped shape the form in its early days commonly mixed sacred and secular. But as the quartet genre spread, the separating line became more pronounced, and religious audiences were very much inclined to forget their Lord's injunction about forgiveness unto seventy times seven when singers strayed from the paths of musical righteousness. Despite this, the lure of pop music—and its material rewards—was strong, and many very good quartet singers crossed over. Soul music, in particular, feasted off gospel quartet music, taking its moves, its singing styles, and its presentation techniques; it is at least a defensible argument to suggest that without gospel quartets, soul music could never have come into existence. (Ironically, hard-style quartet or solo singing is today often referred to as "soul gospel.") The best-known quartet defector is still Sam Cooke from the Soul Stirrers, but many others also crossed over—Wilson Pickett from the Violinaires, Lou Rawls from the Pilgrim Travelers, O. V. Wright and Joe Hinton from the Spirit of Memphis (Wright also sang with the Sunset Travelers), Otis Clay from the Gospel Songbirds, and James Carr from the Jubilee Hummingbirds. Nearly every veteran quartet singer has a story to tell about being offered sums of money (usually large) to sing rock and roll or blues.

The 1970s brought a dilution of quartet music as developments that had been taking place over the previous decade coalesced. Where once the quartets influenced soul music, now the secular influence rebounded. The instrumental sound had by now assumed virtually equal status with the singing rather than serving as accompaniment, and the singing was adjusted to accommodate the change. Harmonies moved to a higher range and became less elaborate, with the bass singer all but ousted by the bass guitar. At the same time, choirs and similar ensembles eclipsed the quartets' popularity. But groups still evolved. The Jackson Southernaires, from Mississippi, were formed in 1945 and started recording in 1964; their 1968 recording of "Too Late" was a national gospel hit. In the early 1970s the second generation of Southernaires adopted an "if you can't beat them, join them" philosophy to combat the rising appeal of choirs and incorporated aspects of choral style into their backup singing. The move came at the urging of group member Frank (Franklin) Williams, who also founded the very successful Mississippi Mass Choir. Williams's reason for the change was entirely pragmatic: "We were trying to develop a type of gospel that would appeal not only to quartet fans but to church people, choirs. There are two totally different audiences."[27] Willie Neal Johnson and the Gospel Keynotes combined choral-styled backing with a hard lead and a frenetic performance style, making sometimes excessive use of high fifth singers. Johnson, who died in January 2001, was also one of the leaders in the bridge-building quartet division of the GMWA.

A long-established quartet that experienced its greatest popularity in the 1990s was the Canton Spirituals, founded in Canton, Mississippi, but now based in nearby Jackson. While the Cantons go back to the 1940s, their success came with a 1993 concert recording made in Memphis that sold more than two hundred thousand copies—compared to the twenty-five thousand to fifty thousand regarded as a good-selling quartet record.[28] At that time, the group had only one original member, tenor singer Harvey Watkins Sr., father of lead singer Harvey Jr. The elder Watkins died in November 1994, but the Canton Spirituals—now an entirely second-generation group—have held their top-ranking position. Other current top groups include veterans and new faces. The Violinaires, from Detroit, date to the early 1950s; Lee Williams and the Spiritual QCs were formed in the early 1960s in Tupelo, Mississippi. Prominent among the younger groups are the Christianaires, led by brothers Tyrone and Paul Porter, from the southern Mississippi hamlet of Sontag, who have absorbed much of the choral style into their singing. Tyrone Porter has also been heavily involved in gospel music ecumenicism as president of the GMWA's quartet division.

The gospel quartets' glory days are long gone, and only a supreme optimist can believe they will return. An annual review, *The Gospel Music Industry Round-Up*, publishes a list of America's top one hundred gospel artists for the year, based mainly on record sales and radio exposure.[29] In the 1999 edition—covering 1998—the list named seven quartets—the Canton Spirituals, the Christianaires, Willie Neal Johnson and the Gospel Keynotes, the Mighty Clouds of Joy, the Pilgrim Jubilees, Slim and the Supreme Angels, and Lee Williams and the Spiritual QCs. The other ninety-three placings went to choirs, soloists, and vocal groups performing in styles ranging from choral to gospel hip-hop and rap. But regardless of the shadow that has fallen over quartets on the national gospel scene, hundreds of amateur groups exist all over the United States. Many, especially the older ones, are organized along quasi-corporate lines, with officeholders, formal rules, and a chain of command.[30] Posts include president, manager, secretary, and treasurer. The president is in charge of the group's business affairs and chairs meetings and rehearsals. The manager is in charge of performance-related matters, ranging from setting up rehearsals to deciding what clothes the group will wear onstage. The positions of president and manager are sometimes combined. Some managers also handle bookings and fees; other groups have a separate booking manager. Many also have a musical director, or "minister of music." Quartets start as local groups, singing around their hometowns; as they develop, some will finance their own recordings and travel away from home. The key event that can turn a local group into a national group is a hit record, providing exposure that enables it to start touring with a name people recognize. With more luck and hard work, this will be followed by top billings, a farewell to day jobs, and a contract with a record company that has national distribution. For nearly all, it will never happen. Even if it does, they won't get a tenth of the money or the fame they could find in rock and roll. But it doesn't stop a host of Stars, Wonders, Mightys, and Sensationals from hoping and trying. And once upon a time, it was the dream of a family-based local group from Horse Nation, Mississippi.

3. Mississippi: Cleave Graham

Horse Nation, Mississippi, doesn't exist today. Traces of it can be seen from the single lane gravel road—the remains of single-story wooden buildings completely engulfed by the trees and undergrowth that have reclaimed the land. But when farmer Columbus Graham and his wife, Josie—the former Josephine Chandler—moved there in 1934 with their family from nearby Woodland, it was a small, self-contained farming community, seven miles from the Chickasaw County seat of Houston, which today has a population of about four thousand. About a mile from the derelict homes, at the intersection of county routes 86 and 85, is the sole remaining active part of Horse Nation, the New Zion Missionary Baptist Church, founded in 1885. It is a tree-surrounded brick building with a covered entrance; this sanctuary was built in 1973, replacing the wooden church that was there when the Grahams came to the area.[1] Today, the church has its own pastor, and services are held every Sunday. But when young Cleave Graham started going to New Zion with his family, full services were held only once a month—on the third Sunday—presided over by a Memphis-based minister who pastored several small north Mississippi churches.

Cleave now lives on Chicago's South Side on one of the streets running off 95th Street. From the street, the brick house looks small, but it is long, running from the sitting room and dining room in front to a den and bedrooms at the back. Cleave and his third wife, Billie—a train driver on Chicago's commuter network—have lived here for about five years. Five television sets are scattered through the house; Cleave explains it's so Billie can keep track of what she's watching as she goes about the home.

"New Zion Baptist Church, that was it. It's in the rural area—it's a country church. Horse Nation was just . . . oh . . . a southern community. Everybody's post office address was Houston. We had two stores—Charlie Verell's store and Dayton Woodruff's store. That's where everybody did their little everyday shopping. Where I was born, you can't get there. You would have to get a mule or a horse and ride up through the woods. I was born . . . the midwife wrote down 1928. But my mom says she put down '28 by mistake because I was born in the first of the year. I've been saying I was born in '29, but she put down '28 and I have to go with what's on my birth certificate—January 8, 1928. My family consisted of four boys and three girls that lived. The whole family was thirteen, but seven lived. Some died at birth or right after. I lost all my sisters. The girls died at a young age. One died at two years old, one died at thirteen, one died at fifteen. My baby sister died at fifty-eight. We were farmers. We rented. They had sharecroppers, but my daddy always had his own farm tools, his own horse . . . horses and mules was the thing back then. What he did, he would rent land and farm it."

A sharecropper grew crops on usually white-owned land for a share of what the crop fetched at market, minus "expenses" and advances. It was a system with great potential for abuse, and landowners usually took full advantage of that potential, leaving sharecroppers trapped in a perpetual debt cycle in which the amount they made each year never quite equaled what they owed in advances and expenses. A farmer who "rented" paid a set fee for the use of a block of land and took the full return from the crop, minus the rent. Clay Graham recalls that his father rented and sharecropped at different times, but Cleave is adamant that "we never did sharecrop, no."

* * *

"My mom and dad sung in church. My mom . . . the church really depended on her. That was before they really had church choirs too much. So before the preacher preached his sermon, my mom had to sing something. My dad, he didn't sing too often at the churches, because he wasn't really a church-going man. But he always saw that we got there. He would hitch the mules up to the wagon and bring it out in front of the house. He always looked out for my mom. He made a seat—got some springs from an old [*Ford*] T-model car and made them fit the side of the seat. So when the wagon would run over rough places, instead of Mom bumping, the springs would make it soft for her. He always had the seat covered nicely with a bedsheet or something to keep Mom's clothes right. And he would pull the wagon right up in front of the church, close as he could, so she wouldn't have far to walk. But a lot of times, he didn't go in the church. He'd sit in the wagon until the service was over. I don't know why. It was . . . I guess . . . he was more or less bashful. He would sit out there and listen to the service. But he'd be there, ready to go home or wherever Mom wanted to go. And we were little kids. I liked to sit on the back of the wagon with my feet hanging out. . . .

"At home was always singing. Even at night when we would come from the fields, we would end up singing. We used to love singing. The whole family, we would sing—the old songs like 'Nearer My God to Thee,' 'Old Ship of Zion' . . . my mom's favorite was 'Come and Go with Me to My Father's House.' My brother and I, we used to be chopping cotton, and we would sing even in the fields. He would be singing and I would try to do the opposite voice [*harmony*] to him. I really didn't know what I was doing, but when I did it in a certain place and it sound good, that's what I stuck with. That was my brother Elgie C.B. In the country they give kids initials for names. Well, C.B. was supposed to have stood for Columbus—Elgie Columbus Graham. But it was just Elgie C.B. He was about ten years older than me. He'd get on a horse to go some place and he had trouble with me because I wanted to go. And he'd throw me up behind him on the horse and take me wherever he went. Even when he was going to see his girlfriend, he'd carry me and let me play with her brothers and sisters while he'd go to courting. We were very close, real close.

"So that was how the group started. Me and Elgie chopping cotton. My oldest brother, Theophilus Graham, he joined later. He had a deep voice to sing bass. And then my cousin-in-law—my first cousin's husband, Willis Johnson—he was interested in singing. He would come to the house and we would sit on the porch at night—we didn't have no music [*instrumental accompaniment*], we'd just sing. And we'd sing until 10:30 at night. And that was very late at night for people back then, especially in the country. We'd have a lot of visitors because we'd be singing and they heard it. And even in the fields in the afternoon, we'd be singing out loud and people in their fields would be listening and they would holler across and request songs. We were young, strong, our lungs real clear—we had good lungs because there was no kind of pollution back then. And oh man, I'd sit in one area and sing and the people would listen at me for almost a whole mile. We had those wide open spaces out there, and it's real quiet. No cars or nothing, you could hear a person a long way.

"Then people started requesting us to sing at little . . . like, somebody giving a party, somebody's birthday. We started doing that, then we started in the church, New Zion. And then people started having afternoons of our singing. They would let me go . . . I called myself singing, but mostly I was just there. I was just a little boy and my voice wasn't ready yet. But I was doing the best I could. We had Elgie with the lead soprano [*tenor lead*]. Monroe Hatchett, my first cousin on my mom's side, he was singing the tenor part. Willis Johnson sang the bass. And for a while, another first cousin-in-law on my mother's side, Alfred Brownlee, came in singing baritone, and now we got a four part harmony."

When the group started singing around Horse Nation, Theophilus Graham and Willis Johnson shared the bass part, with Johnson also singing in the baritone range. The lineup detailed by Cleave dates to the early 1940s, after Theophilus was called into the U.S. Army. At the time, Cleave had no defined role with the group, but he attended the performances and joined in the singing when he could. Eventually, he took his place as a full member of the group.

"This is how I really got to start singing. My cousin Monroe arranged a song, 'Over the River My Mother's Gone.' In fact, he lost his mom and dad when he was two years old. And my mom and dad raised him and his sister as their own. I was about ten years old before I found out Monroe wasn't really my brother. Monroe had arranged this song, and nobody had a high enough voice to do the tenor. And I was praying all the time, because I wanted to be really able to sing. I would ask the Lord, 'Let me be able to sing. Show me how to sing.' And all at once, four-part harmony came to me. And they couldn't lose me, didn't matter what part they put me on or how many different chords they would use. They could put me on tenor, I could do it. They could put me on baritone, I could do that. On bass . . . well, my little voice wasn't heavy enough, but I'd be going, trying to get it out, let 'em know I knew where it was. And all of this just came to me. All the parts came to me.

"And this particular song Monroe had arranged, I said 'I can do it, I can do it.' I kept telling them. My brother called my mom, 'Come and make this boy get out of here.' But another man—I think it was Willis or Monroe—said 'Let him try it.' And sure enough! They went over that song and I reared back and let go. And boy, they grabbed me up! 'That's it, that's it!' And I was in. That was really the beginning of me starting to going with them. In fact, I went to the programs and churches just to sing that one song, 'Over the River My Mother's Gone.' Because they had to have me with them to do that, and that was one of the main songs—the people loved it. By this time they were being called to different churches. We would get on horses and go to programs. And if we didn't have enough horses for everybody to ride, we'd hitch up the wagon. We'd all get in the wagon and go nine and ten miles to sing. At that time, people just called us the Graham Brothers or the Horse Nation boys. So we needed a name. I thought about names; I said 'well, Graham Brothers.' But my brother, Elgie, said 'I'll tell you what, let's name it Pilgrim Jubilees.' Pilgrim Jubilees? That sounds good! Pilgrim Jubilees. And we all agreed to it right there, and that's what we went as. We were the Pilgrim Jubilees."

The formal name for the group was the Pilgrim Jubilee Singers, although the shortened Pilgrim Jubilees was also used from the beginning. Cleave is not sure exactly when the name was selected, but it was probably in 1944—the year now usually given as the group's starting date. Around this time, Alfred Brownlee dropped out—he moved to Chicago soon after—and Cleave took over the baritone part. Around 1945 or 1946 Theophilus Graham returned from overseas military service and resumed singing bass; Willis Johnson went back to singing either bari-

tone with Cleave or bass. "We changed them around," recalls Cleave. "We had two bass singers at times." The group also took its first steps toward semiprofessionalism, obtaining the services of Leonard Brownlee, a distant relative of Alfred's, as manager. Clay Graham recalls that Leonard's father was a prominent white Houston landowner and that as a result he enjoyed a social status that helped the Pilgrim Jubilees when it came to securing engagements.

"Once we got our name, Pilgrim Jubilees, we started booking. And people started calling us . . . man, we had to go up to seventy-five miles to sing. That was big time! We sang in different country churches. Then we started going into the towns. I remember my first program in Woodland, Mississippi, about four or five miles from where we lived. That was the first program actually in town. Oh boy! Nervous to death. We weren't being paid, we were just singing. Sometimes they would raise an offering [*take up a collection*], but it was just for the love of singing. The first song that I ever sang lead on was a song that the Fairfield Four sang years ago, about 'Love Is Like a River.'[2] They'd say 'We're gonna bring up Master Cleave.' Oh Lord, I was so nervous. I was nervous 'til when I raised up off one foot, the heel would be . . . (*he mimics a nervous heel tapping uncontrollably against the floor*). But I sang. And the people gave me an encore. It was a song I loved to hear Mr. Samuel McCrary [*lead singer of the Fairfield Four*] sing lead on. He had a liquid kind of voice—I just loved that. They were broadcasting on the radio then, from Nashville, Tennessee. And we had the old battery radio. We didn't have electricity. But my dad got my mom one of those old Philco radios—it was a big piece of furniture, it was beautiful."

The Fairfield Four had a regular 6:45 A.M. spot on the fifty thousand–watt WLAC in Nashville from 1942 until around 1955. The Grahams enjoyed hearing the group sing, but Cleave doesn't believe its style had any great influence on the young Pilgrim Jubilee Singers. He acknowledges no outside influences, saying he didn't even know most of the major groups of the time, "just the Fairfield Four." "We got that out of the radio. I've heard of the Golden Gate Quartet. But the Fairfield Four. That was the first one I knew anything about." Later, he also listened to gospel music broadcasts from WDIA in Memphis and recalls in particular hearing the Soul Stirrers and the Spirit of Memphis.

"We always tried to mix it up. We always had jubilee songs, and we had some soul songs—as I always say, we had those songs you could get a tooth into. We sang the jubilee things we heard other folks sing, but we would arrange the songs ourselves and make it a Pilgrim Jubilee thing. We just sung, and the folk said, 'You got your own sound.' We got to where every Sunday we had to go someplace. The first time I ever sang on the radio was at West Point, Mississippi. We were doing a program there, and we were making an interview to advertise where we were going to sing. A funny thing happened there. My cousin Monroe . . . one of the kids working at the radio station told him, 'Monroe, don't get too close to that mike.' He knew Monroe didn't know anything about microphones. He said 'That mike will suck you up in it.' And Monroe was standing there trying to figure out . . . 'Now, large as I am, how can that little mike suck me up?' But he was still afraid because the boy had warned him, and he didn't know anything about it. Oh man! He was standing braced up, and when I walked too close to the mike, he pushed me back—'Don't get too close, don't get too close.' He had never seen a microphone. We were from the country—we didn't know anything about electricity and electric guitars and all that stuff. We didn't have electric guitars—in fact we didn't have music at all then. We were just a cappella.

"Then my brother who had been in the army, Theophilus, he came out and said he didn't want to farm. He said 'I can live a little better than what we're doing. And I can get a little bit more rights as a man than what I'm getting.' So he left and came to Chicago. That was in '47. And I married in '47. Three days after I married, I was headed for Chicago. Elgie C.B. and I went together. I married on July the seventh, 1947, and I left on July the tenth or eleventh. Left my brand new wife back there in the woods. I was going to try to get a job to live better than what we were doing. But our money ran out before we could get jobs. We had bought round-trip tickets, so we had to hightail it back to Mississippi. We stayed in Chicago two or three weeks. But really, I was in a hurry to get back to my pretty new wife. Doris, her name was, Doris Hamilton when I married her. So we came back to Houston. And we kept singing. In fact, Clay sang with us on one program before we left Mississippi. By this time, we would go by car to the programs. And that particular night, we had a wreck—a car ran into us at a railroad crossing. My mom hit the ceiling. 'Ooh hoo, my baby! You're not carrying my baby out there no more.' But he made one program in Mississippi.

"Then I went back to Chicago. That was in '51. Elgie and Monroe [*Hatchett*] went about three months before I did and they got jobs. That kinda split the group up. Clay and I went on up about three months later—Clay was about thirteen or fourteen. [*In fact, Clay came soon after Cleave, with their parents—see next chapter.*] And I got a job at a packing company. Man, I was making money! Eighty cents an hour. That was big money. Boy, I got it made! I wasn't thinking about how much rent I would have to pay, how much food would cost. But it was better than I had been doing there in Mississippi. So C.B. is in Chicago, Theophilus is there, Monroe is there . . . now I get there and we've got a group."

4. Mississippi: Clay Graham

Clay Graham is a man of contradictions. Fluent and eloquent, he was by far the most forthcoming of the Pilgrim Jubilees, willing to discuss topics—such as relationships within the group and with other performers—that the others often preferred to sidestep. At the same time, he was the most wary about being the subject of a biography, voicing apprehensions that at times ranged into the fanciful—peaking with a suggestion that "some" of the group thought I might be an undercover agent from the Internal Revenue Service. But these suspicions were flickers in a generally harmonious relationship. That Clay was my main source of information was hardly surprising. Like Cleave, he has been with the group since its inception. He is its manager; he was also the person through whom I arranged my project. He is an extroverted and loquacious man, although occasionally his mood darkens to an aloof remoteness in which he pulls away from people around him, be they would-be biographers or fellow Pilgrim Jubilees. He lives in a tidy bungalow on a street of tidy bungalows off 127th Street on Chicago's South Side. It's a good neighborhood, he agrees, "but not as good as it used to be." The scourge of drugs is starting to affect it, and one knows that not all the black-windowed stretch limousines that pass along 127th Street at surprisingly frequent intervals belong to affluent captains of industry.

Clay and Hazel Graham have lived in the house since the mid-1970s, raising their three daughters, Tichina, Komie, and Latrivia, there. Hazel is the younger sister—by fourteen years—of Cleave Graham's first wife, Doris. Clay and Hazel knew each other as children in Mississippi, but romance didn't blossom until the Pilgrim Jubilees came back to Houston in the mid-1960s for a program. They married in Chicago on July 10, 1965, Hazel's twentieth birthday. "We got married in the courthouse," Clay recalls. "Wasn't nobody there but my mother and Hazel's sister [*Doris*], and she had to keep watch on the car because we couldn't get a proper parking place. So we got married, then we went and had a Chinese meal." Of Clay and Hazel's three daughters, Latrivia has most strongly inherited her father's musical ability. She sings and plays piano, organ, guitar, and drums. She is a paid musician at the family church but, says Clay, is not seeking a musical career—"she's the shy type. She just wants to be the business person."

Only a few blocks from Clay and Hazel's home is the Plaza Inn motel, a utilitarian two-story brick building that was my "home" during my time in Chicago. It was also where all the Chicago-based interviews with Clay were conducted, as he believed we could talk there without distractions. Despite his occasional reservations, he took the interview process seriously and usually had a definite idea of the areas he wanted to cover when he arrived for the day's session.

"The first thing I want to say is we came up in a beautiful life—a poor life, but it was beautiful. I had a praying mother; I had a sanctified daddy. He didn't believe in going to church, but he had a good heart. [*He relates the story also told by Cleave of how their father prepared the family wagon to take their mother and the family to church.*] Church just wasn't his thing. My mother would always pray that Daddy would become saved. But Daddy would just say 'I might go [*to church*] next Sunday.' Next Sunday went for years. He would go to special things that were happening—like Mother's Day, maybe he would go in and sit as far in the back as he could. But when he was seventy-nine, he started ailing. He had bone cancer, so they sent him to the hospital. My mother was praying hard then. And she would sing, because they used to sing duet together a lot of times. Three days before he passed, I took her to the hospital. And when she walked in, he turned his head and looked at her. He said, 'Guess what. Jesus stopped by last night and he saved my soul.' She ran to the bed, took his hand, and started thanking the Lord for saving him. And he said, 'He gave me a song, too.' She said, 'What is the song?' He said, ' "Everything Is Gonna Be All Right." Do you think we could sing that?' And that's what he started singing, and we had church right there.

"But back then, we had a good life. We ate beans and greens right out of the garden. My daddy had the best garden in Mississippi. And when we got a chance to eat some chicken, man, that was caviar! But the only time we got to eat that chicken was when the preacher came to preach at New Zion Baptist Church. He would come from Memphis, Tennessee. He had several churches down through Mississippi, so every third Sunday he'd stay at one of the deacon's houses or one of the mother's houses. Next time, he would stay at somebody else's house. But they would all fix that chicken for him. And Daddy said, 'Don't kill one chicken, 'cause you know the preacher will eat it all. But when that preacher bite off a piece of chicken, I want my babies to be able to bite off a piece of chicken too.' They would generally send the kids out—all the other people's children had to go outside, because the preacher was there. And he'd lay back and eat and cross his legs and lay around the house. And when your father go to work, ain't nobody home but the preacher and the wife. He's laying up there with all the prestige of a king. And nine times out of ten, he'd touch the wife up. So Daddy told all the preachers that came in, 'You're welcome to eat here. Stay all day long Sunday. But Monday you got to be gone.'

"So we were poor, but we enjoyed ourselves. And we were close. Cleave and I argue more than anybody on earth. But nobody else can get in there. Sometimes you'd think we were gonna fight. But don't you jump up and say 'Cleave is wrong.' Because right away, it changes my feeling. I'll be the one that tells Cleave he's wrong, not you. But back then, we hunted, we fished. We'd go rabbit hunting. Possum hunting. We would take the possums and put 'em under the pot. We didn't have refrigerators to keep the meat, so we'd get three or four possums, kill one and eat that, and put the other two or three under a pot. We'd raise the pot just a little bit so they could get air, and give them cabbage leaves and different stuff to eat. And after three or four days we'd kill another one. And the rabbits . . . Cleave had a little old single-shot rifle, and he was the only one that could shoot a rabbit running with a rifle. Everybody else had to have a shotgun, but not Cleave . . . he was just that good with that rifle.

"I went to a little school in Houston. We walked something like twelve miles every day—six there and six back. My teacher didn't finish high school. Her name was Lula Brown, and she was teaching school in Mississippi without a high school education. I remember our mother used to fix our little lunch buckets. We would have sugar biscuits. She would cut that biscuit open, put in a little gravy—she made it up out of flour and grease—and then she'd put sugar in it and close that biscuit up. There was three of them apiece. At lunchtime, I couldn't wait to get those sugar biscuits. Sometimes we'd get a piece of fatback [*pork*]. Man, I couldn't learn anything for thinking about that fatback. Because that was all we knew about. And if you've never known anything better, it's not hard to live with what you've got. The only time you get screwed up in your mind is when you get a chance to know better. They wonder how black people survived in Mississippi. That's how we did it. We ate from the land, we ate from the creeks, we'd go and help the white man to kill the hogs and he would give you pig feet, pig ears, chitterlings, and pig tails. Go in the woods and get plums. I never will forget. I was about ten . . . we lived across the road from a guy named Tot Buckham, he was the home-brew maker there. [*Chickasaw County was—and still is—a dry county, where the sale of alcohol is prohibited.*] I followed him, and I found out where he had his churn, one of those big old cans, buried down in the ground in a patch of that long Johnson grass. So I told my brothers. And when Mr. Tot came back that next weekend, they had made a road to that can. Wasn't no home brew left. I had some myself—and got sick. My momma whipped me! She smelled it on my breath. She said, 'I'm not gonna wait until you get sober. I'm gonna whip your butt until you get sober.' And when she finished with me I was sober. Terribly sober."

Clay's brothers were Theophilus, Elgie C.B., and Cleave. Theophilus was the eldest, born around 1914. C.B. was the next, born around 1920. Clay was born on August 26, 1936, the youngest of the family. Of his sisters, Daisy was born after Theophilus, Mary after Elgie C.B., and Mansavilla between Cleave and Clay. All, apart from Cleave and Clay, are deceased.

"Theophilus was seventy when he passed. C.B. was sixty-five. Mansavilla was fifty-nine. My older two sisters, Mary was seventeen and Daisy was twenty-two. [*Cleave remembers them as being thirteen and seventeen when they died.*] That was tuberculosis. At that time, they didn't know anything about the medicine they have now for curing tuberculosis. The doctor told my mother that the girls would have to go to hospital in Memphis for six months to a year. But my mother couldn't see her daughters going away from her. She was afraid something would happen to them. Sometimes, love can make you make mistakes. I had another sister, she was the first child, before Theophilus. I can't even think of her name—the only name I heard was Black Gal, and I never did learn her real name. They called her Black Gal because she was real black, that beautiful black. And she had long curly hair like my daddy. He had curly hair because he was part Indian. Somehow she picked up a pea—a balance for weighing cotton; it weighed about six pounds—and it slipped out of her hand and dropped on her foot and broke it. Back in that time, there were no doctors for black people. It was a miracle if you got a chance to see a doctor. So most of the black people down South would comb the woods and find different things that would help to cure them. My mother went and got the dirt dauber [*wasp*] nest, and took coal oil and stuff and beat it all up and wrapped a rag around and tied it round her broken foot. And she went into a spasm from the pain and died.[1] They didn't know her foot was broken, they thought it was just a sprain. During that time—I don't remember drinking it, but I know my mama gave it to me—we used to boil cow droppings and drink the tea for malaria and stuff. Because all medicine comes from some type of herb. And cows eat most anything that's there. So during their eating, they find different weeds that will cure things within you. And the black people found out that's what happened. So they would get the cow droppings and boil it and drink the tea off it to take the fever down.

"I was the only one in my family was born under the doctor. Everybody else had the midwife. This lady's name was Miss Angeline. Every time a woman had a baby, they would call the midwife. And she would take down the information down and turn it in. And we found out things that were wrong. I found out I was celebrating my birthday on the twenty-eighth and my birthday was on the twenty-sixth. And my name is not Clay. Well, it is Clay, but . . . down South, whatever the white man said, they did. And when I was born, the doctor said, 'This man here, he's gonna weigh two hundred pounds before he's twenty years old.' I weighed twelve pounds when I was born. And he named me after another doctor in the town. He said to my mother, 'Would you name him Pat Harrison?' Mama said right away, 'Yes. Yes sir.' But when he was gone, she said, 'My baby is named Clay.' But on my birth certificate, it went down as Pat Harrison Graham. And on down through the years, I had to get that straightened out."

Like Cleave, Clay remembers the singing of Elgie C.B. as being at the core of the first incarnation of the Pilgrim Jubilees, and he still pays tribute to his brother in programs today. At a 1996 program in Birmingham, Alabama, issued as a live recording, he tells the audience: "We're going to sing an old song, one that my brother used to sing years ago—the one that organized the Pilgrim Jubilees back in the 1940s. And if you think we can sing, you should have heard him."[2]

"C.B. had a soulful voice. I hear myself sometimes sing different things that sound like him. But it didn't matter what C.B. sang, it'd sound good. He had that little soft voice, but it had something in it. People would be picking cotton or chopping or whatever on the farms beside ours and C.B. would sing—he sang the blues in the cotton field. People would drop their hoes and come across the road to stand and listen at him sing. And C.B. understood audiences. I learned more from him than any professional lead singer I have ever saw. He wasn't considered as a professional singer, because he never did travel. But he understood people. I remember we were singing at a church. We used to sing a simple song about 'I'm looking for that man that don't know Jesus.' C.B. had a little gimmick with it. He'd sing 'I'm looking for that man' . . . and the bass singer would go 'that don't know Jesus.' And then he'd start tipping down through the audience, trying to find that man. But on this day, he found a man that really didn't know Jesus, and he thought C.B. was picking on him. C.B. fell down by him, singing 'Oh I done found that man. . . .' He went into his pocket and pulled that .38 out, said, 'I'll blow your brains out.' And you should've seen my brother tippin' up out of there! And the crowds. I've seen it where they pulled trucks up by the window so people could stand on them and look in. Couldn't get 'em in the church. I've seen a church fall off its blocks because they had too many people in it. C.B. just put a spell on people."

In the late 1940s and early 1950s the Graham family began its piecemeal migration to Chicago, following hundreds of thousands of other black Americans exchanging the feudal life of the rural South for the chance to prosper in the industrial North. The first to make the move was Theophilus.

"Hoppy [*Theophilus*] was in the army, but he missed that invasion and everything, in France, because he played sick. Crazy. There was nothing wrong with him, but it worked. They kept him in the hospital . . . a whole year, in and out of the hospital. What he did, he pulled a little string behind him. Tied it to a little stick. And he carried that little string with him everywhere he'd go. Every time the man said, 'Attention' he'd go to attention and tell the string 'Attention.' He fed that little string . . . everywhere he went, that little string was with him, even in the bed. So he missed all the war. A lot of his buddies were on a ship that got sunk. Hoppy was lying up there in the hospital, talking to that little string. That little string kept him alive.

"When he came out of the army, he came back to Mississippi and did one crop. Then he said, 'I can't handle this. I cannot stand to walk behind a mule any more.' He'd been stationed around Chicago and he'd liked it. So he went back to Chicago. And when he got there . . . this is how long Major [*Roberson*] has been in our family. . . . Major had a barbershop in Chicago then. My brother went into the shop and started working with Major. He worked under Major for a year. Then the store next door became vacant. And right away, Hoppy went and rented the place and opened up next door to Major. Because my brothers—Hoppy and C.B.—and Monroe, all of them could cut hair. So he had a three-chair barbershop. He talked to Major before he did it, because he said, 'Major did me a favor by letting me come in and cut hair.' But after he got the shop rolling good, he would come to the South. He'd pull up in the yard in that Fleetline Chevrolet, and he'd be wearing those jive chains hanging down to his knees, watch in his pocket—decked out. We thought we had the richest brother that ever walked.

"By this time, C.B. and Cleave and Monroe were back in Chicago. Then Hoppy came and wanted Daddy to move to Chicago. Daddy was working real hard, following those mules and he had got arthritis. So my brother came and said, 'Daddy, I want you to come and live in Chicago.' Daddy said, 'Live where, boy?' No way. He's not going to Chicago. So Hoppy said, 'Well, I'll take my mama there for a while, then I'll bring her back.' Mama wanted to go. She stayed three months with Theophilus, left Daddy in Mississippi. When she went back, she told Daddy 'I can't take it down here no more.' And she told him—she knew what would get him—'Columbus, you would love it.' Daddy says 'I'm not going to Chicago.' She said, 'Hoppy's got a nice house. He's got a big television and I was sitting there the other day watching the ballgame.' Daddy used to listen at the Cubs and the Sox and all those down South on the radio. He said, 'I can sit in my house and look at 'em?' That's the only thing got my daddy out of Mississippi. Hoppy came down in his Fleetline Chevrolet. Mansavilla, me, Doris [*Cleave's wife*], Cleave's oldest daughter, Mama and Daddy piled into that Chevrolet and went to Chicago. Hoppy had rented an apartment on Vine Street. And when we pulled up on Vine Street, I said, 'When are we going to the house?,' because I thought we had to go out in the country to get to a house. He said, 'You're at home now.' And I'm looking around at these houses glued together. He said, 'This is your apartment here.' I said, 'This is gonna be fun.' And that's how we got out of Mississippi and came to Chicago, in 1952."

5. Chicago: Major Roberson

Away from what Clay today describes as "our bondage—the plow and the mules," the Graham family settled into Chicago life. Columbus Graham found work in the Chicago depot of the New York Central Railroad; Clay went to school, finishing his education in the tenth grade at Wells High School on Chicago's North Side, then joining his father at New York Central. C.B. and Cleave also worked together, for a packing company. Theophilus was established as a North Side barber. Separated from his Mississippi group, C.B. had been singing with one of Chicago's better-known local groups, the Bells of Zion. But when his family arrived in Chicago, he quit the Bells, and the Pilgrim Jubilees started singing again. Initially the group consisted of C.B., Cleave, Theophilus, and Monroe, with fifteen-year-old Clay starting to play a role as a tenor singer after his mother reversed her Mississippi opposition to him being with the group. "Mom wanted him to sing when he got to Chicago," recalls Cleave. "To keep him off the streets. Because we weren't in a good neighborhood. We were on the West Side, on the 1200 block off of Division and Vine. And in that area you had a bunch of poolrooms and taverns . . . a lot of junk was in that area. But we couldn't afford any better. So him being with his brothers was the best thing that could happen to him as far as she was concerned."

Rehearsals were held in the family barbershop on Larabee Street. But the attractions of Chicago were luring Theophilus, and he was losing interest in gospel singing. Cleave: "He was adventuresome and the lights had kinda got in his eyes, so he wasn't so keen on rehearsing all the time; he was kinda busy." But even after he dropped out, the group continued rehearsing at the barbershop—and the vacancy didn't stay open for long. Cleave: "Major sang baritone. And while we were rehearsing, Major was listening, saying 'Mmmm yeah . . .' He liked our sound better than the group he was with, and he wanted in. He was good to have, because he had been in Chicago a while and he knew his way round. That's how he came to be the booking manager. We were fresh from Mississippi, and he knew the churches, so that gave him the book." The one problem in replacing Theophilus with Major was that it substituted a baritone for a bass. But before starting his own group—which he left to join the Pilgrim Jubilees—Major had been with the Bells of Zion. The Bells' bass singer, Kenny Madden, knew Major and C.B. and was looking for a change. "When Major came, Kenny Madden said, 'I'm coming with you,' " says Cleave. In the new lineup, C.B. continued as the main lead singer, Monroe Hatchett and Clay sang tenor, Cleave and Major sang baritone—with Cleave taking some leads—and Kenny Madden sang bass.

Nearly fifty years after joining the group, Major Roberson is still singing baritone and has only recently given up handling the bookings, although some promoters who have been hiring the group for years still make their bookings through him because that's the way they've always done it. Today, Major lives in a tree-lined suburban street in Dolton on the southern outskirts of Chicago with his third wife, Hattie, and their two sons, Stanley and Sky, both in their thirties. Much of Chicago's housing is divided on racial lines, but the area in which Major lives is integrated.

"It's white on each side of me. And the first thing when I got there, they came over and made me welcome. It's like white here, black there, white here and black there. I happen to be sitting between white and white. But all the way down, they're very helpful and nice people. And you see those people and say 'Why is everybody not like this?' One man said to me, 'I've been here forty-six years, and I'm not about to move.' And they try to help you every way they know and they're real relaxed. It's a nice neighborhood, really nice. But all neighborhoods are not like that. There are some where if a black happens to buy a house, all the white folk put their houses up for sale and move out. I'll tell you something else that's bad. When the television people want to talk about the black neighborhood or something like that, they go to the worst neighborhood, where the houses are all falling down and everywhere you see rats. They won't take the camera into black neighborhoods where everything is in its place like it should be—the lawns are cut and the hedges are cut and the homes are all beautiful. They go in the ghetto, where there's a lot of garbage on the street. So even if you're not prejudiced, when every time you see something about a black person it's bad you'll say 'Well, if he comes into my neighborhood, I'm going to lose the value of my house.' That man doesn't know you, but everything he's seen about you is undesirable. So when you go into that neighborhood, if they can't torment you out, get you back out of there . . . then you start seeing that everybody's got a house for sale.

"I was raised in Clarksdale, Mississippi. I was born in a place called Gunnison, Mississippi. June 11, 1925. When I was a little bitty boy my mother moved to Clarksdale. I have one brother and one sister left. My older brother died last year. My mother and father separated when I was a baby. And they stayed separated until I was twenty-one. Then they got back together. My mother played piano, and she was a great singer. My daddy was a minister in the Baptist church, in Arkansas and Mississippi. And I confessed Christ at eleven years old. I was baptized. When I was five or six years old, I started with the Jew's harp. I played it on up until I got a harmonica. That's what I wanted for Christmas, and Mom bought me one when I was about eight. There was another older boy who blew a harmonica, and he showed me how to change, make my sound and so on—there's a lot of sound you can change with your tongue. Later on, I picked up a guitar, but my patience was too bad. Then I got a teacher for a while to teach me how to play a keyboard. But she put me on middle C; she kept me there so long I never learned to play. Now my mother, she was self-taught. . . . It was a strange thing. She was singing in the choir at our church. And one day, she came down and got on the piano, started playing the piano. She had never played piano before, and she didn't know how it happened. The choir went on and started rehearsing, and from that, she started playing for the choir.

"I started singing, when I was quite young, I guess eight or nine. The first quartet I was in was a quartet out of Helena, Arkansas, called the Glorybound Singers. I got the chance to work with them when one of their guys, Percell Perkins, left to go into the army in 1942. That group . . . it was the best they had down there. They used to broadcast from Helena for Gold Crest flour and stuff like that, over the radio every day. One of the boys that was singing with them, Eulee Vergis, lived close by me. And when Perkins was fixing to go in the army, they had a farewell program at my home church in Clarksdale. My friend said, 'Hey man, this is a good chance for you.' I was singing leads at the time. I can't sing it now, but during that time I had a little high voice. I was only with them for less than a year. We'd go around the county from one church to the other—sometimes we'd do three or four churches a Sunday. And they'd let us in on the program, they'd see a group come up and ask you your name—sometimes you're not even invited, you just go."

Although Major describes the Glorybound Singers as being from Helena, Arkansas—probably because of their radio show there—they are generally regarded as a Clarksdale group. His assessment of them as "the best they had down there" is borne out by other accounts of the group's abilities—in 1989, gospel researcher Ray Funk described it as "legendary."[1] *The Glorybounds made no recordings, but they had their radio show and toured extensively through the mid-South. Percell Perkins became one of the leading quartet figures of the 1950s, singing with the New Orleans Chosen Five, the Swan Silvertone Singers, the Blind Boys of Mississippi, and the Blind Boys of Alabama. He was also a minister and eventually quit quartet singing for the pulpit, becoming pastor of the Galilee Missionary Baptist Church in Helena.*

"After that, we moved away to Indianola, Mississippi. I didn't hook up with any groups for the time we stayed there. We were farmers, and down there you just . . . you farmed. My mother worked in the fields. By this time we all was able to work in the fields, but before that, she had to plough mules and farm the land on the sharecropping thing. The guys [*other sharecroppers*] would go to the barn and get a mule and hook it up and bring it back to her. And in the afternoon they would come by and pick him up and take him back, so she wouldn't have to do that. But the days in the field—she was out there herself. We weren't big enough to do anything like that. Eventually, we went back to Gunnison—I went into the service from there. I was seventeen years old when we went back, and when I turned eighteen, I went into the Second World War. I was in the army air force. After I got my basic training, they sent me to Guam. But I was at just about all the camps in the United States. I was at Fort Benning, Georgia—that's where I got a lot of my basics—and I ended going to San Antonio, Texas, and from San Antonio I went to St. Angelo, Texas. And from there I went to Fort Sheridan, Illinois, from Fort Sheridan to Salt Lake City, Utah, and from there on to San Francisco, California. And from there on the ship to Guam. I was with the Twelfth Air Ammunition Squadron. Very dangerous assignment. We would load the bombs on and off the ships. We would grease the bombs and put pins on them and take them to the airport. Then we would put them on the planes. I was there for the invasion on Okinawa. And after it was over, we had to go and pick up the stuff that was left. But I was blessed and I didn't get hurt. I never was under fire. We were always the clean-up folk. When the bombs fell and didn't explode, we had to go out there and get those bombs and put 'em the truck and take 'em way out and then set 'em off.

"I did have a little group over there. We got a little popular just before I was discharged. And I had a group in the army before I went overseas. In Camp Shelby, Mississippi, with two of the guys I went overseas with. We'd sing sometimes at the chapel. And there were times when they had little contests [*on Guam*] and the winner would get a fifth of liquor and a carton of cigarettes. Lot of fun. We were singing old jubilee songs, 'My God Called Me This Morning,' that kind of stuff. Everybody was doing the same things at that time. I was boxing, too, at the camp. You had a chance to pick what sport you wanted to do. I didn't like football, and I always wanted something a little rough. So I took boxing. I had eight fights. I won seven, and they told me I won the last one, but I didn't accept that because I was out cold. My company commander said it was foul play. I didn't see it. But the guy whipped me anyway. I could tell right away he was better than me. But he elbowed me a little, and I went out just like a light.

"I was on Guam a little better than a year before I was eligible for my discharge. Then I took ship back and took a train from San Francisco to Chicago—my mother had moved to Chicago. When I got there . . . in the service, I went to school to be a heavy equipment operator. I was using a crane to load bombs on and off the ship—I was working all that stuff, cables and booms. But when I came to Chicago . . . I don't know why, but I didn't go in for that. I got one job at the Chicago Pottery Company. Wash basins and all things like that. I was working where you mix together all the different kinds of clay and mold this stuff out. Then I worked at a tannery. But these were all brief jobs, because I never was a person to really depend on a job too much. When I was in camp in Utah, I graduated from barber school. So in Chicago, I went and took my test, got my license and started working for a man that owned a barber shop. About two months after I started working for him, his health went bad and he had to go back to Arkansas. He asked me if I would be interested in the barbershop. I told him 'Yes, but I can't afford it.' He said, 'I'll fix it so you can afford it.' He said, 'I'm gonna walk out that door, and I'm not gonna look back. And the only thing I want you to promise me is that if I ever come back and need a job, you'll hire me. I said, 'Of course.' He said, 'I'm gonna leave my license on the wall, and I'd like you to renew it every year for me.' He left it with me—all free of debt, no nothing. He came about eleven years later. I had moved to a different location, but he found me. And I said, 'Mr. Farley, pick your own chair.' He said, 'No, I don't want a chair. I feel good just watching you, that you still carry it on.' He said, 'Only thing I want is my license.' I went and got his license and gave it to him. He said, 'I'm going back home and I might take my license down and change it over to Arkansas. But I'm never gonna live here again.' I said, 'Can I do anything, do I owe you something?' He said, 'You owed me what you did—just continuing to do what you were supposed to do.'

"I got married the first time in 1941, in Gunnison, Mississippi. Her name was Ruth. She passed [*died*]. She got in the fast life and had cirrhosis. She killed herself, really. When I went in the service, she just went berserk, I hear. She couldn't stop. How I came about her, she got pregnant, and the old folks used to tell you that if you're courting a girl and something happens, then you're responsible for it. They tell you it's yours. So they told me I had her pregnant. And she told them it wasn't me. See, I didn't do it. She went on vacation to Chicago and she got pregnant. They told her she was lying. Her mother and my mother got together and went and bought a license because I wasn't old enough to buy one. We separated while I was in the service. I didn't have any children with her. Then in Chicago, I got married in 1949. She was one of my schoolmates from down South. Her name was Bernice. We had eight kids together. We divorced on down the line, and she passed after that. Then I married Hattie. We've got the two boys. Altogether, I've got twenty-one children. Because I have some outside children. Did a lot of running in my youth days, you know."

In Chicago, Major worked hard to build up his barbering business. But he also wanted to sing and soon joined the Bells of Zion. He stayed with them for two years, then left to organize his own group, the Pilgrim Harmonizers, which "sung around in storefront churches and whatever." But his first contact with the Pilgrim Jubilees came through his barbershop.

"Theophilus—they called him Hoppy—was in Chicago, working in a steel mill. He was one of my customers. One day, he said he could cut hair. I asked him if he had a license; he said, 'No, but I'm good.' So one day after my business grew so big, I was trying to find me a barber. Hoppy came in and I said, 'Do you think you could cut a little bit for me, help me?' He said, 'Yeah.' So he started working for me. He didn't have a license, but I talked to the union people and got a certificate for him. He'd been telling me about his brothers down south, and one day he went back and started bringing them up. And when they all got to Chicago, they wanted to reorganize the Pilgrim Jubilees. So we organized 'em. And they made me the manager and the booking manager. Because the Pilgrim Harmonizers . . . the lead singer was Cleave Mantell. He had just started preaching, so most of the time, he couldn't go on the concerts, and the group was . . . just slowed on down. And with the Pilgrim Jubilees, I had a better group, I had better lead singers, I had the whole nine yards so I said, 'Well, I'm gonna tip on over here.' I started booking the programs in the churches and we would—just like all the other groups—invited or not invited, we would show up at programs just to tighten the group on up. We rehearsed twice a week. And we got a pretty good group."

6. Stepping Out

In 1952 the reconstituted Pilgrim Jubilee Singers were one of many local Chicago gospel quartets. They sang on any program that would have them, but the singing had to be fitted around jobs. Major was running his barbershop; Theophilus Graham's shop next door was providing work for him, Elgie C.B., and Monroe Hatchett, although Monroe was also working at the New York Central Railroad depot, going to the barbershop once his day's work was over. Clay was nearing the end of his schooldays, and new recruit Kenny Madden was running his own car wash business. Cleave was working for a packing company and was finding it hard to make ends meet. He and Doris had two children when they left Mississippi, and the young family continued to grow in Chicago.

Cleave: "C.B. got me a job with him at Kincaid Packing. He worked there a while, and later he started to cut hair at my brother's shop. But my family was growing so fast, I had to have that something steady coming. In the afternoons, after I got off work, I would go to the barbershop. They had started this hair processing thing, where the guys wear their own hair and put the waves in. I learned how to do that, and I would do that after my regular job. And I left the packing company and went with Farmrite Implement Company because the money was better. But by now I had four kids.

So I got a second job, with a can company. I was doing sixteen hours a day for a good while to try to make it better for my family. So I was making $1.50 an hour with Farmrite Implement, plus I had this other job. I said, 'Oh, I'm on my way!' But they say that when it rains, it pours. The government came in [*at Farmrite*] and said that to do this job, you had to be a veteran. And that cut me out. Three days later, the can company let me go. Now, no job! I ran back to the barbershop. My brother had a little shoeshine parlor next door. I'd run in the barbershop and wash the customers' hair and put the relaxer in it and wash it out, then I'd run back over and shine shoes. I was just running back and forwards. And that's the way I kept going until I got another job. But through it all, I found time for rehearsal. And I always tried to arrange it so I wouldn't miss anything my group had to do. Whenever we were going to do something, I was going to be there."

Clay Graham summarizes the group's first couple of years in two sentences: "After we organized, we started to do local shows. Then we became the number one group in Chicago." Chicago in the 1950s was a gospel music heartland. In the quartet world, the city's best-known group was the Soul Stirrers, originally from Texas but Chicago residents since 1937. As the Pilgrim Jubilees rehearsed, the Soul Stirrers and their dynamic new lead singer, Sam Cooke, were cutting a swathe through the gospel world with a potent mix of passionate, skillful singing and Cooke's stagecraft and matinee-idol good looks. Although based in Chicago, the Soul Stirrers weren't competition for the Pilgrim Jubilees. They were a model to aspire to. Competition came from other local groups. "The Soul Stirrers were from Chicago, but they were already out and going big," says Cleave. "The Norfolk Singers, I'd say they were considered the top local group. The Highway QCs were in Chicago when we got there. And the Traveling Kings." Other leading local groups of the time included the Windy City Four, the Holy Wonders, the Bells of Zion, the Pilgrim Harmonizers, the Norfleet Brothers, and the Spiritual Five.

The Pilgrim Jubilees started singing at programs put on by local churches. Their first engagements came through Major's contacts, but soon word-of-mouth advertising was boosting the bookings. **Cleave**: "From one church here, they would want us over to the next church, then the next church would want us. We started out doing Sundays. And then when people got to know us, then we'd be singing sometimes Wednesday nights, Friday nights, Sunday evening on one side of town, Sunday night on the other side of town. Most of the time, we were singing on programs with other groups—when we were beginners, it was strictly with other groups, because nobody knew anything about us. But once we were up here on that program, somebody would want us some place else."

Money was not a consideration—sometimes the group would go to a program without being booked, relying on a cancellation or the organizer's goodwill for a chance to sing. "We sang and we enjoyed ourselves, and the people enjoyed it," summarizes Cleave. Any money made came from collections taken up among the audience, although Cleave recalls that as the group became better known, "the collections started getting a little better—that helped." But the main battle was to get the group known, to establish a reputation. The three key elements in this process were the same for any group—sing as often as possible, sing as well as possible, and have your own sound. Of these, the third is the most important—without originality in singing style and arrangements, no amount of the other two elements will lift a group above its competition. The Pilgrim Jubilees knew this even in Mississippi; in Chicago, they continued their efforts to be unique. Major Roberson's songwriting and arranging skills played a substantial role in this effort

Major: "The big thing we were always trying to stay away from was the sound or the arrangements of other groups. We always wanted to have our own sound. So I started arranging stuff for the group myself, and after a while I started writing songs. At the time, I was the only one in the group writing. My mother and I used to sit down and I would tell her what I was trying to say and she would help me with my arrangements. My mother was good at it. And then I'd bring the song back to the group and we'd go through it. And when I arranged a song—re-arranged it—it didn't sound like the original. I'd take it completely out of context, put it in another style."

Creating your own sound also has three elements; Major refers to two of them—developing your own arrangements and writing your own songs. Having at least one songwriter in the group gives a supply of unique material. But gospel audiences also like to hear old standards. Thomas A. Dorsey's compositions are still found in quartet repertoires, as are spirituals and hymns dating back centuries. Because these are so well known, each group must put its own stamp on its version. One way of doing this is to change completely the feel of a song—as Major says, "take it completely out of context"—by altering the rhythm, the tempo, or even the tune.

The third element in establishing an identity is the sound of the voices in the group—the collective sound and, more important, the sound of the leads. The individuality of a gospel quartet is almost always defined by its lead singers. Classic examples include the silken tones of Sam Cooke with the Soul Stirrers, the piercing wails of Archie Brownlee with the Blind Boys of Mississippi, the hard-edged passion of Julius Cheeks with the Sensational Nightingales, and the distinctive falsetto of Claude Jeter with the Swan Silvertones. The Pilgrim Jubilees' sound was led by C.B. and Cleave. C.B. had a distinctive tenor voice, light but able to power into the driving songs, and with an appealing smoky overtone. Cleave sang leads in baritone and tenor, and his singing was like his stage presence—direct, strong, and authoritative. The group made effective use of the "split lead" technique, contrasting and mixing the two lead voices to provide dynamic layers within a song and build it to a climax. The background vocals were also strong—with six men in the group, the backing never had fewer than four voices, so the leads always had a solid foundation on which to build. Baritone Major Roberson and bass Kenny Madden were prominent in the vocal mix, their voices providing a rich, dense bottom end. It was a sound that obviously appealed to Chicago quartet audiences, and within a short time, the group graduated from hustling for spots at local programs to opening for the big-time professional groups.

Clay: "We were on practically all the professional shows that came through. The Soul Stirrers, the Pilgrim Travelers . . . the Pilgrim Jubilees would open the show for them when they came to Chicago. We were on with the Blind Boys [*of Mississippi*], and at the time they were so hot they would have twelve, fourteen thousand people there. And I remember going up to the mike . . . we were sitting there waiting to sing, and when they called us, I walked up to the mike and didn't have any voice. Hoo! It had popped out the window. My throat was just as tight. . . . We were scared! But we were good. At that time, we were singing all those old songs. 'Happy in the Service of the Lord,' 'God Is Good to Me,' 'It's Cool Down Yonder by the Banks of Jordan' . . . stuff like that. I was tenor singer, then. I wasn't a lead singer. But how I came to sing lead. . . . I was a fan of Rev. Julius

Cheeks. I loved that man's singing. And I used to take my mother to healing services. I'd take her, then I'd go back and pick her up. Sometimes I stayed. And one time, the guy said, 'Everybody that has a special something that they want to be blessed with, I want you to stand. Everybody just stand and repeat in your mind what you want.' So I said, 'I want to sing lead like Rev Julius Cheeks.' I was serious! That was on Friday. Tuesday was rehearsal. I started singing lead that Tuesday. And that next Sunday, we were at a program and C.B. was singing, 'God Is Good to Me.' He got hoarse, and I took the song off him. I tore the church up . . . it was a feeling that radiated to the audience and just bust it open."

At the beginning of 1953 the Pilgrim Jubilees made their first recordings. "Happy in the Service of the Lord" and "Just a Closer Walk with Thee," two gospel standards, were issued on Chance 5004, a 78-rpm disc. Today, the details are vague. Cleave, Clay, and Major—the three present group members who were there—remember little of the experience, recalling only that the recording was made and the songs they sang. Chance, started in December 1950 by Art Sheridan, is today remembered mainly as a blues label, with generally poorly produced records by artists such as John Lee Hooker, Sunnyland Slim, and Homesick James Williamson.[1] But between March 1952 and around July 1954 it issued ten gospel records by an eclectic mix of artists ranging from the bluesy-sounding Mississippi singer Henry Green through quartets—the Golden Tones, the Southern Clouds, and the Pilgrim Jubilees—to soloist Naiomi Baker (the most prolific Chance gospel artist with three issues) and the Wooten Choral Ensemble.[2] Some of Sheridan's issues were what have come to be known as "vanity" recordings, records an artist pays to have made.

Major: "We heard about this Chance Records—that they would do you a session, then charge you so much for so many records. You would pay it and take your records and go on about your business. So that's the way it was. We weren't contracted. We paid them. Then we carried them around under our arms and sold them on the programs. I don't know if he [*Sheridan*] was selling them as well—he might have, because he kept the masters. But we probably sold between five hundred and a thousand in our little circle." **Cleave**: "I believe we did have to pay. But the thing for us was 'We're going to get on record.' That was the thing. Getting on a record. But it didn't go anywhere. A new recording company and young new artists—in the recording business, that's a job for Superman."

"Just a Closer Walk with Thee"—mislabeled on Chance as "Just a Walk with Thee"—features Cleave's lead singing and interpolations by C.B. over a bass-heavy vocal backing that repeats the line "just a closer walk with thee." As the song builds to its climax, a syncopation is added to the background phrasing, and Cleave departs from the formal verse structure to a looser pattern, repeating phrases and ending with a free-form excursion around the phrase "I'll be satisfied, let it be." "Happy in the Service of the Lord" enjoyed a vogue through the late 1940s and early 1950s and was recorded by a number of prominent quartets including the Blind Boys of Mississippi, the Golden Echoes, the Soul Stirrers, and the Spirit of Memphis. Cleave starts the Jubes' version at a slow pace over a "moaned" backing. After sixteen bars, C.B. takes over the lead, the song picks up pace, and Kenny Madden starts a "bom bom bom" pumping bass while the other singers repeat phrases behind C.B. and fill in the sentences he leaves incomplete as he adds vocal ornamentation. Both recordings are confident and competent. The group's jubilee-style roots are apparent, but equally obvious is that the singers have a firm grasp on the then-evolving hard quartet style.

Around 1954 Major Roberson developed tuberculosis and spent some time in a hospital. The Pilgrim Jubilees carried on singing without him, but the loss of his management and booking skills left a gap. To fill it, they obtained the services of Roy Harris, who was managing the Norfolk Singers. Harris played a major role in pushing the group toward its ambition of becoming a professional quartet. He tightened its performing style, introduced a guitar to the lineup, and got the group on radio.

Clay: "By him being the manager of the Norfolk Singers, he had prestige. Because the Norfolks were some bad guys in the city. And Roy taught us a whole lot of things. Such as be at your program on time, and when they call you, make sure you know what you're going sing. And rehearse what you're going to sing before you go there. And another thing he said, 'Don't no one monkey stop no show.' Because we would go to a program and, say, our bass singer might not be there. They'd say 'We see we have the Pilgrim Jubilees here. . . .' Somebody would stand up and say 'We don't have our bass singer tonight. We beg to be excused.' Roy said: 'I don't ever want to hear that come out your mouths again. You're there. If there ain't but two of you, get up and sing.' We started doing that, and it got to where if we had one or two fellows out of the group, we didn't care. And it paid off. After that, Major came back, but Roy stayed for a while. He started us with a guitar. We were singing a cappella. He said, 'You need music. Times have changed.' We got Arthur Crume; he started playing guitar for us. And Roy put us in a position that put us away out front of the local groups. They would go to a little radio station and pay fifteen dollars to get a fifteen-minute broadcast on Sunday morning. Roy said, 'We don't want that little mess.' So we went down town to a radio broadcast company and paid forty-five dollars. That put us out over them because we could be heard in all the suburban towns—we were reaching out there. Those little stations, you could barely pick 'em up in the city."

Paying for broadcast time was a common way of publicizing a group. Artists would pay for a block of time, then broadcast live from the studio. Sometimes they would recoup the cost by selling advertising; often they balanced the expense against the pay-off of more bookings and the status of being radio stars. The station the Pilgrim Jubilees broadcast over was WSBC. Roy Harris knew it because the Norfolk Singers also had a Sunday broadcast there. But when the Pilgrim Jubilees went on the air, they shared their time—and the cost—with another group, the Spiritual Five. **Cleave**: "It was a pretty good station, a powerful station—it would reach two or three different states. And in that area, it was just like having a record. That station was charging forty-five dollars for fifteen minutes. That was a whole lot of money to pay every Sunday morning to do fifteen minutes. The Spiritual Five got the fifteen minutes and they asked us to come and sing a song if we shared that forty-five dollars. And that did it for us, real good! People knew about us over in Milwaukee and some parts of Ohio. Then hey, here comes the mail!"

If the Pilgrim Jubilees' first recording session has elements of mystery, the second is almost a complete blank. The bare bones are that in 1954 the group recorded "Angel" and "Lord, I Have No Friend Like You" in Chicago, and that the two songs were issued on NBC 2003. But Cleave, Clay, and Major have no clear memory of recording the songs and recall nothing at all about the label. In fact, no information about NBC seems to have survived except that it issued at least two gospel recordings, one by the Pilgrim

Jubilees and one by another quartet, the Keynotes. **Major**: "That was another private thing—we bought our way on there." **Clay**: "Well, we did quite a few little things. It probably was a little small label . . . NBC . . . I just don't remember NBC. But we did several little records around then. They cut 'em, you pay 'em and you put it in your hand and run with it." Clay's remark about "several little records," coupled with a vague recollection that "Angel" and "Lord I Have . . ." were made for the small Brewer label, raises the intriguing possibility that other early Pilgrim Jubilee Singers recordings may exist. But none has been found, and group members do not recall any details.

Cleave sings lead on both NBC songs, moving his range up to the tenor register to give his voice a hard piercing edge, more astringent than Elgie C.B.'s and with an underlying feeling of urgency. He is obviously comfortable as a tenor, making frequent use of melisma and grace notes and occasional forays into falsetto to decorate his singing, especially on "Angel." Both songs show the progress the group had made since the Chance recordings. The backing vocals still accentuate the bass end, but the interplay between lead and backing is more confident and adroit than it was a year earlier, and the performances have a more relaxed feel. Arthur Crume's guitar provides an opening chord to set the key and then sits well back, providing only a basic strummed accompaniment but helping to give the songs impetus.

"Lord I Have No Friend Like You" is another standard, but "Angel" is a landmark for the Pilgrim Jubilees—the first time they recorded one of their own songs. Written by Major Roberson, the song is a steady-paced "coming home" lyric—"Angel, get my mansion ready for me / Angel, turn back my bed / Angel, don't bother my pillow/Because Jesus gonna make up my dying bed. . . ." More than forty years after the Pilgrim Jubilees recorded it, the song had a second life when Dottie Peoples recorded it on a 1996 compact disc in a version that—apart from the elaborate synthesizer-dominated backing—is remarkably true to the Pilgrim Jubilees' rendition.[3]

The group's ambition to become a professional quartet was starting to seem achievable. The radio broadcasts were attracting out-of-town engagements as far away as Detroit, and the booking schedule often listed programs on consecutive Friday, Saturday, and Sunday nights, sometimes with others during the day. Inevitably, conflicts arose between singing and jobs. It wasn't so difficult for Major, C.B., and Kenny, as they were self-employed. But Cleave, Clay, and Monroe were working for employers. The Graham brothers had no doubt—the singing came first. But Monroe Hatchett, who was a little older than the rest of the Pilgrim Jubilees, was reluctant to jeopardize the security of a steady income and, soon after the NBC recording session, left the group.

Cleave: "We'd go out in the weekend—I'd go anywhere and back in time to get to work. We could even go to Detroit and do a show and I could get back to Chicago. I'd come back home and go straight to the job. Go to sleep the next night. If I didn't get back . . . I'm sorry. I tried. But I didn't let a job stand in front of what I had to do when it come to that group. If they didn't let me off, I took off. I was going with the group. But Monroe, he was in business with Theophilus in the barbershop. And he had a pretty good job with the New York Central Railroad. He'd work during the day at New York Central. He'd get off at four and come into the barbershop. The barbershop closed at eight, but if you still had customers inside, you've got to do those customers. I've known them to cut hair until midnight."

Clay: "I started off at Beck's Plywood Company on Division Street, right down the street from the barbershop. I was still at school then. In fact, before that I was a shoe-shine boy. My brother had a shoe parlor on the side of his barbershop. Then I started driving a truck for a laundry company. Then I went to work at New York Central Railroad. My daddy was there, and I started working with him. But we were going to different places with the group on the weekend, and we were missing days on our jobs—always missing Monday, sometimes Tuesday. My boss liked me, and he would always see that I could come back to work. But my daddy told me, 'I'd rather for you to quit than for them to fire you.' So I quit and went into the barbershop. At the time, there was a barbershop on the South Side where they were doing the process, straightening the hair. And there wasn't a shop on the North Side doing this. My older brother [*Theophilus*] said, 'We've got to learn this.' So we went and got some of this hair straightener. Then we experimented on each other, trying to get it together. And I was the man that processed the hair and got it in order."

7. Third Time Lucky

In 1955 the Pilgrim Jubilees' initial goal of being the top local group in Chicago was effectively achieved when the Chicago chapter of the National Quartet Convention nominated them to represent it at the national gathering, held that year in Oakland, California. The convention was founded in the late 1940s by quartet doyen Rebert H. Harris to keep the quartet tradition alive.[1] By 1955, when the Pilgrim Jubilees joined, its national gathering—held in a different city each year—was a high point in the quartet calendar, attended by national groups and top local groups from all over the country. The Pilgrim Jubilees were selected to go to Oakland by a vote of the Chicago membership, but they had a head start. "Rebert liked our singing," says Cleave. "And he said, 'I want you to be the representatives of the state of Illinois.' So that put us in the running."

Major: "You have your local meeting. Everybody's there, and they say, 'We've got to send a representative to the convention.' It went on round, then they said, 'Pilgrim Jubilees. Who could do it better than the Jubes?' So they gave us some money for our expenses, we drove out there, and we got to sing on the convention. Oh, we did a job out there!" **Cleave**: "The people liked us so well. They started booking us shows during the week that we were out there. They were booking us all the way down to Los Angeles. We were out there for two weeks after the convention ended."

In Oakland, the Pilgrim Jubilees made a powerful friend in Senior Roy Crain, a founding member and manager of the Soul Stirrers. One convention program was dedicated to the national groups—those with major-label recording contracts and bookings all over the United States. The Pilgrim Jubilees had neither of these qualifications but were selected to open the show. The Soul Stirrers were at the top of the bill—"Sam Cooke was there with them, and they were as hot as a firecracker," Major recalls—and Crain listened to the new group from Chicago.

Major: "He said, 'You need to be recording.' They were recording for Specialty, and he took us there and said, 'I want you to take this group.' The guy said, 'I don't need a group.' Crain said, 'Listen to 'em.' We stood there and we sung. And Crain said, 'You're going to take this group or the Soul Stirrers aren't going to record no more.' So the guy said, 'Go ahead, come on in.' We set up and started singing."

"The guy" was Art Rupe, owner of the Los Angeles–based Specialty recording company, one of the leading black music labels of the 1950s. As well as the Soul Stirrers, its gospel catalog included the popular female group the Original Gospel Harmonettes, the Blind Boys of Alabama, soloists Brother Joe May and Alex Bradford, and the one quartet that could outsell the Soul Stirrers, the Pilgrim Travelers. Crain's ultimatum to Rupe got the Pilgrim Jubilees into the Specialty studio. But a veto from the Pilgrim Travelers' manager and tenor singer, J. W. Alexander, stopped the recordings being issued.

Cleave: "He recorded us. But the Pilgrim Travelers were his top group. And Alexander said, 'No!' He said, 'I don't want that. The names are too close.' Pilgrim Travelers, Pilgrim Jubilees. Well, he had the clout with Specialty. They recorded us and gave us, I think, twenty-five dollars a side. Then the man came back and said, 'I can release you if you change your name.' I said, 'No. No. No. This name is an inheritance. This is a family-given name. I grew up with that name, and we had it before we ever heard of the Pilgrim Travelers.' They were famous, but I wouldn't deny my own name because it was close to theirs. I'm not a Pilgrim Traveler. I'm a Pilgrim Jubilee. And Roy Harris agreed with me. Roy had a lot of spunk. He said, 'We're gonna make it. We don't have to have a Specialty recording contract.' "

The group went home still as the Pilgrim Jubilees and with their reputation enhanced by their West Coast singing—but without a Specialty contract. Shortly before they left California, events took an ironic turn when J. W. Alexander tried to entice Cleave to join the Pilgrim Travelers as a replacement for lead singer Kylo Turner, whose alcohol problems and private life were making him a liability to the group.[2]

Cleave: "I could sing all their stuff—I could do it just like Turner. And they knew it. So Alexander asked me would I consider singing lead for the Pilgrim Travelers. I said, 'I've got a group.' He said, 'Well, would money change your mind?' I said, 'I don't think so.' He went to Roy Harris, said, 'We'll give you two thousand dollars if you'll let him sing lead for us.' He tried to buy me. Roy said 'What did he say?' 'He says no.' Roy said 'That's what it is then.' So we came back to Chicago and went back to what we were doing before. We had our radio broadcasts, and we were running around within the range of them. And just having all kind of fun."

The six songs the Pilgrim Jubilees recorded for Specialty, a mixture of Major Roberson–arranged gospel standards and group compositions, are a snapshot of their repertoire at the time. They show an ensemble that, while not yet as polished as the top professional acts such as the Pilgrim Travelers, the Blind Boys of Mississippi, or the Dixie Hummingbirds, is clearly a cut above the average local group. Had the Specialty recordings been issued, they would almost certainly have given the Pilgrim Jubilees a strong push toward a national career.[3] Specialty archived the full session, and four songs were eventually issued in 1997 on a collector-oriented compact disc.[4]

Cleave is the main lead on all six, soloing on four and picking up after introductory verses by C.B. on the others. Arthur Crume's guitar provides an unobtrusive underpinning, and the backing vocals are carefully and inventively arranged. As on the previous recordings, the bass end is generally prominent, but the singers use a variety of ranges and harmony intervals to vary the sound. On "What Do You Know About Jesus," for example, the backing revolves largely around a repetition of the title. But as C.B. hands the lead off to the harder-toned Cleave, the group harmony also shifts to a sharper edge, accentuating the increase in tension created by the change in leads. On "He'll Be There" the backing tenors of Clay and C.B. are to the fore except at crescendo points, when Major's and Kenny's subdued parts change to an open-throated sound that abruptly shifts the dynamics of the song. "Tell Jesus (What You Want)" is a reworking of the song better-known as "Jesus Is on the Main Line" and starts with a throaty first verse from C.B. before Cleave takes over, lifting the pitch, the tempo, and the intensity. The somber and powerful "Yesteryear," one of the few recorded examples of Kenny Madden's songwriting, is the standout from the session. Over a solid backing that ranges from muted humming to full-throated responses, Cleave gives full rein to his range and vocal strength. Most of the song has a pensive, questioning feel—"In yesteryear / Men would often ponder / Wondering if a man died / His soul, who would gain." But in the last half-minute, it changes to an affirmation of eternal life ("When my work is over / I'm sure gonna live again") and goes into double time to reinforce the influx of optimism. The solemn feel of "Yesteryear" also permeates "Oh Lord," Major's reworking of a song also known as "Lord Own Me As a Child." It was recorded under this name in Chicago a year earlier by the Lockhart Singers, who sang it in a fairly brisk 4/4 time. But the Pilgrim Jubilees' version slows the pace, heightens the intensity, and changes the timing to 3/4.[5]

Back in Chicago, the Pilgrim Jubilees returned to their routine of working by day, rehearsing at night, and singing wherever they could—even if meant taking unauthorized time off the jobs. Soon after the trip to California, they obtained another long-distance engagement, in San Antonio, Texas.

Cleave: "Major had a brother who was a preacher and he had a little church out there. So Major said, 'My brother will book us. Let's go to Texas.' We'd been listening to those Peacock recordings, so we stopped in Houston on the way back and went to the Peacock office. And we got to see Mr. Robey, the owner of Peacock Records. He says: 'Let me hear how you sound.' So we sang right there in his office. After a while, he took his hands from behind his head and said, 'I'll record you. But I would like you to rehearse for two or three days . . .' They had just started drumming [*on quartet recordings*]. The Five Blind Boys made the first quartet record with drums on it. That was with Peacock. So he said, 'I'd like to get y'all to rehearse a couple of days with my drummer.' And one of the fellows in the group said, 'Fiddlesticks. We'll stay down here and rehearse with a drummer? We don't need no drummer to sing!' And we walked out."

The walk out after Kenny Madden's spur-of-the-moment expostulation was probably the Pilgrim Jubilee's most misguided career move. Peacock was the leading gospel quartet label. It was formed in 1949 as a rhythm-and-blues label by Don D. (Deadric) Robey, a black entrepreneur whose earlier occupations included professional gambler, liquor dealer, sports promoter, and nightclub owner. In 1950 Robey expanded into gospel, signing the popular Five Blind Boys of Mississippi. By 1955 he had an impressive roster of powerhouse hard quartets, including the Blind Boys, the Dixie Hummingbirds, the Sensational Nightingales, and the Spirit of Memphis. Robey took an active interest in the production of his recordings and claimed to have been the one who "put the beat" into gospel records, primarily by using drums on his recordings. This started with a basic bass drum and snare behind the Blind Boys' second Peacock session in September 1950. Although Cleave recalls the drums as an innovation in 1955, they were by that time an integral part of Peacock's sound.

But not of the Pilgrim Jubilees' sound. Defiantly drumless—and contractless—the group returned to Chicago, where Roy Harris withdrew as manager, returning the job to Major. "He was a little bit older, and when we started traveling around, he backed away," says Clay. As well, Harris had a well-paid job with Chicago's water board and, notes Clay, "he wasn't going to leave that and go and make those nickels." The other change in the group was more significant. Elgie C.B. Graham had been having problems with his voice since he moved to Chicago, and the Specialty recordings show a throaty huskiness in his voice not present on the earlier Chance and NBC tracks. "Something about the climate didn't agree with his vocal cords," recalls Cleave. Clay agrees that his brother "lost some of his voice by the changing of the climate" and says that C.B., like Roy Harris, did not enjoy the increasing amount of out-of-town travel. But Clay also believes C.B.'s voice troubles were the first sign of the lung cancer that eventually caused his death in the mid-1980s. When C.B. did quit the group, it was on medical advice.

Cleave: "He and I used to talk all the time—we were real close. He said, 'The doctor told me I got to quit. You and Clay can take it.' Clay had started singing a little lead, and he was very effective with it. So C.B. said, 'Clay can sing lead. Train Clay, make him sing. You and him, you can handle it.' Well, I didn't want to hear him saying this. He said, 'I don't want to quit my group. But the doctor told me definitely.' That's when Clay started coming on out with the lead. And then . . . he's so strong and the girls they just went. . . . We decided to give him the stronger songs. What I was thinking was . . . a group needs popularity. Clay's young, strong, tall . . . let's stick him out front. I said, 'He can keep the group popular longer than I can because he's younger.' So Clay went to work."

Despite C.B.'s and Cleave's confidence in Clay, another lead singer, Johnny Felix, joined the group soon afterward, probably in 1957. Clay recalls him as "a little short guy from the North Side" who had sung with the Pilgrim Harmonizers—Major Roberson's former group—and other local groups. It appears his employment did not meet with the complete approval of the Graham brothers. **Clay**: "Me and Cleave were the lead singers in the group, but they were always searching for another lead singer. That was Major's doing." None of the group says much about it, but it seems underlying conflict between Major and the brothers over the addition of extra lead singers existed sporadically until the early 1960s, when Cleave and Clay asserted themselves and assumed the lead roles they have held since. Major has no clear memory of how Felix came to join the group—"I don't know who drafted him or how he got here." But he does point out that until the early 1960s, Cleave was doing the bulk of the lead singing—"Clay wasn't doing much lead at that time"—so room existed for another tenor lead.

In 1957 the Pilgrim Jubilees finally recorded for a major gospel label. If Peacock was a quartet first prize and Specialty second prize, the Jubes ended up with third when they recorded four singles over three years for Nashboro. The Nashville-based label was owned by Ernie Young, who also ran a record shop and a large mail-order business. As gospel historian Anthony Heilbut notes, Nashboro was noted neither for its recording quality nor the sophistication of its record packaging, and its sales were almost exclusively in the South.[6] But Ernie Young knew what would sell to his market, and Nashboro had a significant roster of gospel artists, including Edna Gallmon Cooke, the Consolers, and the Swanee Quintet. In 1957 the Swanees were Nashboro's biggest-selling quartet, but the label also had several other groups, including the Spiritual Five—the Chicago group with which the Pilgrim Jubilees shared radio time on WSBC.

Cleave: "They said to us, 'You need to be recording. Why don't you go down to Nashboro and see if Mr. Young will take you.' Their manager—I can't remember his name—said, 'Come on. I'll talk to Mr. Young. He'll listen to me.' So we went on down there, and sure enough, he took us." **Clay**: "We got a contract. I think it was a two-year contract with a three-year option." **Major**: "Mr. Young was an old Swanee Quintet man—nobody could sing but the Swanees and Edna Gallmon Cooke." **Cleave**: "The Swanees were his money. We were trying to record and he'd say, 'Listen, listen to this.' He'd play something the Swanees had done and say, 'That's the way you're supposed to sound.' The Swanees and us are an entirely different style, but we couldn't say anything. We're trying to get on a record, so we knew better than to say anything. We messed up with Peacock—we weren't going to mess this up. So 'Yes sir, whatever. That's what the Swanees do? OK.' We recorded in his warehouse. Ernie's Record Mart. Sitting in there with nothing to protect nothing. Nothing for acoustics. Just barefaced with a naked mike." **Clay**: "The lead singer and the background singers sang on the same mike. And Mr. Young came out and said, 'Y'all got to cut them Ps out.' When we sang a word with a P in it, it would pop. In the end, he took a handkerchief and tied it round the mike to try to keep the Ps from coming in."

The primitive recording conditions and the pressure from Ernie Young to sound like the Swanee Quintet make the Pilgrim Jubilee's first efforts for Nashboro the least satisfying of their fledgling recording career. Two songs were recorded, "Gonna Work On" and "God Is Good to Me," issued on Nashboro 605. "Gonna Work On" is a remake of the song recorded for Specialty as "Soon Gonna Work 'Til My Day Is Done" and features the low-tenor lead singing of Johnny Felix. His rendition is competent, but it is easy to see why the Graham brothers might not have acclaimed his recruitment, as the Specialty recording is much the better version—a little faster than the Nashboro issue and with a crispness and urgency in the lead vocals that Ernie Young's one microphone and Felix could not replicate. The two versions are fundamentally the same song but with significant variations. Both start with the "work until my day is done" chorus and then go into a verse—but the verses are completely different. And where the Specialty version ends neatly with a third chorus, the Nashboro issue ends with a "vamp," or "drive"—the backing singers repeating the title line on one chord as the lead singer improvises over the top. The backing vocal is well back in the mix—probably because the singers were sharing the handkerchief-wrapped microphone with Johnny Felix—and its arrangement is a little less structured than that on Specialty, with a tentative start that would have been halted for another attempt in a more professional and disciplined recording studio. "God Is Good to Me" is a stronger performance, which Cleave leads with Johnny Felix coming in toward the end for a call-and-response sequence.

"God Is Good to Me" was in the Pilgrim Jubilee's repertoire before they left Mississippi, and Clay describes it as "one of those old songs." But Major Roberson says the Nashboro version is his. The two statements are not as irreconcilable as they seem. A common method of gospel songwriting is to take an existing theme and remodel it. Sometimes the change will be as little as a few altered words; sometimes it amounts virtually to grafting a new song on to an existing title. The Nashboro recording belongs in the "rewrite" end of the spectrum and bears very little resemblance to the song the Pilgrim Jubilees were singing in the 1940s. (No recording of that exists, but the group resurrected it in a 1996 concert recording.)[7] "Gonna Work On" is also a reworking of an established theme recorded in various forms by a number of quartets. Major Roberson recalls it as "one of the old songs we'd sing in church; I fixed it for the group."

Whatever the quality drawbacks of the two recordings, they placed the Pilgrim Jubilees on a national label, boosting their prestige and gaining them more bookings. The record sold well enough for the group to be called back on February 24, 1958, to record another single. Johnny Felix is almost certainly not present; he was another reluctant traveler and left the group around this time. **Clay**: "He started to move away from the singing, and he got himself a job. He was living in the Cabrini [*housing*] project on the North Side. One night he was walking home from his job and he was mugged. They took his pay packet, then shot him twice in the head and he died. That was around 1972." Guitarist Arthur Crume also left the group. He went not long after the first Nashboro recording session to join the Highway QCs, who were starting to enjoy recording success on the Vee Jay label. His replacement in the Pilgrim Jubilees was his brother, Rufus.

The Crumes are a Chicago gospel family worthy of a study in their own right. Brothers Arthur, Dillard, Leroy, Rufus, and Ray worked with many top gospel quartets; two other brothers, Floyd and Peter, also sang. Leroy was a longtime member of the Soul Stirrers from 1955, singing baritone and playing guitar. Ray Crume was singing tenor with the Highway QCs when Arthur left the Pilgrim Jubilees to join them; he also sang with the Soul Stirrers and in the mid- to late 1960s with the Bells of Zion. Arthur stayed with the QCs until the early 1960s; in 1964 he was with the Sensational Nightingales, and in 1965 he joined the Soul Stirrers, eventually becoming a mainstay of the group as its personnel changed over the years.[8]

The Pilgrim Jubilees' second Nashboro session brought Clay into the lead role for the first time on record, singing "John Behold Thy Mother." The sound on this session is more confident than on the first, and the instrumental accompaniment is expanded. **Cleave**: "We had that blind man sitting up there on piano. I can't remember his name. He played the same thing for everybody. When you heard one, you'd heard 'em all. He was [*Ernie Young's*] main man. When you needed piano, that's who you got." Clay's lead singing shows strongly the influence of his brothers, especially Cleave, and the backing vocal is much closer to the usual Pilgrim Jubilees' bass-accentuated sound than in the previous session—partly because Clay's lead role and the departure of Johnny Felix reduced its tenor component. The song was written by Kenny Madden and is a crucifixion narrative, taking its title and first verse from John 19:27, in which Christ from the cross charges one of his apostles to look after his mother, Mary.[9]

The other side of the Pilgrim Jubilees' second Nashboro single—Nashboro 625—was a reworking of "I Heard of a City," a "reward in heaven" standard sung by many gospel artists, including Mahalia Jackson, Clara Ward, and a number of quartets. Cleave takes the lead, and the piano part reveals that his observations on the limitations of "that blind man" are not unjustified. Overall, it is a restrained and controlled performance, but the backing singers—presumably becoming used to the microphone arrangement—make more use of harmony shifts and dynamics than they did on the first session. A third song, "I'll Be a Witness," was also recorded. **Cleave**: "Back then, you'd go to a record company and record one record. Two sides. There were no albums. You might give them something else to put 'on the shelf,' but that release was two sides." The practice of recording more songs than were required for a single 78-rpm or 45-rpm issue gave the company more choice in deciding what to release immediately, and the extra material could be kept "on the shelf" for later use if necessary. "I'll Be a Witness" was never released, and today the Pilgrim Jubilees remember little about it. Cleave sang lead, and it is almost certainly a version of the standard "I'll Be a Witness for My Lord."

The next recording session came a little more than a year later, on March 29, 1959, and again three songs were recorded. Left "on the shelf" was "On My Knees"; today, Cleave, Clay, and Major remember nothing about it. Issued on Nashboro 650 were "Father, I'm Coming Home" and "River of Jordan," both written by Major and with Cleave singing lead. By this time, the Pilgrim Jubilees had overcome their aversion to percussion, and Rufus Crume's guitar is augmented by an unidentified studio drummer as well as an instantly recognizable pianist. Studio facilities at Nashboro had obviously been improved since the first session, as the recordings are well balanced and the group—presumably relieved of the burden of sounding like the Swanee Quintet—sounds relaxed and confident. The songs are both Roberson compositions but are woven from familiar threads—even the titles have a "heard that before" feel. "Father I'm Coming Home" is based on the trust that living right will bring its reward—"When I've done all I can do down here / I want to be able to say, 'Father, I'm coming home.' " "River of Jordan" deals with maintaining religious faith in the face of adversity—"If you don't meet me at the river of Jordan, I'll stand there anyway." It has no connection with the well-known "Got to Cross the River of Jordan," but two of its verses borrow heavily from other well-known songs—"Job," the oft-recorded story of the Old Testament victim of a trial of strength between God and Satan, and "Touch the Hem of His Garment," a hit in 1956 for the Soul Stirrers.

The combination of familiar and new appealed to listeners, and "River of Jordan" was the Pilgrim Jubilees' most successful Nashboro recording. The group did one more three-song session for the company, on November 10, 1959; the issued recordings, on Nashboro 695, were the fast-moving Major Roberson composition "Jesus Help Me" and a slower rendition of the widely sung "Done Got Over," both with Cleave singing lead. But for unknown reasons the group's relationship with Ernie Young was souring. **Major**: "The last time . . . I don't know whether he was disgusted with us or whether he just didn't care for us or what. But he'd always given us fifty dollars to record—that was up-front money. This time, it was 'Y'all can record, but I can't give you fifty dollars this time. I'll give you twenty-five.' So that's where we ended, with that particular session." But if the end of their time with

Nashboro closed one door, others were opening. "River of Jordan" was the catalyst.

Major: "We got our start with that song. Edna Gallmon Cooke took sick and her manager, Barney Parks, wrote me a letter saying 'we'd like to have you come out and work with us.' Because he'd heard the record. So it was a good chance. I told all the guys, 'Hey, we got a chance to go on the road.' So I accepted."

The chance to travel with Edna Gallmon Cooke was a breakthrough for the Pilgrim Jubilees. The soulful-voiced Cooke was at the peak of her popularity and was—with the Swanee Quintet—one of Nashboro's top-selling artists. Through most of her career, her soft mezzo-soprano was backed by quartets, including the Radio Four, the Singing Sons—her main group—and the Southern Sons. Madame Cooke, as she was respectfully known, had frequent bouts of poor health and was only forty-nine when she died in 1967. Her manager and husband, Barney Parks, was singing baritone for the Dixie Hummingbirds when they made their first recordings in 1939. But soon after this, he decided his talent lay in managing gospel groups rather than singing with them.

Cleave: "Edna Gallmon Cooke was having [*health*] problems. She had a package going and she was booked up for six months—deposits paid, everything. And Barney Parks was wondering what he was going to do. Edna needed somebody to stand for those shows because she wasn't able to do them. 'River of Jordan' had got us booked in Jacksonville, Florida. The promoter there . . . she and Edna Gallmon Cooke were close friends. So Barney Parks was wondering what to do, and Mrs. Jackson—that was the promoter—says, 'Let me play you something.' She played that record. He said, 'Hey, they sound good.' She said, 'Do you think they could help?' He said, 'Could they do it?' She said, 'Yes, because they're ready.' That's what started us on the road."

The Pilgrim Jubilees' job was to sing on the bookings Parks had secured for Cooke. Cleave recalls that Cooke traveled with them but because of her illness did not perform, although she may have sung a few numbers on some shows. Cleave, Clay, and Major all say the tour was not lucrative. But it put them on the road as professional gospel singers. Day jobs were abandoned—"I didn't have time for no job," says Cleave. "Everywhere we went, the people wanted us back." The group was already building a reputation through its recordings and performances, but the association with Edna Gallmon Cooke accelerated this process, providing six months' worth of almost guaranteed audiences. As well, they were able to meet some of the top names in gospel music—artists and behind-the-scenes career-makers—on an almost equal footing as associates of another big name rather than as a relatively unknown group trying to break into the big time. This paid its biggest dividend when the Pilgrim Jubilees went with Cooke to a major gospel program in Atlanta in 1959.

8. Stretch Out

Clay: "We went to Atlanta with Edna Gallmon Cooke, and Barney Parks got us a two hundred dollar guarantee. But the man [*the promoter*] wasn't going to pay us. Barney said, 'Well Edna's not going on until you pay them.' So the man paid up and we hit that stage. And we were like little wild children up there, man." **Cleave**: "At the City Auditorium. With the Swan Silvertones, the Davis Sisters, the Soul Stirrers, the Blind Boys [*of Mississippi*], the Swanee Quintet. Oh my goodness, you know that was something! We were the new guest group. And they had our record ["*River of Jordan*"] on a loudspeaker [*mounted on a vehicle to publicize the program*] going down the street. I went across the street from the hotel to the restaurant to have some breakfast, and they came by with the loudspeaker and the song playing. The man from Peacock, Dave Clark, was sitting there. And when they went through playing our record, he asked the man at the restaurant, 'Do you know what group that is?' I said, 'I know them. That's the Pilgrim Jubilees. That's my group.' He said, 'I'd like to meet the group. Here's my card. I'm Dave Clark from Peacock Records.' I said to myself, look at this joker sitting up here pretending he's somebody. I took the card and I'm sitting there and all these people are coming in and 'Hi Mr. Clark', 'Hi Mr. Dave.' I said, 'Heyyy!' So I told him, 'My booking manager is in the hotel, in room 212—I'll never forget the room. He says, 'I'd like to meet with y'all and we'll get something together.' "

Major: "They brought me the news and I said, 'No, no. Not Peacock.' Because we were down there. . . . But he came by the hotel and said, 'Do you want to record for Peacock?' I said, 'Everybody would like to record for Peacock, but they don't want no Pilgrim Jubilees.' He says, 'Forget that. Do you want to record?' I said, 'Yes.' 'If I send you a recording contract, will you sign it?' 'Yes.' When he went out, I said, 'That man is phony! Walking around with his funny-looking clothes and Stetson hats and stuff.' So we were out for about another week, and when I got home, there's the envelope from Peacock. Opened it up and there's a contract. Everybody's rejoicing. We didn't read anything. We didn't think about an attorney. Lordy, if you could record for Peacock, you were top stuff! Everybody in the group put their name on the dotted line, and we sent it on back to him, right quick."

The skepticism about Dave Clark, while appearing to confirm that this was a group with a death wish when it came to recording success, was understandable. He wore stylish and costly clothing in outrageous combinations—"If you didn't really know clothing, you would think he was a bum," says Cleave—and had a speech impediment. But even in 1959 he was a legend in the recording industry, and his sixty years in music covered virtually every aspect of the business. Born in Jackson, Tennessee, in 1909, he graduated from college in 1934 and became a writer for *Down Beat* magazine. In 1936 he joined Jimmy Lunceford's orchestra, initially as a musician, then as an advance man, going ahead of the band as it toured to publicize its performances. In 1939 he graduated from Juilliard School of Music and went into record promotions work. He joined Peacock in 1954 and stayed until 1971. His main job during this time was promotions, but he also served as talent scout, producer, and songwriter and was as much identified with the label as was its owner, Don Robey. "When I say I want you, Mr. Robey's gonna call you," he told Cleave; the boast was also the truth. From Peacock, Clark went to Stax Records in Memphis until 1976, after which he joined the R&B and gospel label Malaco in Jackson, Mississippi, staying there until his death in 1995.[1]

The arrival of the contract ended any doubts about Clark. The Pilgrim Jubilees started preparing for their first Peacock recording session, even rejecting bookings generated by their appearances with Edna Gallmon Cooke to allow more rehearsal time. The main song they worked on was an up-tempo piece called "Stretch Out," which they had been singing for a while. Major had worked out its arrangement one evening when he and guitarist Rufus Crume were waiting for the rest of the group to arrive for rehearsal.

Major: "We were in the barbershop and the boy was shining somebody's shoes. I heard the ruffling of the rag—tipa, tipa, tipa [*he imitates the shuffle of the shoeshine rag*]—and I started thinking. I said, 'Rufus, get the guitar.' He said, 'Man, I don't feel like doing it now. Wait till rehearsal.' I said, 'No, I got something in my head. I'm gonna get it right now.' He said, 'Oh man, you're always doing stuff like this. If I like it, you're gonna have to give it to me.' I told him, 'If you'll help me with it, you can have it.' And that's how he got the biggest record I ever had in my life."

Because of Major's promise, Rufus Crume is credited as the writer on the Pilgrim Jubilees' recording of "Stretch Out." But he didn't write it, and the song wasn't Major's to give away. It has been in gospel repertoire since the mid-1940s under two names, "Stretch Out" and the original "In These Dark Hours of Distress." It was first recorded by Rosetta Tharpe with the Sam Price Trio in New York on July 1, 1947. Tharpe is credited as the arranger; no writer is named on the Decca label.[2] Over the next five years around a dozen different recordings—nine by quartets—were made of the song. The version Major acknowledges as his direct influence—"I used my version of it . . . but I used her words"—was made in 1957 as "Dark Hours" by the Chicago-based Roberta Martin Singers, with writer credits to Helen Shedrick and Z. R. McEachen, who registered it for performing rights with Hill and Range Songs, now part of Warner/Chappell Music, in 1951.[3] Pre- and post-1951 recorded versions have the same verse and chorus.

Oh Lord, we come now
Just as humble as we know how
With our hearts laying bare
As before Thee we bow
Dark clouds hover over us
Nowhere is there rest
Lord only Thee can save us,
In these dark hours of distress

Let us stretch out, stretch out, on God's word
'Til His comforting voice is heard
God giveth strength to go onward
In these dark hours of distress

On early recordings, the verse is universally taken at a slow, careful tempo, but treatments of the chorus differ. Soloists tended to sing the whole song at the same steady pace; quartets often livened it up with a sharp increase in pace for the chorus. But nobody gave the song the jet-propelled thrust of Major Roberson's shoeshine-derived arrangement.

The Pilgrim Jubilees' first Peacock recording session was held late in 1959 in Chicago. Although Peacock recorded a lot of its material in Houston, it also contracted producers and studios in other cities to avoid the expense of bringing artists from distant hometowns. In Chicago, the venue was Universal Studios on Ontario Street; the producer was Willie Dixon, a three hundred–pound titan far better known as a musician, songwriter, talent scout, and producer in Chicago's very active blues scene. Born in Vicksburg, Mississippi, he moved to Chicago in the 1930s and started singing and playing double bass with the Five Breezes and the Big Three Trio vocal groups. As Chicago blues evolved into the tough, strident electric sound pioneered by Muddy Waters, Dixon concentrated more on songwriting and studio session work. He played bass and produced sessions for most of Chicago's leading blues names, including Muddy Waters, Howlin' Wolf, and Little Walter. As well, he wrote hundreds of songs, many of which have become blues standards. Dixon started recording gospel through Dave Clark, whom he knew from a time when both worked for United and States Records in Chicago. "Don Robey would send me a letter to get the spiritual groups together and record 'em," Dixon says in his biography. "Just about every group they had I recorded."[4] Dixon also supplied backing musicians. His main stalwarts were drummers Clifton James and Odie Payne and pianist Lafayette Leake, all—like Dixon—much better know for their blues playing than for their gospel sessions work.

The Pilgrim Jubilees rehearsed their material carefully and arranged to meet at Universal. Cleave, Clay, Major, and Rufus arrived, but none of them knew that as well as being the day of their first Peacock session, this was the day Kenny Madden had decided to quit.

Major: "We're sitting there waiting for Kenny. And at that time, you weren't allowed but four hours for a session. We stood around looking at the clock, and it's dropped thirty minutes already. Willie says, 'Do you want me to call the man and stop your session? 'Cause you know Don Robey's gonna get mighty mad if you don't get this thing.' I said, 'We'll give him a few more minutes.' But he didn't show up. Then I said, 'Hey, what is this sitting in the corner?' He said, 'It's a bass fiddle.' I said, 'Who plays it?' He said, 'I play it.' I said, 'Why don't you try to play it with us?' He got it out and we started up. Oh Lord! That thing was going like a bullet. There weren't any groups on the road singing with a bass instrument until then. But after that, everybody fired their bass singers."

Cleave: "Major said, 'Hey, is there anybody here can play that thing sitting over there?' Willie Dixon says, 'I can.' We didn't know nothing about Willie Dixon. But man, we got on the song and . . . in fact, we recorded the rehearsal that we did. Clay just hit it, and that was what came out. The first take! And it was one of the biggest hits we had. That's what really put us on the road for good. Because we were the first that really made that bass thing popular. Groups just used to have bass singers, going poom, poom, poom with their mouths. Then we came out with that. And there was such a beat that they had it in the juke joints and everywhere. People were dancing to it."

Clay: "It was a mistake . . . no, it wasn't a mistake, it was the Lord's will. If our bass singer had been there, we wouldn't have used the upright bass. But he didn't make the session. And when that sucker [*the record*] hit the streets, it was wide! I was so glad Kenny Madden stayed home."

The reasons for Madden's departure appear to be twofold. He did not enjoy the Edna Gallmon Cooke tour because it paid poorly, and he also doubted that the Pilgrim Jubilees could succeed as a professional group. But as well, it appears, he had clashed with Major over his management. **Major**: "He didn't want to stay on the road. You see, when the doors were opened through Edna, we went out. But we weren't making any money, and he couldn't take it. That's the way it goes. Most of the first group you have, you'll lose it when you venture out. If it's not fruitful right away, somebody will say, 'You can't give me no money, so I'm going.' " **Clay**: "Kenny didn't think we could make it. He didn't want to leave his job to take a chance like we did. Also, he was mad at Major. He said, 'I wouldn't follow Major across the street.' When I met Kenny, him and Major were buddies. But when the Pilgrim Jubilees started moving, he said, 'I don't follow him.' But we weren't worried about what Kenny said. We worried about getting where we wanted to be. If we had listened to him, we wouldn't have gone anywhere. We'd have been at home. So we kept right on stepping. And following Major."

The Pilgrim Jubilees' recording of "Stretch Out" is a dramatic departure from previous versions. The first five seconds are low key, as Rufus plays three ascending guitar chords—A, C, and E—and Clay calls the opening "Oh Lord." But as he hits the next word, Willie Dixon ignites a three-minute musical explosion, propelling the singers on the rocket blast of his booming double bass. Clay sings the verse twice then goes into a free-form drive that builds in intensity as it progresses. Behind him, Cleave, Major, and Rufus try a couple of combinations, then settle into a response that alternates between three short "oh, oh, oh" syllables and one long "ohhh."

Oh Lord (Oh lord)
Jesus (Oh)
I call (Oh, oh, oh Lord)
My friend (Ohhhh)
I call (Oh, oh, oh)
'Cause you help me (Ohhhhh)
When I'm in trouble (Oh, oh, oh) . . .

The use of this section instead of the usual chorus means that, although the Pilgrim Jubilees called the song "Stretch Out," the words "stretch out" do not appear anywhere in it. Behind the vocals, Rufus Crume lays down a dense pattern of mainly open chords, and Dixon's bass plays a quick-fire walking pattern that he sometimes varies by playing down through the progression instead of up.

The use of double bass in gospel music was not new. In 1955 Willie Dixon recorded behind Rev. Robert Ballinger, a Chicago preacher, pianist, and singer; the pattern he used on Ballinger's fast-moving "This Train" is not too far removed from his playing on "Stretch Out." Guitarist and singer Maurice Dollison, who later played with the Pilgrim Jubilees before going on to minor secular fame under the name Cash McCall, described Dixon's approach to gospel bass: "It's like a I-VI-V-VI-I-VI-V-VI . . . it just keeps going. It would fit through all the changes . . . in any kind of quartet melody."[5] The use of double bass in quartets was not new either. The Golden Gate Quartet started using bass on its recordings in 1946—with piano, guitar, and drums—and several other quartets used the instrument through the late 1940s and 1950s. What made "Stretch Out" different was the prominent and aggressive role the bass played in the arrangement and, more important, that it replaced the bass singer. Even the Pilgrim Jubilees did not initially recognize the impact of what they had done and hired a replacement for Kenny Madden. But when the record hit the market in early 1960, they got the message. **Major**: "We were in Washington, D.C., when we first heard it. They played it, I guess, about ten times from eight o'clock that morning until about one or two in the afternoon. That was all you could hear. Then it was on all the jukeboxes. . . ." **Cleave**: "It was the one that just changed the whole feel . . . they called us the 'rock and roll Jubilees.' "

The other side of Peacock single 1819 was a much more sedate gospel standard, "Evening Sun"—also known as "Life's Evening Sun"—which came from the repertoire of Major's former group, the Pilgrim Harmonizers. "It was their song," recalls Clay, "but we liked it." The double bass is again prominent, but the feel of the song is almost leisurely, giving Clay space to ornament his lead vocal part while the backing singers echo each line. Apart from "Stretch Out" and "Evening Sun," details of what was recorded at that first Peacock session will probably never be known for certain. Documentation doesn't exist, and Cleave, Clay, and Major can't recall specifics of other songs, although all believe more were recorded—a four-hour session was usually expected to produce four songs. Based on the sound of the recordings and the vocal and instrumental lineup, it seems probable that the Pilgrim Jubilees' other two songs were "Steal Away," a standard with roots going back to spirituals, and the Major Roberson composition "Jesus Come Help Me," a remake of the last Nashboro single. These two were issued in 1962 as the Pilgrim Jubilees' third Peacock single.

"Stretch Out"/"Evening Sun" changed the lives of the Pilgrim Jubilees. They'd been on the road for six months before the session, but that was under the patronage of Edna Gallmon Cooke. Now, the "rock and roll Jubilees" were in demand on their own account. The first move was to hire another bass singer. **Clay**: "We still had it in our minds that we needed a bass singer. So we got Mack Robertson. He was with the Bells of Zion. Mack didn't have the best bass voice, but he had that superior look. He was six foot two, very handsome. He had beautiful teeth, and his mouth was full of gold. When he walked on the stage, people would be looking at him. He gave the group a little prestige. But after we started to travel . . . well, every person can't just jump up and leave a job like we did. Mack just couldn't see leaving his job and going on the road. So when he dropped out, we didn't look around for another bass singer. Because it had got to where if you heard a bass singer in a group, it made them sound old."

One side effect of the popularity of "Stretch Out" was that it put the final dampener on Clay's alternative plans for a career as a professional boxer. "They called me the Black Eel, and I had three professional fights. But my manager kept telling me, 'Clay, you've got a lot to learn. Slow down.' I wanted to fight a boy named Cedell Simon. My manager said, 'You couldn't beat him.' I said, 'I can beat him.' He said, 'I'll tell you what, do you think you could whip me?' He was an old man! He said, 'Tomorrow, we'll go two rounds. I just want to show you something.' I went in the ring with him, and I never did touch him for two rounds. And my eyes were swollen, lips were busted. That was so devastating to me . . . a man that age and he knew that much more than me and here I am turning pro—I've got too far to go. So I went on and pursued my singing."

A group with a hit record, especially a new young group, was in big demand, and bookings flowed in for the Pilgrim Jubilees. Venues varied widely, just as they do today, from small programs in school halls to much grander affairs in auditoriums seating several thousand. Then as now, a program usually included several groups, and promoters would sometimes assemble several acts into a package that would make hard-driving swings through large areas, traveling hundreds of miles by day and singing nearly every night. Bookings came either directly from local promoters or through agencies acting as intermediaries between artists and the people wanting to engage them. The Pilgrim Jubilees were soon sharing stages with some of the leading quartets—and discovering that some groups weren't entirely happy about the prospect.

Clay: "An agency in New York wanted to take two artists—us and another of the main artists [*a quartet*] from Chicago. We said, 'We're gonna make some money now!' Then all of a sudden it went dead, and we couldn't figure it out. Didn't hear from them again. Two years later, we were working in Chicago with a lady called Isabel Johnson [*a promoter*]. She said, 'I know what happened. The artists that were signing up with you told the man at the agency . . . he asked about the Pilgrim Jubilees and they said, 'Well, they're all right, man, but all of them carry guns, and they don't stand no mess.' So here's a man who doesn't know us very well, but he's going to book us. But here's eight niggers got eight guns? Who'd want to be bothered with them? Of course we didn't have eight guns. But that was their way to reap all the benefit by themselves. A lot of different things like that happened to us."

Finances were another area in which reality fell well below the dream. The group set itself what it thought was a realistic goal before accepting the invitation to tour with Edna Gallmon Cooke. **Major**: "Before we went, we all talked. If you're leaving home, you're leaving everything. Now, what's the least we could work for? And we all came to the same point—if we could make ten dollars a day or fifty dollars a week . . . at fifty dollars a week [*each*], we could make it. But wasn't ten dollars a day. Sometimes a dollar, dollar and a quarter! You pawned your rings, pawned whatever you had to buy some food. Once we recorded for Peacock, the guarantees got a little bit bigger, and so it was a little easier. But even then . . . you'd sing and take what they gave. The biggest guarantee I was getting was fifty to a hundred and fifty dollars. I remember the first ten thousand people we sung to, in Newark, New Jersey. We got a hundred and fifty dollars. For singing to ten thousand people! Ronnie Williams was the only promoter there at the time. You came to Ronnie or you didn't come to New York. So he paid what he felt like. We worked hungry more times than anything else. There was hardly anything to send back home to your family."

The guarantee was a minimum payment, agreed when the booking was made. In theory, the final payment could be above the guarantee if the program was successful; in practice, the guarantee was almost always also the maximum. Promoters paid none of the groups' expenses. Travel, accommodations, food—all had to come out of the fee, and artists quickly learned which were the best cheap motels and restaurants. One way of supplementing the guarantee was by selling records at programs. On a trip soon after "Stretch Out" was issued, the Pilgrim Jubilees sold all the copies they had and had to find more. **Cleave**: "We were going through Nashville, so we stopped at Ernie's Record Mart. When we went in, Mr. Young said, 'Why wouldn't y'all give that to me?' We'd tried our best to give him 'Stretch Out.' But he said, 'Who ever heard of anything as ridiculous as stretch out on gospel, stretch out on God's word?' And he would not accept it. So when he said, 'Why wouldn't you give that to me?' I said, 'Mr. Young, we tried our best to give you that song. But you didn't hear us. You were talking about what the Swanees sound like.' " Ironically, Ernie Young's favorite group recorded a version of the song, "Let Us Stretch Out," for Nashboro around 1954.

Travel for the groups on the road was by car, even if the booking was in California or Texas. Flying was far beyond the budget of any gospel quartet. The Pilgrim Jubilees' first car was a De Soto limousine, bought for the 1955 trip to California. "We bought it at a good price from an old white man," says Clay. "It was kinda old, but it was comfortable." When they went on the road with Edna Gallmon Cooke, they were using a Dodge owned by Kenny Madden. When he left, he let the group keep the car. "We wore it out, all the way out, on the road," says Major. The Dodge was eventually replaced by an Oldsmobile, the Oldsmobile by a Buick. The one thing all the cars had in common was that they were large, powerful, and reliable—large and powerful because they had to carry five or six men and their baggage on journeys covering hundreds of miles, reliable because today's four hundred–mile journey could be followed tomorrow by another just as long or longer. **Cleave**: "We would average more than a hundred thousands miles in a year. Usually about a year and a half was about as long as you could keep a vehicle—to have it in good shape and be confident it would take you where you were going. You're putting a lot of pressure on it, hauling loads and people, and it's got to be in shape. Cross that hundred thousand, it's ready to be traded."

The success of "Stretch Out" kept the Pilgrim Jubilees busy through 1960. Toward the end of the year, they returned to Universal in Chicago to record a follow-up single. The group had expanded again, with the addition of lead and tenor singer Percy Clark. "He'd been singing with two or three groups in Chicago," says Cleave. "I can't think of their names, except I know he was with the Holy Wonders." Again, it appears the move to hire him came from Major. **Cleave**: "We had one man that felt like that [*that*

Clark was needed]. We didn't need another lead singer. But he had a beautiful voice and was very highly liked. And we let him in for . . . even more strength, I guess. But we didn't need him." The main song for the new session was "Walk On," written by Peacock's Dave Clark. It was common practice for record company executives to hijack authorship of songs as a form of kickback, but in this case it appears Clark probably was the author. Cleave is a little skeptical, saying, "Dave Clark wrote it—or he went in the name of writing it, anyway." But Major believes Clark wrote the song. "It's Dave's," he says. "We hadn't heard that before Dave." The other side of the new record was a Kenny Madden composition, "I See a Man," led by Cleave. The accompaniment once again featured Willie Dixon's double bass, with Rufus Crume playing guitar and one of Dixon's blues-playing associates on drums. A pianist was also used—almost certainly Lafayette Leake, who Cleave and Clay recall as the pianist on all their Chicago recordings through the 1960s.

"Walk On" starts with a spoken introduction—the Pilgrim Jubilees' first recorded use of a technique that would later become a staple of their performances. Over a hummed backing vocal, Percy Clark intones, "I'd like to tell you a story 'bout Moses when he was leading the children of Israel across the Red Sea . . ." going on to tell how when the Israelites were trapped between the pharaoh's chariots and the Red Sea, "Moses walked off a few paces and looked up toward heaven and I believe this was the voice (that) descended from above, saying these words . . ." and moving into the song—"Walk on, in my name / You don't have to be uneasy, walk on. . . ." The accompaniment is dominated by the bass, and Rufus Crume does not play. He is present on "I See a Man," setting up a riff that is the basis of a strongly rhythmical calypso-styled accompaniment featuring clattery woodblock percussion. The two songs were issued as Peacock 1830 in 1961. The record didn't have the impact of "Stretch Out," but it sold well, with "Walk On" initially attracting radio play—not surprisingly, as its author was also responsible for promoting it. But its popularity created a problem when Percy Clark quit after only about six months as a Pilgrim Jubilee.

Cleave: "We cut him on that 'Walk On'—and I don't know why that happened. They should have come back out with Clay, because he had a two-side hit. But Percy did it, and then he quit the group about a week before it was released. [*Clay remembers the departure as being a month after the* *record came out.*] He was married and he had a baby, and he had domestic problems. So he quit to come home. But they put that record out, and 'Walk On' was the plug side—the side they told the DJs to play. But the Lord blessed us, and the DJs just happened to flip it over to 'I See a Man' with that kinda calypso beat. And it just took off!" **Clay**: "So they weren't playing 'Walk On' any more. And it was a blessing to us. Because people didn't miss Percy. If the DJs had kept playing Percy, people would have been wanting Percy. That's when I opened my eyes. I said, 'Now anybody else that comes in here is going to have to be secondary.' And I said to my brother, 'Cleave, I know we're not the baddest lead singers in the world, but I think we've got enough lead singers.' "

From that time, no one was ever again hired as a lead, although other singers did join the group. Percy Clark was replaced quickly by a singer whose time with the group was brief and unmemorable enough that only Cleave remembers him being there at all. "There was another boy we got to sing tenor. I can't think of the kid's name. He was just there for about eight or ten months." That Clay doesn't remember this singer is not entirely surprising, because in 1961 he had another problem to handle—the U.S. Army. He had become eligible for the draft in 1954 but had never registered. Now time was running out.

Clay: "I thought you were supposed to register when you were twenty-one. But it was eighteen. And when I found that out, I was twenty-one. So I ducked and hid and ran. One day I came home and there was a note on my door from a detective downtown. I went to his office and he said, 'Hey Clay.' I said, 'How do you know it's me?' He said, 'I've been following you for two years.' He said, 'You're a good guy. That's why I called you in here. I could have come and picked you up. But now I can say you turned yourself in. Now, I want you to go down to the draft board and register.' So I went down and they told me to come back five days later to do my tests—the physical and all that. And I used my little gimmick that I had, that was given down through the years from black boys. And they turned me down. [*He is initially reluctant to reveal the 'little gimmick' but eventually relents.*] I got some sulfur. This trick saved a lot of guys. See, away back, the white man would have two or three [*black*] families living on his farm, and they would have two or three sons apiece. When the army called for his sons, he would substitute one of the black boys for his son. So they started learning tricks to keep from going into the army and taking the white boy's rap. They would get sulfur and a couple of hours before their physical, they'd sit over that sulfur can and inhale it. You light it and sit over it and breathe that yellow smoke. It stuff your lungs up. They become congested and tight, and it sounds like you got asthma. After a while it goes. But when the doctor's checking you, it's wheezing."

After two successful singles, the Pilgrim Jubilees were ready for their next recording career move, their first album. Peacock PLP-105 is very much the Pilgrim Jubilees as before, with Willie Dixon's double bass as the foundation of the accompaniment and a mixture of traditional and group-composed songs. Dave Clark's involvement is obvious. Instead of being named for the group's hit, the album is titled *Walk On*, and neither "Stretch Out" nor "Evening Sun" is on it.[6] **Cleave**: "They should have come out with a 'Stretch Out' album with that big national hit on it. But Dave Clark made the album and called it *Walk On*." As a substitute for the hit, the group included "Stretch Out No. 2," a loosely assembled pastiche that rectifies the omission of the title phrase from the original record by making it the dominant part of the backing vocal. The song is lively and up-tempo but sounds underprepared and disjointed. It is credited to Rufus Crume but was assembled by Major Roberson, who today is scathing about his creation. "It was the ugliest thing you ever heard. It was a mess. I thought I could come back with Part Two and get another big record. But the feeling isn't there. There was nothing to it." "I See a Man," the successful B-side of "Walk On," is on the album, as is "Steal Away," probably from the group's first Peacock session. Percy Clark leads on "Separation Line," an adaptation of a standard that made its first appearance on record in the 1920s. Although the album has twelve tracks, only eleven are by the Pilgrim Jubilees. The twelfth is "King's Highway" by Rev. Robert Ballinger. Its appearance on the album is a mystery, but it was recorded at about the same time as the Pilgrim Jubilees' tracks, and tapes of the two sessions were possibly sent to Houston together.

Although the Pilgrim Jubilees' use of double bass instead of a bass singer created a wave that swept through the quartet world, they did not have their own bass player—and concert audiences wanted to hear one. **Cleave**: "The recording companies put on extra instruments. Then when you go on stage, you don't have all those instruments so you don't have that sound you had on that record. That caused singers to start adding on more and more. . . . We used to tune the regular guitar down low to run the bass line. And we went that way until we found somebody we thought had what we wanted as a bass player. That was Roosevelt English. Roosevelt was with Edna Gallmon Cooke when we first heard him. But he wanted to be a Pilgrim Jubilee. What drew him to the group was our beat . . . the beat and our way of singing. We sang the way he felt it should be done, so he could do his best, he could let himself go with it. Not just in a professional way, but in a soul way. That's why nobody could beat him doing what he was doing." English was a guitarist when he joined the group and initially used a regular six-string guitar tuned low. But within a short time, he was using a proper bass instrument. Not a double bass, as used by Willie Dixon, but an amplified bass guitar. With this heavy propulsive beat anchoring it, the Pilgrim Jubilees' sound was fully established. **Clay**: "He was the best 'drive' man that's ever been on the road—everybody will tell you that. Roosevelt English had the drive, he had the Jubilees' stomp."

9. The Drive

"The drive," "the beat"—these are the phrases the senior Pilgrim Jubilees use to define the elements that make their music different. None of the group members has any formal musical training, so their arranging of their songs is largely an intuitive process of trial and error, guided by past experience and balancing the traditional Jubes' style with the need to keep the sound modern and of interest to today's audiences. But all of the Pilgrim Jubilees agree that the core of their musical identity lies in the rhythm, the blueprint for which was drawn up at the first Peacock recording session. And all believe the blueprint has been studied carefully by the quartets that followed them. **Clay**: "We didn't realize what we were doing. Struck gold and didn't know it. 'Stretch Out' set the trend for that beat. If a quartet goes into a drive, it's going to end up Pilgrim Jubilees.[1] That's what's kept us alive so long—they're still hanging around our style. You can't get away from our beat." **Major**: "I started arranging for the Jubes years ago. And my thing was to be sure that if I took a song somebody else wrote, that the Jubes didn't sing that song like the writer or anybody else who had an arrangement of the same song. I'd bring the song in, and all the guys would sit down and listen. And everybody would be picking on it. When we finished with it, it didn't sound like anybody else. Whether it sells or not, it's not going to sound like anybody else's stuff." **Cleave**: "Just about everybody out here's got something of the Jubilee beat. Everybody! Well, not the real old groups that had already made their way—the Dixie Hummingbirds, or the Sensational Nightingales. But the rest? Every last one of them that come up after us."

Obviously this claim is not going to attract any great support in a field where each group prides itself on its individuality. But one unreserved endorsement comes from the Canton Spirituals, who invited Cleave and Clay to join them in 1999 when they recorded a live album and videotape in Jackson, Mississippi.[2] In an interview inserted into the video segment in which the Graham brothers appear, Cantons' singer and guitarist Cornelius Dwayne Watkins talks of the influence the Jubes have had on his group and on quartet singing: "Their sound and their style is so much a part of me till it'll never leave. You can hear their style in much of our music. . . . Our music has always been influenced by the sound of the Pilgrim Jubilees. I don't think there will ever be another group that will come into the gospel arena . . . they gave all the groups a style to sing." On their previous CD, the Cantons recorded Major Roberson's "Father I'm Coming Home"—recorded by the Pilgrim Jubilees for Nashboro in 1959.[3] Their concert recording of "Mississippi Poor Boy" ends with a drive that has too many similarities to the Jubes' "Don't Let Jesus Down" to be coincidence, whether it is unconscious imitation or deliberate tribute.[4] "The fact of the matter is that a group can't hardly do a beat without running into the Jubes," says Major. "The Jubes brought the beat out here."

Cleave offers the closest to a musical analysis of the Pilgrim Jubilees' style with the apparently enigmatic statement, "The best thing that happens to us is on the 'one.' Bam! There! Foot, there. That's Jubilees." He's referring to the stresses in a bar, defined by the foot-operated bass drum. Where most groups usually accentuate the second beat of a bar—One TWO—the Pilgrim Jubilees more often accentuate the first beat—ONE Two. Most of the impetus in the Jubes' music comes from the bass guitar rather than from the drums. The group used drums—played by session musicians—in the recording studio from 1959, but on the road its only accompaniment in the early days was guitar and bass. Today, the Pilgrim Jubilees can't remember when they first took a drummer on the road with them—or who that drummer was—but it wasn't until the late 1960s. Major Roberson recalls that, despite the widespread use of drums on recordings, few groups used them onstage until at least the mid-1960s. "The Clouds [*Mighty Clouds of Joy*] were the first I know that started using drums. And they were so noisy that we used to laugh about it."

Of all the vaguely remembered figures who have played transitory support roles in the Pilgrim Jubilees story, drummers are the most ephemeral. **Cleave**: "Now drummers, they're bouncy. I haven't seen a real drummer yet that wasn't flaky. We've had a lot of drummers—I can't even call their names." **Clay**: "Drummers always come and go. It's hard to find a drummer that'll settle down for a long time." Despite their seemingly peripheral status, drummers are now a key part of the Pilgrim Jubilees' sound. Once they became a regular part of the line-up, the relationships between instruments—and the relationship between instruments and singers—became more elaborate. Discussing the playing of former and would-be Jube drummer Greg "Bobo" Harris, Cleave said: "He's a good drummer. But he's used to playing that leaning-forward beat like the Violinaires. With us, he's got to lay back. A lot of our stuff calls for simplicity with the drums. Keep it simple." Much of the character of the Pilgrim Jubilees' sound comes from the way the bass guitar propels the rhythm while the drums simultaneously hold it back—a push-pull effect that creates a dynamic tension within the song. The lead singers then have the option of singing on the beat with the bass or fractionally behind with the drums. But it all comes undone if a drummer starts pushing. **Clay**: "He has what we call a pocket that he has to get in. The songs seem to be going faster than they are, but we always tell him to get in the pocket, to kinda back off—lay back." Failure to "lay back" gives a double push to the song instead of the desired push-pull, the tempo starts to accelerate, and the singers find themselves trying to fit into an accompaniment that is no longer providing the foundation they need.

That foundation is laid when the group starts learning a song. Creating an accompaniment is ultimately a collective exercise, but one of the attributes necessary for being a Pilgrim Jubilee musician is the ability to do as one is told. **Major**: "Every song I write, I give the musicians the sound. You don't just automatically come up with the music for the Pilgrim Jubilees. The song brings the music. So I make the music with my mouth, say 'This is the way this music goes.' And be sure he [*the musician*] does it just like that. Don't let him substitute anything. Get your basics first. Then if he wants to add a little something—go! Because when a song comes to me, the words, the arrangement and the music all come to me at the same time, and I put it all in place. So when I get to the guitar—or whoever I want to lay it down with—I already know how it goes. All he's got to do is listen to me. Because if you carry it through the way I say, it's gonna sound like the Jubes. It's the same with Clay's songs. He knows what he wants with the music. And sometime it takes three weeks or a month to get the musicians on to the music that you want."

Roosevelt English was able to give the Pilgrim Jubilees exactly what they wanted. So was Rufus Crume. But soon after the *Walk On* album was issued, Rufus left the Pilgrim Jubilees.[5] Another Crume brother, Dillard, joined the group; he traveled with it for a few months but didn't make any recordings. He was followed by Dewheel Wallace, brother of Richard Wallace, longtime guitarist for the Mighty Clouds of Joy.[6] Wallace was with the Pilgrim Jubilees for only six months before being called into the army. The next guitarist was Chicagoan Maurice Dollison, a talented musician who could play guitar and bass and sing most vocal parts. But he couldn't reach the high fifth Rufus Crume had taken, so the group also took on another singer, Charles Green. "When Charles came to the group, he didn't know anything—we had to tell him everything," says Clay. "But he had the voice and he wanted to be a singer. His cousin, Robert Dixon, was a singer [*with Chicago's Salem Travelers*], and that's what he wanted to be."

Despite his lack of singing experience, Green made an immediate impact on the Pilgrim Jubilees. **Clay**: "I give him credit for the look, the dressing of the group. Charles was a very handsome guy. And when he came in, we were still wearing Fruit of the Looms, cotton socks and stuff like that. But when we saw the silk socks and things he was wearing, the Jubes went to the silk socks. We went to the silk shorts and bikinis and spit shined shoes. We were looking at all this, and we're not going to let anybody come up and out-dress us. And first thing you know, we were the dressiest things on the road."

In recent times, the line between gospel and secular has become ill-defined, as young gospel performers borrow extensively from pop music's sounds and presentation. In this environment, the traditional-styled quartets who still sing deliberately about and to God stand almost as paragons of religious virtue. But in 1960s it was the quartets who occupied the ambiguous territory between sacred and secular, wrapping their religious message in all the showbiz trimmings. Matching tailored uniforms, onstage choreography, techniques for evoking audience reaction—all were (and still are) part of the worldly side of the business of singing gospel music. For some groups, even the physical appearance of the members was an element to be considered.

Major: "We had a thing when we first went on the road. If you wanted to be in the Pilgrim Jubilees, we had a couple of songs you had to be able to sing. And you had to weigh so much, you had to be so tall, and you had to look so good, or else you couldn't be a Jube. That's the truth. You had to pass all those tests, your qualification had to be . . . first, look at you. The appearance had to be there. Then we had a song, 'So Good,' a smooth musical thing. And if your voice didn't blend in that song, you were out!"

The young Pilgrim Jubilees were undeniably handsome men, and under Charles Green's tutelage they concentrated on dressing and looking their best when they went out to sing the Lord's praises. Today, Clay believes this was one of the reasons they had problems with some of the older groups with whom they were sharing stages. "We never did get support from any of the artists on the road. The Pilgrim Jubilees were always downrated. And I figured it out after the years passed why those other artists were like that. Because of jealousy. The Pilgrim Jubilees were the sharpest-dressing group on the road. And we were noted as the best-looking group on the road. That's not bragging. It was just fact."

Comments like this provide ammunition for critics who say the quartets too often succumb to show-business glitter and temptations and lose sight of their spiritual mission. Not all quartets, particularly in the heyday of the style, were faithful to the tenets they sang about. Howard "Slim" Hunt, a member of the Supreme Angels since 1958, says many quartet artists—including him—in the 1950s and 1960s were "shaking and faking—just going through the motions." "We could jump around on the stage, and the old people would think we were happy. But I wasn't happy in the Spirit, I was just happy to be on the road." Hunt became a committed Christian when he was saved in 1979 and now pastors his own church in North Carolina as well as singing with his group.[7] The Pilgrim Jubilees also know of gospel performers who are not saved. **Major**: "Like Sam Cooke. He said,

'No, I never belonged to a church. Ain't never been baptized. I just sing.' There's a lot more like that. I'm not judging them, but they admit it. You've got 'em in the pulpit. There's some ministers preaching and they haven't been saved. They feel they want to do the job, somebody told them they've got the talent to do it. And they go out and they find they got a way to drag people in—and they do. And then some of them go for the money they can get out of it."

While the gospel music world does contain artists whose commitment to Christianity and its lifestyle is somewhat less than might be expected, some of the criticism leveled at professional quartets is based on idealism or even naïveté. It can be argued that no professional gospel quartet can fulfil the expectations of the truly devout, as turning professional immediately compromises the idealistic focus on spirituality. As well as singing for the Lord, the professional group is singing for its livelihood and therefore has to concern itself with worldly matters such as presentation, appearance, and pleasing the crowd to ensure a steady flow of bookings and preserve that livelihood. To some hardline church folk, seeking payment for singing gospel music is wrong; for the professional group, it's a necessary preliminary to paying the rent and eating. Often the mere fact that a group has continued to sing gospel music is testimony to the religious commitment of its members. Many quartet artists—including most of the Pilgrim Jubilees—have rejected lucrative offers from secular music, indicating that something stronger than the glamour of driving thousands of miles for payments far below what they could earn in R&B or pop music is keeping them on the gospel highway.

The Pilgrim Jubilees are all Baptists. Cleave and Major are members of the Greater Whitestone Baptist Church; Clay worships at the sanctified North Side Church of God in Christ—the church his mother joined soon after she came to Chicago—but still regards himself as a Baptist. All three made their commitments to Christ during childhood in Mississippi, and all regard themselves as being under the guidance and protection of the Holy Spirit and on a mission to glorify it.

Clay: "We pray and we've got business. That soul is there within us. We do wrong stuff—every night, I have to say 'Lord, why did you let me do this?' But I ask for forgiveness. I never asked Him for anything yet that it didn't work out. I never got in a tight place, a strain or didn't know what tomorrow's gonna bring that it didn't work for me. It might look like I'm fixing to drown, then all of sudden here comes a boat to pick me up. It took me some years to realize it. I thought it was just happening. But He's really got something for me to do. And I know it. Sometimes my feet get dirty, then He washes them off and 'Now don't you go back and step in that mud again.' I try to go around that mud, but then I find another puddle. [*He laughs*.] But we're all God's children."

Cleave: "People come to your shows for different reasons. And those that come to admire, I don't want to turn them around. Let them come on and admire. When they get there, I've got something good to tell them. I've got something they need to know. So I've got to get what I'm doing, what I'm about, over to them. I don't want them to run them away before I can say what I want to say. And God knows, I'm thankful for every moment He gives me. He made it possible for me. The Lord has blessed me to be here, and I give Him the praise for it.

Major: "What we're doing, it's very important to be saved. It's very important to keep yourself to a certain thing so you can be spiritually led."

The Pilgrim Jubilees spent much of the 1960s traveling. Clay recalls it as "the same kind of program we do now"—a succession of small-town venues paying two hundred or three hundred dollars each, with the occasional larger show yielding a better payday. Through most of the 1960s and into the 1970s they played the annual gospel extravaganza at one of the premier African American venues, the Apollo Theater in New York—three performances a day, four a day on weekends. These shows featured the top gospel acts; the Pilgrim Jubilees were the headliners only once, "but we were there in the show—we must have worked the Apollo for ten years," says Major. The success of the *Walk On* album sustained them through 1962; no singles apart from "Steal Away"/"Jesus Come Help Me" were issued in that year. In 1963 three singles were issued. Although the group now had Roosevelt English and his electric bass, the first two 1963 releases have Willie Dixon playing double bass and were probably "on the shelf" recordings from around the time of the *Walk On* album. "Unmovable" (Peacock 1872) is credited to Major Roberson but is an up-tempo reworking of the spiritual "I Shall Not Be Moved" featuring Clay's lead singing. Cleave takes the lead on the reverse side, "This Morning," a slower-paced Roberson composition built around the traditional giving thanks theme of "the Lord woke me up this morning . . . ," frequently heard in song and prayer. "I'm On the Right Road Now" (Peacock 1894), also written by Major, revisits the calypso lope of "I See a Man," with guitar, double bass, and drums. Major cannot recall whether he or Kenny Madden wrote the song on the reverse side, "Restless Soul," but it bears all the hallmarks of Major's writing, taking its opening line, "Oh Lord, you know I have no friend like Thee" from the traditional "I Can't Feel at Home in This World Any More" and using it as the basis for a new song.

The electric bass made its first appearance on a Pilgrim Jubilees' record on 1963's third release, Peacock 1899. The up-tempo side is "Wonderful," a song that Major Roberson brought to the group. "I'm not the original writer," he says. "I just rearranged it. I'd heard it sung around me for years." The song is a version of "Won't It Be Wonderful," recorded in 1955 by the Davis Sisters, a Philadelphia group led by the powerful contralto of Ruth "Baby Sis" Davis.[8] Their version moves at a steady pace; the Pilgrim Jubilees' reworking takes the song into overdrive, pushed by a driving bass line and overlaid with tinkling piano fills. The bass owes much to Willie Dixon's "Stretch Out" sound, but Roosevelt English uses the characteristics of the electric instrument to create a denser and more flowing sound than is possible on the acoustic bass.

Although "Wonderful" was the "hit" side of Peacock 1899—Major recalls that it sold more than fifty thousand copies—the other side had a greater long-term effect on the Pilgrim Jubilees. "True Story" introduced another new direction for the group, one that has been a core part of its performances ever since—the "sermonette." Sermonettes, which gained in popularity from the early 1960s, are a form of narration with preaching overtones. They start with a story told by the lead singer in semipreaching cadence while the rest of the group hums or sings softly in the background. Often, the last line of the story is also the first line of the song it is introducing; if it isn't, the story line will lead into the song.

Sermonettes, especially those of quartets, sometimes involve "testimony," in which the singer tells of a personal religious experience or of surviving a life-threatening incident through the grace of God. Composed narratives are drawn in broad stereotypical sweeps; while story lines vary widely, they are populated by an abundance of gray-haired old mothers and ministers, wayward children who finally find the right path, and dutiful children who reap the rewards of not straying from it. Common to all is the theme of overcoming or dealing with adversity through Christian faith. In a study of New York City quartets, Ray Allen points out that sermonettes, whether testimonies or composed tales, fulfill a number of functions.[9] In the mechanics of performance, they provide a bridge between songs and introduce variety into the group's program. More important, they personalize the performance and the songs, building a rapport between singers and audience and giving the song immediacy by tying it to a story of events or circumstances with which the audience can relate. **Major**: "You have an audience for that type of stuff. They get off into that story when you start to tell it. So after a while, you hear a reaction in the audience. That's because that person has been through this, or they know somebody who's maybe going through it at this time."

One of the most popular sermonette performers was—and is—Dorothy Norwood, a onetime member of the popular Chicago female group the Caravans, who started recording her "stories" in 1963. Another ex-Caravan, Shirley Caesar, has also had several successes with sermonettes. The leaders in quartet "preaching" are Clay Graham—who writes all the Pilgrim Jubilees' sermonettes—and Mighty Clouds of Joy lead singer Joe Ligon, both of whom made their entries into the field in the early 1960s, not long after Dorothy Norwood. Clay believes the foundations for the style were laid by the popularity of Detroit preacher C. L. Franklin, who between the early 1950s and the mid-1970s had more than seventy sermons issued on record. But Clay's "preaching" style is strongly influenced by Rev. Julius Cheeks of the Sensational Nightingales. "He used to do a lot of explaining of his songs. Not making up big long stories, but he would emphasize and paint a picture. And he did it so well. So I started talking onstage and presenting my songs. I found out I had a preaching voice that had soul in it, and I just went further and further. And it was real popular. It's faded out now, to an extent. But people still wait on that Pilgrim Jubilees album or that Clouds album to see what Clay's saying, what Joe's got to say."[10]

"True Story," Clay's first sermonette, is a slightly tentative entry into the field, as the story takes only about half the record's two minutes and forty seconds. A more usual ratio is two-thirds story to one-third music; on some, just enough singing is crammed on to the end to establish what song the story is illustrating—although onstage, story and song can continue for as long as audience and singer want. But despite its relative brevity, "True Story" follows the formula as Clay sets the scene, presents a main character who will draw listeners' sympathy and with whom they can relate, details with vivid imagery the hardships the character has endured, and then offers reassurance with the song "He Won't Forget":

> I had a conversation the other day,
> With an old friend of mine, who was about eighty-four or eighty-five years of age.
> He says "Son I've had many things to happen to me in life."
> Said, "I've been pushed back further than any country trail."
> One more thing, he said, "I've been hit harder, I've been hit harder than baseball
> And knocked further than any home run."
> Said, "Son, I've been a slave for man down through the years."
> Says "Son, you should see my back, my back bears more stripes than any zebra mule."
> Said, "But listen, it's one thing, it's one thing, I would like to know
> When I come down, when I come down to die,"
> Said, "I wonder will the Lord, will the Lord forget me?"
> You know what I told him?
> I told him, I told him these words
> [*the song starts*]
> "He won't forget you . . ."

Clay: "This was a guy's life. He was on the North Side of Chicago at the time, and he was talking about the different things that had happened to him. He was telling me how hard things had been and how he had been mistreated. I just wrote those kind of lyrics. And I put in the little bit about the zebra mule and baseball. Those are my lines. I wrote the song, too, that's mine."

The group's next recording success came from another change in direction. The Pilgrim Jubilees' reputation was built on full-speed-ahead drive material, increasingly written within the group and performed in solid 4/4 time. "Old Ship of Zion," a song the Graham brothers had been singing since their early days in Houston, had none of these attributes. It was a traditional slow hymn, which the Pilgrim Jubilees recorded in 3/4 (waltz) time, adding an organ to their accompaniment for the first time. Clay sings the lead, abandoning his declamatory drive style for a sinuous near-croon, laden with vibrato, spoken asides, and excursions into falsetto. The delivery is slow and reflective; when he interjects "I want everybody to listen to me" after the first line, it is more plea than instruction. "Old Ship of Zion" was so successful that it has remained in the Jubes' repertoire ever since, and they sing it virtually every time they perform. "I don't care where we go, I have to sing 'Old Ship of Zion,' " says Clay. "If I don't, they'll run me out of the city." Over the years, he has turned it into a virtual sermonette, prefacing it with a narrative telling how he found Jesus "at a little old church set back in the woods . . . called New Zion Baptist Church."

When the second Pilgrim Jubilees album came out in 1964, "Old Ship of Zion" was the title track. The album is a mix of old and new. Six of the twelve songs, including "Old Ship," are traditional gospel songs; five are by Major Roberson. No sermonettes are included, although Cleave does a spoken introduction to "Jesus I Love You" that almost qualifies, both in delivery—he uses the hoarse, urgent delivery of a sermonizing preacher—and in the content, which evokes a memory to link singer and song:

> . . . I used to hear the old people a long time ago when they would have what you call a testifying service.
> And I could see my mother and father as they would walk down the aisle.
> And over in the Amen Corner, somebody would be over there.
> And they would be singing the old different songs.
> But most of all what I like to hear them sing,
> Was this old song that set my, set my sinful soul on fire
> This is what they said . . .

The last line leads into the song—"Jesus, I love you"—with the backing singers singing the melody and Cleave singing a harmony over it. His description of the testifying service as being "a long time ago" and involving "the old people" invokes a common theme in gospel music—that the people were more religious and sincere, that the church services were more devout, that the singing was more inspired in the good old days. It may be true, but on the other hand, the lament is now into at least its third century. The song fades out well before its logical end, which, coupled with the rough-hewn phrasing of the introduction, suggests some ad-libbing. **Cleave**: "That happens to us often. You'll be standing there singing and things come to you. You ad-lib. You minister to your song. Many times you don't have planned what you're going to say. . . ." **Clay**: "We ad-lib a lot in the studio. In fact, we find ourselves better ad-libbing. Every time we write it down, it seems like it just doesn't work. When you ad-lib, you bring yourself into it."

The album's one song that is not traditional or written within the group is "You've Got to Wait." It is solid, up-tempo, classic Jubes with a rolling bass line and an extended drive at the end. But the opening line, "You can't hurry God," and the background refrain of "He's right on time" reveal it as a version of the Original Gospel Harmonettes' 1952 hit "He's Right On Time," written by their leader and lead singer, Dorothy Love (later Dorothy Love Coates).[11] It is writer-credited on Peacock to Major, and he regards the song as his own but at the same time acknowledges its origins.[12] "Dorothy Love Coates did it back in the days with the Gospel Harmonettes. But I rearranged it, and it did very well." His proprietary regard for the song arises from his arranging work—the tune and tempo are different, and a Harmonettes verse about the afflictions of Job is dropped to create room for the drive at the end. One of the oldest traditional songs on the album, "Wicked Race," undergoes a similar Roberson-engineered transformation. The song was already well established when the Norfolk Jubilee Quartet recorded it in 1923, delivering it in the staid and mannered style of the times.[13] Many other soloists and groups have subsequently performed and recorded it in a variety of arrangements, but only the Pilgrim Jubilees seem to have seen it as a vehicle for a full-out bass-propelled frontal assault.

Soon after the release of the *Old Ship of Zion* album, guitarist Maurice Dollison left the group. His musical interests had extended into the secular even while he was playing with the Jubes, and when the leading Chicago blues label, Chess, offered him a job as a songwriter and session musician, he took it. Chess later issued rhythm and blues recordings by Dollison, renaming him Cash McCall. His departure came during a tour the Pilgrim Jubilees were making with Rev. Julius Cheeks and the Mighty Clouds of Joy; a replacement was quickly found. **Clay**: "We met Bobby McDougle through June Cheeks. He was playing for Rev. Julius Cheeks. We were in High Point, North Carolina. I told Cleave, 'He's got big fingers and he looks clumsy. But he's strong. That'll be our guitar man right there.' He had the tone the Pilgrim Jubilees needed. And he's a good person. If you can't operate with Bobby, you can't operate with anybody."[14]

10. Bobby McDougle

Bobby McDougle is living in a motel room. Room 152 at the Motel 6, 17214 South Halstead, on the southern outskirts of Chicago. It's not his first choice of residence—a man who sees as many motel rooms on the road as he sees doesn't want to come home to another one. But he's been caught in a house deal. He and his wife, Rosemary—they've been together since 1968—sold their home and signed to buy another. With the new house deal about to be closed, they agreed to leave the home they'd sold so the new owners could move in. Then legal complications arose and their deal fell through.[1] Now Rosemary, an evangelist, is staying with one of their four daughters, and Bobby is sitting at the small table in room 152. "A lot of time I need to get by myself—I have my little den that I go into at home," he explains. "So I came out here, where I can get some music together. Then my wife comes over later, and we go and play with the kids [*their four grandchildren*], and then I come back to the hotel." The room has the everything-in-its-place neatness of the frequent traveler; the small, open-fronted closet is crammed with a line of suitbags, each containing a Pilgrim Jubilees uniform. As we speak, Bobby warms to his subject and the interview process and frequently leaves sentences unfinished, the last words implied as he skips to the next sentence and the next thought. The unusual spelling of his surname is his preference; some people in his family spell it that way, others use the more conventional McDougal. He was born in Valdosta, Georgia, on August 26, 1944, the seventh of twelve children—seven boys and five girls—of Ananias and Rosie Mae McDougle.

"We were farmers. We owned our own land—still have it there today. We mostly raised crops, vegetables and stuff like that. We lived off the land. And we were a churchgoing family. Absolutely. That was something we must do, even when we were little. We had to go to church—Daddy would see to that. That was Morning Star Baptist Church in Valdosta. It became a part of us. And I just grew up in the church. All my life I've been in church. My father played guitar a little bit, not very much—he was gospel also—and he always had an old acoustic around the house. I was between six and seven when I started playing. I was just gifted—the Lord blessed me with that talent. It was a gift from God. Music was in me. We had a thing they used to call 'Vastapol,' open tuning. And boy, I used to work out with that one finger. [*"Vastapol" is usually tuned in D—DADF#AD. Because the open strings form a chord, it can be played in a basic fashion by fretting chords with one finger up and down the neck of the guitar.*] I started playing for my sisters in a group—we were a big family, and practically everyone in my family was a singer, so we had about three groups with all my brothers and sisters. We were on a show, locally, and one of the other groups on it was the Smiling Jubilees from Fort Lauderdale, Florida. One of their guys showed me how to tune into the natural E [*standard guitar tuning, EADGBE*]. From there, I started out finding things on my own, finding chords, putting patterns. . . . I began making a little sound that was interesting.

"Then I worked with another group [*in Valdosta*], the Sensational Singers. I was about eight or nine. I'd been with my sisters, and they were singing in the women's style. But with these guys, it was a bit different—quartet sound. That's how I got into quartet. Then I moved to Fort Lauderdale, where the Smiling Jubilees were from. I had relatives there, my mother's sisters. I was almost ten at the time. What happened was . . . I was going with my cousin to spend a week, visiting during summertime. And I got there and I kinda got a little excited with it all being different. So I called home and asked my mom and dad could I stay a little longer. They said, 'Well, you can, but you'll have to go to school.' I ended up staying there for about a year and half, and that's when I ran into the Smiling Jubilees again. In fact, the lead singer, I came to find out, was my cousin. So I started playing a little for them. For about six months. Then I moved back to Valdosta and back to school there. And I joined a group called the Swanee Jubalaires. Stayed with them until I was about thirteen years old. Then I was with another group called the Five Converted Singers. We were all in the same church. I was still only young, but people used to say to me, 'You act so grown.' The reason for that was that I was mainly around grown-ups because I was playing for different groups, and they were older guys. And they'd take me with them when they'd go to eat and stuff like that. They treated me real well. They taught me things school didn't teach me, like how to be independent."

The teenage prodigy learned his craft in a combination of on-the-job training and listening to the big-name quartets on radio, on record, and in person when they visited Valdosta. Asked his favorites, he says: "Oh, I had quite a few. There was the Dixie Hummingbirds. Howard Carroll was one of my idols. Also the Sensational Nightingales, one of my idols was Jo Jo Wallace. And the Swan Silvertones, which was Linwood Hargrove. He was another one of my idols. I loved all gospel. But musicians were . . . ooohh! I was all ears and eyes. Looking and listening. And enjoying. I could just see myself with them." The individuals he names are the guitarists with the three groups; all—especially Wallace and Carroll—were widely respected and influential quartet instrumentalists. Bobby McDougle does not sing—"He didn't bless me like that, but I'm still grateful"—so all his efforts went into improving his instrumental skills. He was only fourteen when he got the chance to join and travel with a professional group, The Five Singing Stars. They were led by Tommy Ellison, a gospel veteran who got his professional start singing for Edna Gallmon Cooke's backing group, the Singing Sons. In 1959 Ellison formed the Five Singing Stars—later Tommy Ellison and the Five Singing Stars. The group recorded sporadically through the 1960s, making six singles and an album, but didn't consolidate its reputation as a national group until the early 1970s, when it joined Nashboro.

"Tommy Ellison and the Five Singing Stars were having a program there, in Valdosta, along with the Consolers. At the time, Tommy had a musician who had to go backward and forward to the doctor. So Tommy was asking at the program if there were any good musicians in Valdosta. Most of the guys considered me as pretty good guitar player. . . . So he sent for me and I came down and met him at the motel. He asked me about . . . I said, 'You'll have to get permission from my mother.' Because my father had passed when I was nine. So he went and talked to my mother. She said if he would personally look out for me and take care of me, she would let me go. Tommy said he would. And he did. Like I was his son. So I moved from Valdosta, Georgia, to New York. In Harlem—I was staying off 127th Street and 11th Avenue with Tommy. It was the experience of a lifetime! All the tall buildings . . . you know how a country boy is. But I still took the Lord with me. I left Valdosta but He was still with me, I was with Him. In fact, I didn't take Him with me, He brought me through.

"We spent a lot of time traveling. In those days we would do shows two and three weeks at a time, for a month or even two months. Two months before you get back home. But I was getting experience. For real! I didn't make much money. Only experience. But I was still happy—I was doing something I loved doing. I was with Tommy for two years—I recorded 'Been in the Storm Too Long' and 'Let Me In' [*Peacock 1890, issued in 1963*] with him. That was my first time recording, my first time going to a studio. I was scared then and excited. But by then I had learned his style and his type of music. I grew up a lot with Tommy, because he gave me so much confidence. He was that kind of guy, and he was a wonderful person.

"Then I met Madame Edna Cooke—we were working with her. And she approached me . . . at the time, her organist was Sammy Stevens; it was his idea because he liked the rhythm I had. So Edna listened one night and asked me how would I like to become her musician. I said, 'I think it would be fine, but I must talk with Tommy first.' That was out of respect—he was like a big brother or father to me. So I talked to Tommy, and he said, 'Well, if that's what you want to do, I wish you blessings.' Because she was doing a little more traveling than we were. So I became a member in the Singing Sons. I was sixteen. I didn't do any recording with her—I was only with her for about a year. But I loved her to death. She was so beautiful. She was like a mother away from home. We did a lot of traveling . . . places I hadn't been. And it was experience, especially playing with Sammy Stevens. It was my first time playing with organ. It was something entirely different—it was like playing with a band. It felt wonderful, because the sound was just there all the time. And that took me to another height. I said, 'Oohh, wow! Look at this.'

"And then . . . we were working with Rev. Julius Cheeks and the Four Knights. We were traveling, doing two weeks at a time in a package. At the time, Rev. Cheeks's guitarist was going back to school to learn trades for something else he wanted to go into. We were in Huntsville, Alabama, and Rev. Cheeks said [*he imitates Cheeks's raspy tones*], 'Madame . . .'—he always called her Madame—'why don't you let me have your guitar player?' Madame said, 'I don't know—I like him myself. But you can ask him.' So Rev. Cheeks came to me, said, 'I would like to have you as my musician.' I said, 'I'll have to ask Madame Cooke and see what she thinks.' Because . . . it's how you're raised; you're raised to respect. And I like to leave my job open, so I can go back. So I talked with her, and she gave me her blessing. And she told me, 'If you ever want to come back, your job will be here waiting.' So that's how I began with Rev. Cheeks. I was with him for two years. He said he liked the way I played because it looked like I was thumping my guitar. So he nicknamed me 'the thumper.' And that's what everyone started calling me, Thumper. I made one record with Rev. Cheeks, for Peacock, at Erasmus Street in Houston. 'The Last Mile of the Way' and 'Turn Your Radio On' [*Peacock 1875, issued in 1963*]."

Cheeks's career had passed its best by the time Bobby joined him. As lead singer of the Sensational Nightingales, he had enjoyed a reputation as one of the hardest of the hard quartet leads. He paid a price for it, and when left the 'Gales in 1960 his voice was shredded. But he continued touring and drawing audiences, and his recordings through the 1960s and 1970s produced occasional successes. "Last Mile of the Way" was one of these. The song has been recorded by a number of quartets and is usually done in a soulful style, but Cheeks turned it into a grinding tour de force of emotionalism, especially when he recorded it again in a two-part version for Savoy around 1975.[2]

"We were in High Point, North Carolina. Us and the Mighty Clouds of Joy and the Pilgrim Jubilees, on a tour together. In September 1964. And the Jubes were scorching hot. They had 'Old Ship' out then and 'Won't It Be Wonderful.' Oh man! They were setting this country afire. They were hot! And we . . . well, we were hanging in. So Cleave and Clay approached me and asked me about joining them. At the time, they had a guy named Maurice Dollison, but he was getting into studio work, and became a musician at Chess studio. I told them I'd have to let them know later. I talked to the Pastor—I always called Rev. Cheeks the Pastor—about it. He and his wife . . . his wife was Marge Cheeks, she played piano . . . they were like a family, too. They said, 'Well, those are nice guys you're going with. They're really nice guys.' He said, 'You know I need you, I really hate to see you leave. But if you would like to go with them, you have our blessing.' And I wanted to go, but I just hated leaving. But these were younger guys, near my age. I had been around a while, but I was still young—I was nineteen at the time. So that's where I became one of the Pilgrim Jubilees.

"I had to change my whole sound. I had to learn the Jubes' sound. That was from what Rufus and Maurice . . . well, actually Rufus Crume. I had to get into his head, learn what he was playing, from the records. I used to sit with my guitar at night and listen to him on my record player. And if I missed something I'd back it up and correct it until I got him down pat. Then when it was time, I played it like that, with the help of the guys in the group. They'd say, 'Put that in . . . No, something like this will do' and all that. And I said, 'OK.' I was never hardheaded, I was always a good listener. Then I just sat in on that pace until we got into rehearsal for new material. And then I gave it the same flavor, but I had some little different things that could be eased in there. When they wrote new songs, I'd try to hold the flavor of the sound but I kept easing different things in there."

Even with the new sounds that he "eased in," Bobby McDougle remained faithful to the guitar style defined by Rufus Crume. When he joined the group, he and Roosevelt English were its only musicians, so the guitarist had to maintain a full chord-based sound with occasional single-note riffs. One of the devices Bobby developed was a fast-moving riff that, although constructed differently, is not dissimilar to the riff popularized by Chuck Berry in songs such as "Memphis." Blues influences do creep into his playing—he is a big fan of B. B. King, and the other Jubes tell how at rehearsals, he occasionally provides light moments with extremely accurate King imitations—but Bobby McDougle credits Rufus Crume with originating "his" riff.

"Rufus used a little of that back in his day. He just didn't use it as much and as effectively as I do. I put it in those little holes to catch up any little slack in there. Because I'm not really fast [*he mimics playing a flurry of fast guitar notes*]. I just use that little touch-up thing. It sounds just enough, and I get back into my rhythm. Keep the rhythm going, the groove. I let my second guitar player make those fast runs. I just keep that drive tight.

"Soon after I got in the group we started rehearsing the songs for the first album I was on. I would get with Major and come up with some music—he would be singing, and I'd find some music to go with what he's singing. Or else maybe I heard a sound in my head and I've got some music together already. I would give it to him and Clay to put something with this, say, 'Why don't you write something to this sound?' Then we would bring everybody in and start working on getting the background and . . . little pieces at a time. Everybody sharing and helping put in their ideas to work. Major and Clay do the most writing. They already have the idea how they want it to go, but they want some help, too. So if you see something that'll make it sound better or make a little different. . . . The Pilgrim Jubilees is a group where everybody does a little touching up in a song. We put our heads together, and we come up with something. And we try to perfect it as we go along."

11. Ups and Downs

The second half of the 1960s started with the Pilgrim Jubilee Singers as stars of the gospel world and ended with them struggling to survive. In 1965 "Old Ship of Zion"—song and album—ensured a full schedule of bookings. It became even more full and more lucrative when they were selected to tour with James Cleveland and the Caravans. Cleveland was a Chicago singer and pianist who started his professional gospel career in 1950. In the early 1960s he began working with choirs and in 1963 had a major hit with "Peace Be Still," a soaring epic in which his hoarse baritone fronts the Angelic Choir.[1] Cleveland later established the Gospel Music Workshop of America and is widely regarded as being responsible for choirs gaining the prominence they now have.[2] After "Peace Be Still," his next album with the Angelic Choir produced another hit, "I Stood on the Banks of the Jordan," and he decided to capitalize on its success with a national tour.[3] He engaged the Caravans, with whom he worked as a pianist and singer in the 1950s, and decided he also wanted a male group.

Clay: "So James Cleveland calls, says, 'We want you in the package, but you've got to have a Cadillac.' Because he was big time. He had a Cadillac, the Caravans had one. They weren't traveling in buses and vans then. If you were big time, you had a Cadillac. So he wanted the artists that were working with him to have Cadillacs when they pulled up on the ground. It was time for us to get a new ride anyway, so . . . we had a '64 Buick Electra 225; we traded it in and bought a new white Cadillac." **Bobby**: "That was our first time for making what you could call big money. We had been mostly doing schools and auditoriums. But when we got with James Cleveland we went to the big places."

The tour ran through 1965; in 1967 Cleveland used the same package for another series of bookings. The first tour wasn't a full-time engagement—it would do a series of performances then disband until the next block of bookings was assembled—but it did provide much of the group's work in 1965. Romance blossomed during the tour, and Charles Green of the Pilgrim Jubilees married Delores Washington of the Caravans. And Clay Graham discovered an unexpected hazard of being with "the best-looking group on the road."

Clay: "I know you've heard the publicity on James Cleveland that he was a bisexual, he went both ways. [*Cleveland was, in fact, a homosexual, as were some members of his entourage. His sexual orientation was an open secret in the gospel world; it became public knowledge when he contracted AIDS. He died in 1991.*] On the last night, we were in the dressing room and [*Caravans' leader*] Albertina Walker walked up to James Cleveland and said, 'James, the tour is over, and I want my money.' They were laughing about it, and we didn't know. . . . We had been paid. But Charles Green was married to Delores Washington. And Delores told Charles that James Cleveland owed Albertina a thousand dollars because she had bet him that his fellows or him would not touch a Pilgrim Jubilee on the tour. She said, 'Those are men, you won't touch none of that.' And he bet a thousand dollars that before the tour was over he would. I do remember that he invited me to breakfast. I went to the breakfast, and he offered me a brand new car. I left the breakfast table and went back to my room. I saw where he was coming from—I said to myself 'Puh-lease. I don't need no boy nothing.' So she collected that money. And after that, I knew he really was that way, which . . . to each his own. Who am I to judge? But he offered me a brand new car. I didn't accept it, and a lot of people called me crazy. I told them you can call me crazy about women if you want, but I don't want none of that. The Pilgrim Jubilees are thoroughbred men!"

* * *

A more widespread and sinister danger stalking the gospel highway was racism. Although the Pilgrim Jubilees lived in Chicago, their main support was—as it is today—largely in the South. In the early and mid-1960s the area was a tinderbox of racial tension, as black Americans fought to claim their civil and human rights. Large modern cars with northern license plates and carrying young African American men were prime targets for southern law enforcement officials. "If you were from any of the northern states and you were black, they had their eyes peeled for you," says Cleave. "Any little thing . . . they'd make up things." More than thirty years later, the indignities, the powerlessness, and the danger of that era still burn and hurt, and it was a subject Clay Graham wanted to talk about, arriving for the interview session with his opening sentences worked out.

Clay: "I want to speak a little bit about integration and segregation and certain things that the group went through during those tedious years which were in the '60s. We had to do a lot of touring before Martin Luther King did the marches. And we weren't able to stay in Holiday Inns or Best Westerns or any name motel. We mostly stayed in little rooming houses. We would carry our own TV and radio because they didn't have TVs in those rooms. Paying $2.50 or $3.00 a night. It was very prejudiced then. I remember we were out in Texas, on our way to Houston. This was in 1961, I believe. Our taillight was cracked, but we didn't know it. And the police pulled us over. It was very, very cold, maybe fifteen degrees. He said, 'Where are you boys going?' We said, 'We're going to Houston, Texas.' 'What y'all gon' do down there?' 'We're going down there to sing.' He said, 'Your taillight is broke out.' One of the fellows got out, looked and said, 'Yeah, it's cracked.' He said, 'It's broke out.' I said, 'OK, it's broke out.' He said, 'You boys sing? Y'all get out and sing me a tune.' We were traveling with the Highway QCs. We had two cars and we just split up between them. So we made up a group there on the highway and got out and sang. He said, 'Since you boys sing so good, give me another one.' We sung him another. With that anger inside of you, but you knew you had to do it. He said, 'All right, I'm gonna let you boys go.' We got down the highway ten miles and the lights flashed on us again. The same police. Pulled us over, said, 'I want the judge to hear you boys.' Took us about eight miles to a little shanty . . . one little building, like a trailer house. He knocked on the door and the judge got up. The police said, 'I got some boys here can sing pretty good.' So the judge sat back and we sang a song to him. He crossed his legs and asked for another song. Then he got up and got his book, said, 'Well, since y'all was so nice and sang a song, I ain't gonna charge y'all but forty-five dollars for that broke taillight.' We paid the forty-five dollars and hit the highway.

"That wasn't all. I tell people right now, Texas is just about the most prejudiced state in the union. Even worse than Mississippi. People in Mississippi are noted for it. But Texas is awesome. During the sixties and the later part of the fifties it was so hard on the groups that were out there traveling and had to depend on the facilities. Because there weren't any open. I remember . . . we pulled up in a service station and they had a black restroom and a white one. And the water fountain was white. Round the corner, there was hot water coming up out of a little spout with a sign, said 'niggers.' And . . . I'm a little bullheaded. Been that way all my life. I went to the white fountain and started to drink. The guy ran out of the service station with a jack handle in his hand. He said, 'That ain't for no nigger to drink out of.' I said, 'Y'all crazy. You better put that jack handle down.' He said, 'Are you threatening me, nigger?' I said, 'Yeah, come on.' So he made his pass, and when he made his pass I tripped him up, took the jack handle from him, kicked his ass, and we left. Police never did find us because he didn't get our tag number and we were gone."

Cleave: "Back then, well . . . the country was mad. Oh, we ran into a lot of things. We got run out of a place down the east end of Georgia. Our group and a group from Little Rock, Arkansas, the Loving Sisters. We were traveling together. It was late at night and we couldn't find too many places that were open—especially back then for black people. This particular place was supposed to be a public place, it was like a truck stop. So we pulled in to get something to eat. We started in to the restaurant. And boy! All hell broke loose. And we were hollering 'We're sorry, we're sorry, sorry.' That was the only way we got away without getting mauled. I didn't see any sign, but you didn't have to see signs saying 'white only.' The ones that put up the 'white only' sign were the ones trying to save you embarrassment. You were supposed to know. If you didn't see a black person coming to greet you, you knew you weren't supposed to be there. What it really does, it disgusts you and makes you angry. But you say, 'If they knew better, they'd act better.' I just feel like they were pure ignorance. It was the way they were raised, and they just didn't know any better. A lot of ignorant stuff went on like that. Different things happened to you just because you were a different color."

Bobby: "We used to go to Clarksdale, Mississippi. And each time we went, the police would follow us until we got to the city limits. They had a curfew time there. But the DJ was known around there pretty good, so they would let us sing and everybody could come and hear us. But they would escort us out of town each trip. [*The DJ was pioneer African American broadcaster Early Wright, who also promoted gospel programs. He started broadcasting on WROX in Clarksdale in 1947 and was widely respected by blacks and whites in the town.*[4]] We've have some times. . . . times we had to go through the back to get food. If you didn't get mad, you weren't human. It was just so degrading, so unkind. So rude. Just like you ain't nothing. It was hard to understand the way we were treated when God made us all."

Major: "That was a bad time. You had to go to the back door. That's for the white restaurant—you go to the back door and order your food. You couldn't go in and sit down. And in the public places where the drinking fountains were, they had 'white' here and 'black' there. Washrooms were the same. I never understood it. Even up until today. It just never made any sense to me. For what? I haven't done anything to you. I didn't make my skin any more than you made yours. Whatever it takes to keep me alive, that's what it takes to keep you alive. But that's how it was. It was bad. You had a few places where you dare not stop. And even today, we've got places like that. We still run into it. You've got some places in some of these cities you go though . . . like people think you're safe when you go to Chicago. You're not. Chicago is one of the most prejudiced places you can go in."

Clay: "Even after Martin Luther King opened it up, there have been several things happen to the Pilgrim Jubilees. We have been in motels . . . one lady would check us in and the boss would come in later and find out they had a black group there. He'd say the rooms were already rented and we would have to leave. They talk about America being a free country, but it's one of the most prejudiced countries in the world. You find it anywhere you go. It has changed. But segregation and prejudice will be here until doomsday. It's not going anywhere."

Incidents such as these and others the Pilgrim Jubilees relate—Cleave Graham spent a weekend in a Louisiana jail for a driving offense; Clay fled for his life after his "bullheadedness" led him to make a sarcastic reply when refused service—were commonplace, and other groups have similar or worse tales. What made southern race hate especially difficult for the touring groups was that they met it usually far from home, away from the support of family, friends, and community, and they had to keep going back into the same hostile environment time after time, knowing that something as petty as a cracked taillight or a minor car accident—as Cleave says, "any little thing"—could expose them to potentially life-threatening harassment and degradation.

In 1965 the group started recording its third Peacock album, *We Are in Church* (Peacock PLP-133). Bobby McDougle remembers doing it in Houston, Texas. Major Roberson says: "I thought we did it in Chicago." The album reveals the reason for the contradiction—at least two different recording sessions were involved. The distinctive piano sound of Lafayette Leake places six of the tracks at Universal in Chicago; the backings on the other five have an organ instead of the piano and a drummer who is more tentative than the Chicago blues players and are presumably the Houston recordings Bobby remembers. The album is very much the mixture as before. Most of the material comes from Major—his own compositions, reworkings of traditional songs, or in-between songs that are not fully original but are more than rearrangements. The album opens with one such song, "My Soul," which takes the line "My soul looks back in wonder [at] how I got over" and uses it as the refrain for a story of religious faith overcoming childhood deprivation. The line is best known from Memphis composer W. Herbert Brewster's "How I Got Over," but it comes from a traditional spiritual; an earlier "How I Got Over," using the same refrain as Brewster's but different verses, was copyrighted by Rev. C. H. Cobbs in 1936.[5] Brewster's influence also appears in "Shout," a reworking of "Shout All Over God's Heaven," which uses his famous "move on up a little higher" line as the foundation for the end-of-song drive.[6]

The album's big success was the sermonette "A Child's Blood," written and related by Clay. The group recorded it twice, once for the two-part single Peacock 3087 and then again for the album. **Clay**: "We cut that song, and when it came out it sounded so bad to us that we called Peacock and told them to cancel it. Then we did it again. But DJs that got the first one kept on playing it anyway, and that song bust the country open! We could hear all the mistakes, but it was what the people wanted." The album version—the second attempt—is the better recording. The organ, in the background on the single, is moved to the fore, providing a mournful vibrato-laden foil for the story line. The bass guitar is fattened from the overtrebled wooden thud of the single. Clay has refined his recitation, honing the story so the album version takes around four and a half minutes, compared to the more than six minutes of the single. But in either version, "A Child's Blood" ("The Child's Blood" on the album) is a classic of the sermonette genre. Its song is Thomas A. Dorsey's "Precious Lord"; its story is implausible even by sermonette standards—a father beats his little girl to death for defying him by going to church and discovering Jesus. But Clay says it comes from real-life incidents and believes the topicality of its subject is the reason for its enduring popularity. "Child abuse. People can relate to it every time you play it because it's happening every day. When I wrote it . . . we were in Dallas, Texas, and this preacher was talking about the abuse of kids. And in Chicago, a man on Clybourn Street whipped his little girl until . . . she didn't die, but she stayed in the hospital unconscious for almost two weeks. That's the way I came up with it."

Clay's delivery is closely related to preaching. He uses the heavy rasping breathing common to many preachers as they approach the climax of a sermon and reiterates phrases as the story builds in intensity. In places, the influence of Rev. Julius Cheeks's tense and hoarse delivery is obvious. "A Child's Blood" has never left the Pilgrim Jubilees' repertoire. "It was the biggest thing we've had for continuously selling," says Clay. "It wasn't a big overwhelming hit, but it always sells. They call them moneymakers. Every time you turn around you get a little check from them."

The recordings for *We Are In Church* were the last the group made for more than four years. Today, the Pilgrim Jubilees say Peacock did not issue any records of them in that time. In fact, four singles came out between 1967 and 1969, but none were new recordings, and the discs were not promoted. The first coupled "My Soul" and "I Don't Mind" from the *We Are In Church* album, the other three were "on the shelf" recordings probably made around the time of the album sessions. The drought followed a rift between the group and Peacock owner Don Robey. The Pilgrim Jubilees were unhappy with the contract they had signed and the lack of royalty income from their records; Robey was annoyed when he discovered the group had been approached by other labels and was trying to leave Peacock. Cleave, Clay, and Major all freely admit that their eagerness to be on Peacock overrode any sense of caution when they signed the contract, and they did not notice that it bound them for life with no options for termination or renegotiation. They also say that apart from the twenty-five dollars they were paid as advance money for each song they recorded, they made no money from their Peacock records—even from "Stretch Out."

Major: "To us, it was fame, not fortune. It was fortune to Don Robey. But we didn't make any money. The only thing we made was in personal appearances. We got our name known through the record. But there weren't any financial rewards. He had us down [*in the contract*] for a 3 percent royalty. Then the cost of the session, he deducted that off your 3 percent. And by the time he got all his money back, it's time for you to record again. So you go back in the studio and build up another bill. Then he started cheating. When the Dixie Hummingbirds went in there three weeks after 'Stretch Out' came out, he showed them the invoice. He'd sold eighty-five thousand. In three weeks. Now that's selling records! When Tucker [*Dixie Hummingbirds lead singer Ira Tucker*] saw us, he said, 'Y'all got the biggest record Don Robey had in a long time.' So I went down there [*to Houston*], and he showed me something that said we had sold eighteen hundred records. And he said, 'Y'all got to do something a bit better than this.' Eighteen hundred was all he gave us credit for. That thing was on fire! At the programs, we could only sell a few because everybody already had it. That thing was like an R&B record, it just went. All the jukeboxes across the country were playing it. He told us we had to sell fifty thousand copies before we'd be eligible for a royalty. But we had no way of knowing if we'd sold fifty thousand. It was whatever he said. If he said we didn't, we didn't."

Cleave: "He was a rich man. And he had that foolproof contract. It wasn't really against the law, but it wasn't really lawful. Now who do you think's going to win? That's the problem, that's what we were up against. Mr. Robey was a hard cold businessman. He took advantage where he could. And then when he found out we were trying to do better, trying to get out from under him. . . . We were being approached by different companies—Savoy, Columbia, and what have you. And when he found out that we wanted to leave, that Columbia wanted us . . . oh my God. He said, 'I made you, and now you want to go over to those people?' He said, 'I'll see you dead in the street.' "

Major: "That man pulled a gun on me twice—.357 Magnum. He wouldn't record us and he wouldn't release us. I got angry and I told him 'You're starving my group to death.' He said, 'I'm not gonna turn you loose until I'm ready for you to go. If you try to get away from me . . . we got some boxes for every man in your group.' So I went into his office, and he jumped up and put that gun on me. I went back another time, I said, 'Will you just please give us a record?' He said, 'I'm thinking about it. But I ain't got it down yet. I don't know what I'm going to do.' I walked inside his door, he jumped up and drew the gun on me again. The girl that worked there, she called me and said, 'You can't handle Mr. Robey like this. He's bitter with your group because you've been trying to go somewhere else. Now just take it real easy, and I'll see if I can't get him to release a record on you.' [*"The girl" was possibly Evelyn Johnson, a leading executive in the Robey empire.*] We knew we were being mistreated. But we didn't look at the dotted line before we signed. We just thought everybody was in good faith—we thought everybody would do you right. When we found out the contract was round like an apple, with no way out, we said, 'Let's get a lawyer.' We got three different lawyers at different times. When they would write him a letter, he would contact them and buy 'em out. He used his money's strength. And the day I heard he had passed . . . Miss Johnson called and said, 'Mr. Robey died and we're burying him Friday. It would be nice if your group could come down here and sing.' I said, 'Do what?!' I said, 'I'm glad—that's the best news I ever heard in my life, that he's gone.' 'Oh you shouldn't say that about Mr. Don. . . .' I said, 'I'm glad he's dead. I bet he couldn't take that money he took from us in the grave with him.' " [*Robey died at the age of seventy-one on June 16, 1975.*]

The Pilgrim Jubilees soon started to pay the price for their escape bid. The *We Are In Church* album and "A Child's Blood" sustained them for a while, and the 1967 James Cleveland tour provided work and income. But without new strongly promoted records in record stores—and, more important, on radio—their market value plummeted. From around mid-1967 bookings dried up, and when they did get engagements, promoters would not pay as much as they once had. Major Roberson was the first casualty. He had kept his barbershop going when the group started traveling, employing people to run it for him. At the end of 1966 he sold it, telling himself, "Now I'm committed to the road." Within months, the road had turned so rocky that he could not support his family. He got a job as a security guard in Chicago and stopped singing, although he continued to handle the bookings. Charles Green also quit. Delores Washington had left the Caravans, and they had started a family. "Money wasn't flowing in like it should," recalls Clay, "so Charles came home and got a job." Roosevelt English followed for the same reason, and by the end of 1967 the Pilgrim Jubilees were a trio—singers Cleave and Clay Graham and guitarist Bobby McDougle.

Cleave: "It got tight, but . . . the Lord is always there. You just have to have faith. You can't figure out how He's going to do something—you just know within your heart, He's going to do it. We were just three. But we had programs booked, so we kept going. For about two years. Sometimes somebody from another group would be at a program, and they would help us. But it was just the three of us for a good while." **Bobby**: "It was rough. We went hungry many days. Eating soda crackers and baloney—if we could get it. We just loved singing and it was just in our hearts to continue. Just dedicated to singing, singing, singing God's praises."

Two events helped turn the group's fortunes sufficiently to enable it to keep going and eventually recover. The first was the 1968 booking for the annual Apollo Theater gospel season; the second was a new song.

Clay: "We got a call for the Apollo Theater. But the promoter found out there wasn't but three of us. So he called Major, said, 'Those three fellows can't go on here like that.' " **Major**: "The man at the Apollo called me, said, 'You got a piece of a group here. Where are your men?' " **Clay**: "Major called me and Cleave, and we said, 'Tell him to take us for two days and if we don't work out, cast us off.' At the Apollo, you started . . . it depended on your prestige. So we were the opening group. If the opening group was too strong for the second group, they switched spots. And I think there were about five or six groups, and when we finished at the weekend, we were sitting next to the top, which was the Mighty Clouds. And they were worried. That's when they were burning up hot and there wasn't but three of us. We gained a lot of recognition from that." **Major**: "After the second show, the man at the theater called me back and said, 'Hey, Major, it's OK. The three of them are bringing it down.' " **Clay**: "In other words, we were getting over. Cleave had thought of a song . . . he came up with 'Too Close.'

'I'm too close to Heaven to turn around.' And folks liked it. It hit across the country from us singing it. We didn't have a record, but this song carried us. They were booking us for that song—people went nuts over it."

Cleave: "That was something the Lord blessed me with. Rev. Alex Bradford recorded it, and he got a good hit. I listened to it, said, 'Mmm hmm, that's a good song.' But I didn't think anything more about it. Then the Davis Sisters did it. I said, 'Oohh, the Davis Sisters are putting a hurting on that!' Then the Blind Boys of Alabama did it. But with all these people doing it, I don't never remember . . . like, you hear a song and sing it to yourself—I never remember humming that song to myself. Until one night, we were in Newark, New Jersey. When it came time for me to sing one of my songs, I couldn't think of anything. The only thing that was in my eyes and my mind was 'I'm Too Close.' I turned around and . . . I always tell my fellows to just watch me. If something comes to me onstage I might change in the middle and do something different. So I just reared back and hit that song, and I tell you, the anointing got so high in that place that my fellows say that when I left the floor I stayed in the air for a good while before I came down. And man! Wherever we went, it was just like we had a brand new hit record. We did it in Philadelphia one night and Rev. Bradford was on the show. 'Too Close' was his biggest hit, so naturally there was a demand for him to sing it. Which he did. And there was some political maneuvering among the artists on the show. They knew how the people liked me doing 'Too Close.' So they put the man that wrote it right before us. The people loved Bradford doing 'Too Close,' so those groups knew I wasn't going to do it behind him. But when they called the Jubes, I spoke to him onstage. I said, 'Rev. Bradford, this is your song. You wrote it. But if ever somebody wrote something for somebody, you wrote this song for me. Because I never have in my life sung a song that fits my feelings the way this song does.' He said, 'Sing it! Sing it, sing it!' And I reared back and sung 'I'm Too Close' and the people just jumped up! It was something the Lord gave us to keep us going until we had records again."[7]

The Pilgrim Jubilees' version of "Too Close" eliminates much of Bradford's lyric and strips the song to its basic theme—"I'm too close to Heaven to turn around." Both versions are slow, but Cleave Graham replaces Bradford's easy delivery with the driven intensity of a hard quartet lead. "I'm doing it a little differently," he says.

From the low point of around 1968, the group started reclaiming its position in the gospel world, bolstered by the Apollo performance and "Too Close." **Cleave**: "If we performed for an audience, eight times out of ten we'd get booked back. They always seemed to like our performance. And the promoters, too, they liked us." The bookings and the fees improved, and from 1969 the trio began to expand again. Charles Green returned for a short time, but the comeback was not a success. "He did a couple of programs, but he had lost it," says Clay. To fill the vacancy, the group fulfilled the dreams of ex-Mississippi singer Ben Chandler by hiring him as a Pilgrim Jubilee. In 1970 Major returned to singing duties, and young Michael Ray Atkins came in to relieve on guitar while Bobby McDougle was away on family business . . . and stayed on as bass player. The core of the Pilgrim Jubilees for the next thirty years was established.

12. Ben Chandler

The anniversary or homecoming is a gospel quartet's big day. For local groups, it usually marks the date the group was started; for national groups, such as the Pilgrim Jubilees, it can be a founding-date anniversary or a special return to the hometown. Local groups usually organize their own anniversaries, with other singers donating their services in the knowledge that the favor will be returned when their anniversaries come around. For professional groups, the event is more commonly organized by a promoter who assumes the risk and pays the artists—either an agreed fee or a percentage of the door. Whatever the status of the group or the way the program is organized, it is a special day, a combination of commemoration, thanksgiving, promotion, and revenue raising—a once-a-year occasion. Except for the Pilgrim Jubilees. They have two homecomings each year, one in Mississippi on the first Saturday in June, the other about a month earlier, on Mother's Day in May, in their adopted hometown, Chicago. In November they have another Chicago program, which they refer to as their anniversary. Although Chicago is a major gospel center and the Pilgrim Jubilees' home base, these two programs are the only ones they perform in the city. "Just two shows a year," says Cleave. "We don't want to do any more than that. When we come to Chicago, we will draw good as anybody operating because we don't wear the people out."

The Chicago programs are held at Mercy Seat Missionary Baptist Church on Roosevelt Road on Chicago's West Side. The building is an old movie theater, converted to a church in the 1960s by former gospel singer Rev. Amos Waller, some of whose sermons were issued on record. It seats around fifteen hundred people but is not ideal for gospel music programs because the space between the front seats and the pulpit area is too narrow to accommodate the singers, the musicians, and their equipment comfortably. Despite this, Mercy Seat is one of Chicago's main gospel music venues. **Clay**: "You don't have a stage—you're singing on the steps and your knees are touching other folks right in front of you. But, oh man, you say you're at Mercy Seat and you've got some people. They love that West Side. Most of our followers live on the West Side. And people out west won't come to the South Side. But if you go to the West Side, folk from the South Side will go to the West."

Today, three o'clock is approaching, and Mercy Seat is almost ready for the Pilgrim Jubilees' homecoming. On the narrow stage area, the sound crew is setting up microphones, and musicians are finding room for amplifiers, keyboards, and a drum kit. People are arriving, most in their Sunday best—some have stayed on after the morning's church service—handing over the tickets they bought in advance for seventeen dollars or paying the twenty-dollar door charge, described euphemistically on the posters as the "donation." As well as the Pilgrim Jubilees, today's program includes national groups the Christianaires and the Jackson Southernaires—both from Mississippi—and top local groups the Victory Travelers from Chicago and the Virginia Aires from Norfolk, Virginia. All have been booked by the promoter, Chicago gospel DJ Kathy Lockett, although for an occasion like this, she consults the Pilgrim Jubilees to see if they have any preferences on who appears with them. A room to one side of the church is the kitchen and dining room, where chicken is the featured item on the menu. Most of the people seated around the tables are gospel singers and musicians; some have traveled hundreds of miles. One such long-distance traveler is a Pilgrim Jubilee. Ben Chandler's group is based in Chicago, but he lives 750 miles away in Atlanta, Georgia.

* * *

"I left at 6 o'clock yesterday morning, and by 6 o'clock [*in the evening*] I was here at the hotel. We've been driving up and down the road for years, so it doesn't bother me. In fact, I'd rather drive than fly. If we have to go California, that's just too far and I'll fly. But most of the time I drive my van or my car . . . I kinda enjoy driving by myself. [*He has a Dodge van and a Cadillac, both bought because of their suitability for long journeys.*] I leave in plenty of time so I won't be in no stress. That's why I bought my van. If I get tired, I can make a bed and go to sleep. I pull into a rest area, somewhere I think it's safe for me, and go to sleep. And God will take care of you. . . . When I leave home, I tell Him to take care of me, take care of my wife and bring me back home safely. Then everything will be all right. I go in God's name, and I know He's going to take care of me.

"I was born in West Point, Mississippi. December 26, 1938. . . . I'm a Christmas boy. I was almost born on Christmas Day, but it was a little bit after midnight when I was born. I finished school there, at North Side High School. I think it was 1955. I've been singing all my life. Ever since I was about five years old. Started out with my sisters. We started singing in church. As a matter of fact, my father was a minister, Rev. Henderson Chandler. I didn't know him—he passed away when I was three months old. He had twenty-one children with his first wife and had four by my mother. All of them have passed except me and my three youngest sisters. [*Both of Ben's parents had previous spouses who died. His mother, Laura Harris Chandler, had five children from her first marriage and four—three daughters and Ben—from her second.*] We organized our own little group, me and my sisters. Bernice, Loreen, and Ozella. We called it the Chandler Four. We were singing . . . some of the old groups like the Fairfield Four, Soul Stirrers, Pilgrim Travelers. We didn't know anything about writing and arranging, we were just singing because this was what we grew up in church doing. My older brothers were singing with another group, singing around in different churches, so I was listening to those guys and taking patterns. Our church was Old Saint Peter Missionary Baptist Church. And that's where I confessed Jesus Christ. At the early age of nine years old. Because my mother . . . by my father passing away when I was about three months old, she raised nine children by herself. She taught all of us to go to church, go to Sunday school and get an education. She instilled in us to stay with God, stay in God's will

. . . she always told us, 'Don't let nothing separate you from the love of God.' That's what I try to tell the young people today. I found out since I got older and grown that what she told us was the gospel truth.

"My whole family sung. My mother sung. She had a beautiful voice. So I was born to do it. When I was in high school, I won a talent show. I was about sixteen, and my teacher asked me to participate on the talent show at the fairgrounds. And I won. I sang one of Brook Benton's songs, 'Poison Ivy.' They gave me fifty dollars first prize. I didn't know how much fifty dollars was at that time. But I've dedicated my life since I was a very young man to singing gospel. I sang with my sisters until they all grew up and started getting married. That left me by myself, so . . . I had another brother on my dad's side. His name was Willie Chandler. He sang with his sons—he had about four boys—and I joined his group. I never quit singing. I was surrounded by singing. And people always told me 'You're gonna make something out of yourself by singing gospel. You're going to get out there, you're gonna travel, you're gonna make records.' And that's what I wanted to do. But it took me a real long time to get with the Pilgrim Jubilees. I wanted to be with them from a young man because . . . their first big hit record was 'Stretch Out,' and that thing burned the country up. My older brother had it and he played it all night long. And we used to sing it. By then I had organized my own group, the Southern Wonders. The Jubes came through our town, and we opened up the program for them. I thought that was the biggest . . . I said, 'Man, I'm gonna sing with these guys one day if it's the last thing I do.' "

Soon after he left school, Ben married Carrie Fields, mainly because "my mom had decided me and my wife had to be married." The young couple had two children, Ben Jr. and Robert, but the marriage didn't endure. Ben was working as a mechanic, and he and his wife sang together. But Ben wanted to be more than a Sunday-at-church singer, and the marriage became a gospel music casualty.

"I wanted to travel. I wanted to be big time. She didn't want that so there was a split. I left and went to Chicago. I wanted to get out of Mississippi anyway to sing with the Pilgrim Jubilees. In Chicago, I worked at a chemical plant, then I went to the Sweetheart Cup Company. I was a machinist. I always like to work on machines and fix things. I like fooling with cars. That's my hobby. I like to make them run right. I went to school for that in Chicago, at Illinois Institute, to learn mechanical work. But I still wanted to get with the Pilgrim Jubilees. I would call them every week. Most times they'd be out of town, but sometimes I would catch Clay in town and Cleave or Major. But at that time, the group wasn't taking on people. So I started singing with Martin Jacox in the Swan Mellarks. [*The Swan Mellarks later made a few locally distributed recordings but never achieved any great prominence outside Chicago. Martin Jacox was a hard-driving lead singer who sang with a number of groups and as a soloist; he died in 1998.*] After that, he and I organized another group called the Mighty Wings; I think they're still singing. Then he left and went to the Soul Stirrers. And he said to me, 'Ben, you need to be on the road traveling like me.' I said, 'Well, I tried to get with the Pilgrim Jubilees.' He said, 'I'll help you any way I can.' So he called Howard Hunt, of Slim and the Supreme Angels and told him about me. Slim called me, and I went to the rehearsal and fitted right in. I recorded with them—we were on Nashboro records—but I didn't sing too much lead. Just every now and again; I always like to sing in the background. I stayed with them for about four years, from '63 to '67. Then I came back off the road. Things weren't working out like they should have, and I didn't want to go through the hassles of being treated the wrong way. It was money problems. Once we started making a bit of money . . . I wasn't treated fairly. And it wasn't really what I wanted to do anyway. I left Mississippi to join the Pilgrim Jubilees. I learned a lot from the Supreme Angels—that was my first step into becoming a professional gospel singer. But I wasn't satisfied—I didn't really want to be there in the first place. So I went back to my old job in Chicago.

"Then Bobby . . . I knew him better than I did Cleave and Clay and Major because he used to come around and we would shoot a little pool together. He said, 'Come and sing with us.' I said, 'Man, I've been trying to get with this outfit for ten years.' He said, 'Come to the rehearsal.' So I went to rehearsal. They had about four guys there trying to sing the tenor part. And I was sitting there listening to them . . . I knew the Jubes' songs, I knew them down. And Bobby said, 'Try Ben.' They said, 'Can you sing our songs?' I said, 'I can sing 'em better than you.' They said, 'We'll sing this one. . . . ' I can't think of the name of the song, but I fitted right in. They said, 'This guy can sing. Let's sing another one.' We sung 'The Old Ship of Zion' and

'Won't It Be Wonderful' and man, we just fitted just like a hand in a glove. And I felt comfortable, they felt comfortable. Everything just grooved in; we just fit like we should've been all the time.

The bond between Ben and the rest of the Pilgrim Jubilees was strengthened when Cleave realized that their new singer was a second cousin to him and Clay through kinship between their mother and his father. "She called my daddy Uncle Henderson," Ben recalls. "And when she saw me, she had a fit. 'Look at this boy, look at him. That's Uncle Henderson.' I said, 'Well, I'm his baby boy.' "

"When I got with the Pilgrim Jubilees, I felt . . . just comfortable. Everything fell into place. Because I wanted to be here for so long, and when I got the chance to join that group, I was very excited. I enjoyed it, and we have stood together through good and bad times. Back then we would sing every night. They used to have the Clouds of Joy and the Jubes, the Gospelaires, Davis Sisters, or the Caravans . . . sing every night. And we would put it on. And the Apollo Theater. Oh man! That was something. We would sometimes stay out on the road for three weeks or a month at a time. We didn't make much money. We made some, and things were much cheaper, but gospel singers in our age bracket never made a whole lot of money. It was dedication. We came up the hard way, and we knew what hard times were about. We wanted to make money, but it just wasn't there. So we took what we could get and made the best of it.

"Our style was something we created, and we are so close. . . . Clay and I talk a lot in the background. When we're singing in the background we might have a conversation and nobody knows it. 'Let's do this, let's do that. OK.' We might come up with anything on the spur of the moment. We call our style 'homemade.' Like the old folks bake a cake from scratch. You put your own recipe into it and nobody can duplicate it unless you tell 'em how its done. So this is the way the Jubes have a special sound. We sing old-fashioned, but it's up to date. It sounds easy to sing, but it's not—we get people who say 'Oh I can sing your style,' but they can't. It's what the Jubes put together. And it's different, because we don't want to sound like anybody else. So when you hear us on the radio or you play a tape or a CD, you can tell the sound from anybody else. You know that's the Pilgrim Jubilees. We try to keep that flavor."

* * *

In 1975 Ben married again, to Pheola, and left Chicago to live in Houston, Texas. He is reticent about the relationship and the move, saying only that he moved to Texas "to do a little better." The couple had one son, but again gospel singing proved incompatible with married life. "By me staying so far from the guys it was a big problem and one thing led to another and we couldn't get along, so we divorced." In 1979 Ben returned to Chicago. Six years later, love again blossomed, this time at a program in Georgia.

"Her name is Gloria. We were doing a concert and she told her sister, 'I like that guy there. I want to meet him.' I didn't meet her that time, but later we were singing in Cordele, Georgia, about thirty miles from her home town. She came to the concert, and a friend of hers introduced us. We dated for about four years, then we got married. She lived in Atlanta, so I left the fellows alone—let them have Chicago and I moved to Atlanta. We dated for so long because we wanted to make sure this was what each one of us wanted. Didn't want to make a mistake and be tied down. It can be hard if you're married to the wrong person that doesn't understand your life. They've got to understand your life. You'll be away from home. Because this is God's work. And this is what I'm dedicated to doing. But if you haven't got that right woman or that right wife in your corner, there's always going to be a confusion. But I believe there's a woman for every man. Sometimes we marry the wrong people, and it doesn't work. But when you marry the right person, it jells together.

"I moved to Atlanta because it was better for Ben. I found a good wife. And I'm still close to the guys. Sometime I feel closer because I think about them, I call them and we talk. I never liked Chicago in the first place. I moved to Chicago to get with the Pilgrim Jubilees. But a lot of times I miss the guys because I'm not around them. When we have rehearsals, I might go to Chicago, or they might come down south. And we're still close together—if something happens, they get on the phone and call me and if I can get there any way possible, I'll be there. And I've enjoyed it and I'm still enjoying it. I'm blessed. God has kept His arms around us, the Pilgrim Jubilees. It's up to us to treat each other right and look out for one another. Because we have been together so long. God has kept us for a reason. We stayed here through the storm, through the hard times, the good times, and the bad times. We're still here. And we're going to stay. Until God separates us."

13. Michael Atkins

Rush hour traffic on the I-90 and I-94 freeways through Chicago is nose-to-tail by five o'clock in the morning. From then until well into the night, it's just a question of how busy and how clogged the roads will be. People drive them every day, so obviously it can be done. But as a foreigner hurling myself onto them, I felt an immediate affinity with the little steel ball in a pinball machine. These highways are the most direct route to Michael Atkins's home in northwest Chicago. It's an expedition I'm not looking forward to—and one Michael doesn't think I should make. "You'd have to drive fifty miles, and you'd never find it," he assures me—which is why his large form is dwarfing one of the two chairs in my South Side motel room. It's much easier, he says, for him to come to me than for me to try to find him. Michael is the Pilgrim Jubilees' bass guitarist and the only member born in the city they now call home. He replaced Roosevelt English, and his admiration for his predecessor is almost unlimited. "Nobody," he says in his resonant, slow-spoken baritone, "could play the drive like him." English's playing has had a strong influence on him, and he has built on its foundation. But Michael Atkins is much the better bass player of the two, and the style he has developed is today almost as much an instantly recognizable part of the Pilgrim Jubilees' sound as the lead singing of Cleave and Clay.

"In 1970 was when I first did a concert with the Pilgrim Jubilees. I was playing guitar at that time. I was about fifteen years old. Clay and I met through a friend of Clay's. His name was Hughie Hawkins, and I was playing for his group, the Gospel Clouds. I was over at Hawk's house, and I was playing and Clay came over. He said, 'Man, you sound pretty good.' I said, 'Thank you,' and I'm thinking, 'This is Clay, one of the Pilgrim Jubilees!' I was really excited. Later on, he called me and asked me if I would like to do a recording session with them. I couldn't even sleep that night. Then he asked me if I would like to make a trip with the group. That came about because Bobby was in Valdosta, Georgia—his mom was sick. We went to Buffalo, New York, and, I think, Niagara Falls, and Erie, Pennsylvania—a three-day thing. From there I came back home and continued back at school.

"Roosevelt English is an idol to me. I think that maybe on the slower songs, I probably do better. But when it comes to driving, Roosevelt is the man. I came in playing bass while he was away from the group. Then he returned, so I played drums for about eight months or so, because I was determined to still be a part of the group. We didn't have a drummer, so the guys said, 'You think you can handle the drums?' I said, 'Yeah, I can do that.' During the time I was playing drums, Roosevelt was schooling me on the bass as well. Then he decided he wanted to do something else, and that's when I returned to being the bass player. His family has a group—I think they were called Plain Old English—and Roosevelt was there, helping his family.

"I have four sisters and three brothers. I was born in Chicago [*on May 20, 1955*]. But I spend so much time in the South that they tease me a lot about being from the South, from a little-bitty town my mom is from, called Pelahatchie, Mississippi. When I first told the guys about Pelahatchie, they had never heard of it, even though they're from Mississippi. It's about twenty-four miles from Jackson. I spent a lot of time down there. My dad is from Alabama. Allen Atkins. He passed away March the third this year [1999]. He used to work at a tanning company. Then he worked for a lamp company . . . he was a polisher and buffer. When he retired from that he opened a store on the West Side. Food and liquor, groceries. When he decided to stop doing that, he turned the business over to me. That was about '95. But it was hard to deal with the group and that business. And my first love was the Pilgrim Jubilees, so I said I'll leave the food store alone and I just went out of business. Stayed with my group. My calling.

"I got my start in gospel music from my dad. He was a singer with a group called the Davis Spiritual Five. Clay and Cleave's older brother, Elgie C.B. . . . him and my dad were very good friends. Dad made sure we knew about Jesus and His love, even from a very young age, and he always carried me to church with him. I got into the habit of going with him, so every time he was getting ready to go somewhere, I wanted to go. I would even go to his rehearsals, and I'd be eyeing that guitar. And I appreciate the Davis Spiritual Five. They didn't tell me one time, 'Don't touch that. Leave that alone.' They would say, 'Try it.' I would watch the guy's hands and say, 'OK, that's how he's doing it,' then they would place my fingers on the guitar. And there was another guy, named Eddie. He used to play for a group called the Golden Wings, from the North Side. He taught me a couple of chords. And from there, I just kept practicing and carrying on. We had the records of the Pilgrim Jubilees, and I remember when my dad would take us down south, he would sing 'Old Ship of Zion.' My sisters and I would do the background, and Dad would be singing the lead part. And I remember going to St. Louis with my dad—his group was singing there. I was about nine years old. Back in those days, we would go to the radio station to advertise the program, and they let me play the guitar while they were singing on the radio. Man, I was straight struck! After that, I said, 'This is what I want to do.' "

As well as the Pilgrim Jubilees, Michael listened to other top quartets on radio and on records. The Blind Boys of Mississippi, the Sensational Nightingales, the Gospelaires from Dayton, Ohio, the Mighty Clouds of Joy—"by my dad being in the gospel field, we had [records of] *a variety of the groups." The first national group he saw in action was the Violinaires. "They were singing at the Coliseum. And when I saw them, I said, 'Man!' This was totally different to what we were doing. Their sound, their delivery, their playing . . . it was a professional thing. Up a level in the way that they were doing it. So I said, 'Well, I can take it a step further, too. If they can do it, I can do it.' " As he developed his bass guitar playing, he listened to other gospel bassists and to the best in secular music, includ-*

ing the groups Earth, Wind, and Fire and Sly and the Family Stone. From all these influences and his own experimenting he developed a style that ranges from an unadorned drive behind the fast hard numbers to intricate arrangements in which the bass sometimes plays a melodic counterpoint to the guitar.

"My playing is smooth, but driving. Sometimes I use lead guitar riffs and licks on the bass. And when I hear something . . . I might be just messing around and I'll find something, say, 'Yeah, that sounds good.' Then I figure out how to use it with the Pilgrim Jubilees. I like to thump when it's in order. But there are certain pieces where you don't need thumping, where you have to be smooth, smooth as silk. But if it comes to a point where I need a thump right there, I'll thump it and then come back to that smoothness. And Bobby and I have to work in together. I always have my head cocked to one side so I can make sure I can hear where he's coming from. But for a drummer . . . he has to know what he's doing to deal with us. A lot of them, I guess they're excited because they have all these different pieces up there and they want to hit 'em all. But you don't have to do that. I like that solid lick.

"I sing more now than I used to. I do baritone. Major has such a unique way of doing his baritone—it takes a real person to try to fill his shoes because he has a style of his own. Cleave and Clay will sing in the background and then sing lead, and sometimes it's hard for them when they've been out there singing lead wide open to come back and be a laid-back blender. Sometimes when they come back and they've been driving real hard out there, they have to settle down. So I'll sing the part for a couple of bars. Then they say, 'OK I got it,' and I just back on out and they continue singing.

"In our style . . . well, first off, thanks to God that He has blessed us to put all these different minds together to come up with one sound. I stay away from everybody's style. The Jubes have always had this driving force style, and when I came in, I had to learn that style. But as time went on, I created a style of my own. It all came through prayer, because I would pray—I believe in prayer and practice. I tell a lot of the young guys when they come up and ask me about playing, 'just pray and practice.' A lot of times when we rehearse, I just get the fundamental points of what's going on. Then when I get home, I practice again by myself. Because then I have a direct line to Christ and the vision comes. He guides me through that—and through every situation. I acknowledge Christ, then He directs my path. And He doesn't lead me wrong.

"When Major or Clay, Cleave or Ben write a song, they just have the lyrics on paper, and they basically know what they want. So they'll just come and maybe tap a pencil or something to whatever tempo, whatever rhythm they hear. So we just bump to this rhythm, and they start singing to it. Then they get to a part where they say, 'I need to make a change here, what do you hear?' And we put the ideas together. When we're rehearsing, the average person would listen to us and say, 'What in the world are these guys talking about?' It is totally Jubilee language. Like one will say, 'I want it to go a-bop-a-loo-bop-bop-a-da-da-da. And then you draw back on it and make it go da-da da da-da-ta-da.' And he'll say, 'You draw back and then set it on outside of the bar'—all of this kind of talk. What they want you to do when you set it outside the bar is to draw back in the music instead of punching it, standing on top of it. It'll be laid back but steady keeping the groove at the same time. Or else they might want you do an abnormal change, something different—'outside of the bar.' Then there's 'goose it' or 'put some flavor to it.' I can understand exactly where they're coming from when they say that. But I always tell them, 'If somebody came in here now, they'd say, "These cats are crazy. What are they talkin' about?"' Because some of the guys live out of town, we'll set one week aside and say, 'Every day this week, we're going to rehearsal.' So we'll go out and do a weekend, then when we come back we go into rehearsal every day. Not always in Chicago. Sometimes we do it there, and lately we've been doing it in Mississippi, either in Columbus or Meridian. At hotels where we stay often, they know us and if they have a little banquet room or something like that, they'll let us use the room to rehearse. Or if they have an empty room all the way at the end of the hotel, they'll let us use that room so we won't disturb the other guests."

When Michael joined the Jubes, their popularity was rebuilding after the slump of the late 1960s, and bookings were heavy. Away from home and families for weeks at a time on a schedule that blurred the days into a routine of ride and sing, ride and sing, the group members became themselves a traveling family.

"Sometime we would stay out three weeks to a month. Sometime we were on our own, and sometimes we were working with packages. We would sometimes work through the week by ourselves, and in the weekend we would meet up with a package. Sometimes we would work all week long with the package. When we're working steady, we're around each other more than we are our families. Therefore we become closer. Being on the road, you're away from your home, your children, your wife—your whole family. And sometimes you're away for holidays . . . when my children were growing up, I never was around for Easter, because we would always be working. [*He has seven children—two sons and five daughters—ranging in age from twenty-eight to six. He is married but is separated from his wife.*] Sometimes you get a bit down because people like to be around their families. So all we have is each other, and that takes up the slack. So we become a very family orientated organization.

"We have fun. Bobby McDougle . . . he doesn't play like anybody else. When he's onstage, what you hear is totally Bobby. But when we're having fun, this guy can play so close to B. B. King's style it is amazing. Cleave can play guitar—he plays that old Lightnin' Hopkins type of stuff. He can whip it. And he has an ear for tuning a guitar. He says, 'Get it here . . . you guys' ear is off.' Clay plays, Ben plays a little bit—when he plays, we laugh. A lot of people see us and put us on this pedestal. Some of them are afraid to talk to us because of who we are. But these guys are such fun guys to talk to—just down-to-earth people. And Cleave and Clay—I've heard a lot of people say, 'I would like to speak to them, but I'm afraid.' I say, 'Why? These guys will crack you up. You'll be in stitches in five minutes.' Cleave . . . well, all of the guys, they love to go fishing. We have been on the way to a program and seen a body of water and these guys will say, 'I bet there's some fish out there.' They'll have their fishing gear in the vehicle, so we hit the side of the highway, and here we go on to the bank, digging for bait. I wasn't into fishing at first, but when I saw how much fun they were having I got into it."

As well as the close relationship within the group, the Pilgrim Jubilees have formed friendships with many of the artists with whom they perform. The relationship between the touring groups is a mix of rivalry and comradeship. They are in competition for bookings and for audience acclaim. But they also have the common purpose of spreading their gospel message, and the rigors of the gospel highway are a shared and unifying experience. Because they meet so often on the road, they come to know each other's music, so it is not uncommon for a musician in one group to take the stage with another on the same program if that group needs someone to help out. The Pilgrim Jubilees, for example, do not have their own keyboard player. But they appear on few programs without one. At the Mercy Seat homecoming described in the previous chapter, they had two. One was from the Christianaires, a group with which the Jubes often perform; the other was with the Jackson Southernaires but had been with the Jubes in the 1980s.

"It's not only when they see us at a concert that we talk. Sometime we go to a town where some of our buddies live, so we call them up and we get together. And it's the same way when they get here. Sometimes we call one another long distance. The Violinaires are some of my favorite people to be around. That group . . . we go a long way back. Robert Blair, the lead singer for the Violinaires, he's a great person and one heck of a singer. [Robert Blair died on March 19, 2001.] And Joe Ligon with the Mighty Clouds. I remember several times we have worked together, and after the concert we would sit and just talk. I have played behind the Clouds, Shirley Caesar, Inez Andrews, Dorothy Norwood, the Salem Travelers. The Violinaires . . . I've worked with those guys plenty of time, standing in. We were working with them one time, and we worked from Sunday up until Thursday, then the Violinaires had Friday, Saturday, and Sunday to work. Something was happening with their bass player, and they didn't have a bass for those days. So Blair told me, 'Hey, man, you're going with me this weekend.' So I went on our bus and said, 'Blair needs me to work the weekend. Is that OK with you guys?' They said, 'Sure, man, go ahead.' So I got my gear and went out and did the weekend with the Violinaires."

14. "Please Don't!"

An underlying reason for the camaraderie among traveling professional quartets today is simply that not too many are left. Quartets are not quite an endangered species, but times have changed since the days when they ruled the gospel circuits. Then, competition was fierce, as new groups worked to climb the ladder and those already on its top rungs battled to maintain their positions. The Pilgrim Jubilees quickly found that the meek inherited very little in the gospel music business.

Major: "When we first came on the road, we tried to stay in different hotels to the older groups so we could learn our way without finding ourselves in any situation. Because sometimes they would have a little gathering in that circle . . . they liked to have fun. We didn't want to be part of that. We stayed away and would just show up at the program. Women couldn't get close to us. No women. And as far as drinking and stuff like that—nobody drinking. Our rules were strict. Then we found out they were talking about us, saying, 'The Jubes are stuck on themselves.' So we said, 'Let's loosen up a little bit. But no drinking, no messing around.' So we loosened up a little bit so they would like us more. Because some groups didn't want to work with us. And every time they could tell a promoter something ugly they would. They would say, 'Don't fool with the Pilgrim Jubilees. They like

An early Peacock publicity picture from around 1961. From left, rear: Major Roberson, Cleave Graham, Clay Graham; middle: Percy Clark; front: Rufus Crume. Picture courtesy of Joann Reel.

From left: Cleave Graham, Maurice Dollison, Major Roberson, Roosevelt English; front: Clay Graham, circa 1964. Picture courtesy of Major Roberson.

Rear: Roosevelt English, Major Roberson, Clay Graham; front: Cleave Graham, Charles Green, Bobby McDougle, probably taken soon after McDougle joined the group in 1965. Picture courtesy of Clay and Hazel Graham.

By the early 1970s, the long-term core of the Pilgrim Jubilees was established. From left: Bobby McDougle, Michael Atkins, Ben Chandler, Clay Graham, Cleave Graham, Major Roberson. Picture courtesy of Joann Reel.

Shannon Williams and Clay Graham pose for a publicity picture as the Pilgrim Jubilees sign with Nashboro in 1976. Picture courtesy of Opal L. Nations.

The Pilgrim Jubilees on Malaco. Rear, from left: Major Roberson, Fred Rice, Marco Atkins, Michael Atkins; center: Ben Chandler, Cleave Graham, Bobby McDougle; front: Clay Graham. Picture courtesy of Jerry Mannery, Malaco Records.

Founding members Cleave (left) and Clay Graham. Picture courtesy of Joann Reel.

Backstage at a gospel music program . . . As local groups sing on stage, Pilgrim Jubilees drummer Greg "Bobo" Harris (left) and Violinaires bass player Dwight "Tito" Arthur play dominos in an office converted to a dressing room at the Monticello High School gymnasium in Mississippi. Photo: Alan Young

New Zion Missionary Baptist Church. The church was founded in 1885; the wooden building at which the Graham family worshipped was replaced by this brick structure in 1973. Photo: Alan Young

On stage at Mercy Seat Missionary Baptist Church in Chicago. From left: Fred Rice, Michael Atkins, Clay Graham, Cleave Graham, Ben Chandler, Greg Harris (obscured, rear). Guitarist Bobby McDougle was on stage, far right, but is not in the picture. Photo: Alan Young

Carrying the message . . . Clay Graham goes into the audience while singing "Old Ship of Zion." Photo: Alan Young

Stepping out . . . Bobby McDougle plays his finale to "Too Close." Photo: Alan Young

Bobby McDougle. Photo: Alan Young

Cleave Graham. Photo: Alan Young

Clay Graham. Photo: Alan Young

Major Roberson. Photo: Alan Young

Ben Chandler. Photo: Alan Young

Michael Atkins. Photo: Alan Young

Eddie Graham. Photo: Alan Young

Fred Rice. Photo: Alan Young

Gregory "Bobo" Harris. Photo: Alan Young

to fight promoters.' Or somebody [*from another group*] would say, 'Man, you got a good group. I'm going to get some dates from you so we can work together.' He'd take the dates; after a while, I'd call him. 'We're working on it,' he says. The dates get a little closer, I call him again. He says, 'You're on. Here's the promoter's phone number.' So I call the promoter and he tells me the other group is on the show, but we're not. And you were depending on those programs. And another thing they'll do. A promoter wants a concert. He calls another group, says, 'Hey can you get the Jubes?' 'Yeah man, I can get 'em.' 'Well, we'll have you and the Jubes.' And they won't even call me. And if the promoter doesn't check . . . some promoters are very strict, and they'll call and check. But some don't—they just take the word of the other group. And that guy hasn't called you, hasn't told you one thing. The fans think you've let them down. They say, 'That's the second time the Jubes haven't showed. I'm never coming back to their show.' Now, that is killing your group."

Clay: "Some people protect themselves real highly to keep the prestige around their fellows. These groups held the Pilgrim Jubilees back for a long time. I'll call their names . . . people like the Swanee Quintet, Soul Stirrers, Harmonizing Four, Blind Boys [*of Mississippi*]. We were going to work a package with the Caravans and Shirley Caesar, and the Blind Boys said, 'We'll work in the package if you don't take Major Roberson's group.' That was at its worst back in the '60s, after we got 'Stretch Out.' Then after a while, we were preferred over them. Because we were singing a better message than they were. And we were younger. Now we've gone right past them. Only two weeks ago, a guy called me, said, 'Clay, we're not doing too much right now. I wonder if we could do a few dates.' 'Hey man, no problem. We can hook up for a week or so.' He was happy, but my mind went straight back to him that put his foot on me. That was the Swanee Quintet."

Cleave: "If there's someone else in the same business you are, you always have that rival thing. Everybody wants to see everybody do good, but they don't want 'em to do better than they're doing. I've known some things to happen on stages that were a little bit sneaky. We've had people pull the plug on the electricity. A lot of the time it's jealousy. They know that if they cut you off, that's gonna throw water on your program. And I've had people do different little things to try to halt the group performance on stage. Some would get up and walk through the audience, simply to draw people's attention."

Major: "One group would try to take the whole show and all the praises. But that is not a good intention on the stage. They're out there to try to get a message over to somebody. Maybe to save somebody. And anybody I can't save, maybe the group following me will have a song that will take. But no, some of them want their songs to take care of everybody. And if their songs don't take, they don't want people to listen to your songs."

Not long after Major Roberson's second gunpoint meeting with Don Robey, the Peacock recording drought broke, possibly through the intervention of Evelyn Johnson with Robey. For the first time in four years, the Pilgrim Jubilees returned to Universal in Chicago. The session wasn't a success. The group was using a bass player today remembered only by his hometown, St. Louis, Missouri. Bobby McDougle and Michael Atkins—on his first outing with the group—were playing guitars, the drummer was an unremembered session musician, and Lafayette Leake was playing piano. The producer was Willie Dixon.

Clay: "The boy that was playing bass for us got to the session late. That's how Michael started playing bass. Michael was hired as a guitar player, but when that boy didn't come, he started playing bass. Now, if you put a man on bass that has never played it before, you're not going to get anything solid. And Leake and Willie Dixon weren't jelling too well that day. I remember Willie Dixon telling him, 'Put both hands on it, Leake. Get your elbow off the table.' That session was so poorly that when we sent it to Peacock, they killed it. And I'm kinda glad it didn't come out."

Some months later, the group traveled to Peacock's headquarters in Houston, Texas, to try again. The tardy bass player from St. Louis was gone, replaced by Michael Atkins, who had adapted quickly to his new role. "Too Close" was an automatic selection for one side of the new single; the other was a Major Roberson composition, "Let Me Come Home." Against expectations, the gentle and melodic "Let Me Come Home" rather than the powerful "Too Close" was the hit. Today, Clay Graham realizes that the group had been performing "Too Close" so extensively that "it was worn out—when we released it, everybody had heard it." "Let Me Come Home" is written in Major's trademark style as a new song built on a traditional line—"I haven't been to heaven, but I've heard the streets are paved with gold"—and is an almost wistful yearning for the joys of heaven. Unusually for the Pilgrim Jubilees, it has no lead singer; instead, the group sings the song in quartet harmony. The record did well but didn't lead to more recordings. Peacock's recording activity had slowed, and in 1973 Don Robey sold the label to ABC-Dunhill.

Major: " 'Let Me Come Home' came out, and because we hadn't had a new record in four or five years, everyone in the world played it. It warmed us right back up, and we got going again. So Don Robey didn't mess with us after that. Of course, we didn't try to get away from him, either. And the next thing, I was getting a call from ABC, telling me they had bought our contract. They bought Peacock, and our contract was in that. The man said, 'I have your group. But the contract you're under is a slave contract, and we don't recognize slave contracts. So we want you to sign a contract for us.' But we weren't ready to go back under a contract. So we asked them, 'Could we do a couple of sessions without the contract?' 'Sure.' So that's what we did."

Before the group recorded for ABC-Dunhill, it hired another singer, Charlie Brown, from Detroit. He was a utility—someone able to sing any part and, as a bonus, adept on a number of instruments. "We had heard him singing with different local groups, and he was excellent," Clay recalls. "He could do any part and play practically any instrument, too. He was a great help to the Jubes." Brown stayed with the group for about three or four years; he later became a long-standing member of the Violinaires.

The new album, *Don't Let Him Down* (Peacock PLP-193), reflected changes in the group, in technology, and in society. For the first time, more of the songs were written by Clay than by Major. For the first time, Clay sang more leads than Cleave. For the first time, Bobby McDougle multi-tracked his guitar, laying down a basic part and then going back and adding in other parts. And amid the social turmoil of the early 1970s, the album included a number of songs commenting on the state of the world. But that wasn't a "first." The Pilgrim Jubilees ventured into social commentary in the mid-1960s when they recorded Major's "Mr. President," although it was left "on the shelf" until 1969.

I've heard of wars, and rumors of war, ever since I was born
But I can't understand the laws of the land, why don't they leave our boys alone?

Please, Mr. President, or somebody, tell me what's wrong, tell me what's wrong
Why should our boys lose their lives away from home, before they're grown?

The First World War I can't recall, I can tell you how the second one started
On December the seventh, Nineteen and Forty One, that's when the Japanese, they bombed Pearl Harbor

Please, Mr. President . . .

Now, I have a question, in my heart I'm sincere
Before our boys could pull off their uniforms, they had to go back and fight a war in Korea.

Cleave sings the song in a relaxed baritone over a backing that is almost pure country music, down to a Sons of the Pioneers–style "clip-clop" guitar part. Although it was issued at a time of mounting opposition to America's involvement in Vietnam, the genesis of "Mr. President" was in the Korean War of the early 1950s, and Major did not view it specifically as an anti–Vietnam War song. "My baby brother went to the Korean War. And I was depressed about that. After one war, here's another war. It came and picked my baby brother . . . because, see, he was the closest to me. I'd just come out of the war, here's my baby brother going back into the war." (Major's brother, Jack, survived the Korean War.)

"Mr. President" was an anomaly in the Pilgrim Jubilees' recording career when it was made and seems to have been an experiment in content and style. They have never performed it onstage, and the songwriter credit on the Peacock label is "H. Blount"—the name of Major's wife, Hattie, before her marriage. But the *Don't Let Him Down* album is a deliberate mix of social comment and admonition on the need to live a Christian life. Of the album's ten tracks, one is by Major; another is his reworking of the traditional baptizing theme "Take Me to the Water." The other eight are by Clay. The most trenchant piece of social commentary is "Trouble in the Streets," which in its first verse appears to be a message of support for the police. The second verse makes it brutally clear that it isn't.

We are having a lot of trouble in the streets y'all.
Even the policeman that are on the beat
They are tired of being called pigs and shot at
And I don't blame them for not liking that

Now ain't that right (Ain't that right)
Now ain't that right (Ain't that right)
Now ain't that right (Ain't that right)
That's right, yes it is, yes it is, yes it is

Policeman will tell you to obey the law
In the cruel meanest way that you ever saw
They will raid homes and shoot men without a cause, y'all
But they don't know that one day they're gonna pay for it all

Now ain't that right . . .

There's one thing we all should do
We should stick together if we want to make it through
There is one thing I believe in most of all, y'all
Together we'll stand and divided we'll fall

Strictly speaking, the song is not gospel, as it has no religious references apart, perhaps, from the ambiguous suggestion that "one day they're gonna pay." The reggae-styled "It Isn't Safe" does offer a religion-based solution to the problem it details, but its view of the world is no more optimistic:

It isn't safe, anywhere, any more
It isn't safe, anywhere, any more

It isn't safe to walk the streets alone
You don't even feel secure in your own home
There was a lady on her way home from church
She was attacked by two men
You see

It isn't safe . . .

We should treat sin just like dirt
With the broom of faith we should sweep it aside
Just remember, this is the only way to survive
Do unto others as you would have them do unto you
I declare this is all we have to do

Other admonitions are delivered in "Don't Turn Back," which urges perseverance; "Two Sides of Life," which exhorts Christians to always look on the bright side of life—a difficult injunction for anyone who's just listened to "Trouble in the Streets" or "It Isn't Safe"—and the "later than you think"–themed "No Time to Lose." The up-tempo "Don't Let Him Down," with its repeated plea "Don't let Jesus down," was the album's most successful song, aided by an ABC-Dunhill promotional push, which included issuing it on a 45-rpm single with the same recording on both sides. "We thought it was crazy," says Clay, "but they had their sense. They had confidence in the song, and they did it to stop the DJs from confusing the people by switching between songs. And it worked."

The album didn't sell as well as the group's earlier albums, but at least it did better than its successor. *Crying Won't Help* (Peacock PLP-59216), recorded in Chicago, went on sale in 1975. Again, Clay was the dominant songwriter with five songs. Major wrote three, and the other was an extensively reworked version of the standard "Swing Down Sweet Chariot." With this album, the Pilgrim Jubilees decided to update their sound. **Bobby**: "We used a studio second guitar. His name was Barringer . . . I can't remember his first name—we just called him Barringer. He's the one that started that modern sound in gospel—that crying and that noise like [*the movie*] *Shaft*. We were the first ones to come out with that type of sound, but they didn't play it too much because they said we sounded too rockish." **Clay**: "That was a pretty good album, but I don't think they sold two of them. It sold in one city, Baltimore. Other than that, nothing." The accompaniment on the album is a great deal more "rockish" than on the Jubes' earlier recordings. Barringer uses most of the effects available to a mid-1970s' rock guitarist—wah-wah pedal, distortion, and the "crying" technique in which a note is picked with the guitar volume off, after which the volume is turned up so the after-ring swells up without the sound of the initial pluck. Top blues, R&B, and jazz session musician Sonny Thompson plays piano and probably organ, and Michael Atkins's bass lines are busy and strong, revealing his funk influences.

It wasn't only the accompaniment that made disc jockeys wary of the album. The Pilgrim Jubilees had recognized a developing trend and were making a cautious move toward a softer form of gospel music, one in which direct "God and Jesus" evangelizing is replaced by more diffused "inspirational" messages. Its proponents say they are broadening the appeal of their musical advocacy; critics say the style is aimed principally at achieving a crossover hit in the secular market. The most overt nod in this direction on the Jubes' new album was "Sunshine"—usually known as "Hello Sunshine." Although the song is listed among Major Roberson's BMI compositions, it was partly composed by blues and jazz saxophone player "King" Curtis Ousley and had already been a recording success for three other Chicago gospel acts—organist and choir director Maceo Woods, choir leader Jessy Dixon, and the Soul Stirrers—when the Pilgrim Jubilees recorded it. Their version, led by Cleave, is powerful and spirited, but the song contains no religious references at all, unless the sun is considered to be allegorical.

Gospel roots are strong in some songs. Major's "Call Him Up" reworks the "Jesus Is on the Mainline" telephone-to-heaven theme into a new song, and Clay's "Put On Your Shoes" is a direct invitation to "take a walk with me. . . . We're on our way to see Jesus." Also still strong is the admonitory tone and pessimistic worldview of the *Don't Let Him Down* album. Major's "Exit 100" moves the traditional "Ninety Nine and a Half Won't Do" message into a modern setting by using freeway exits as an analogy—"Exit 100" is "where the good people go," but those who drive too quickly and don't follow the signs find themselves getting off at "Exit 99," from where they have to go "all the way back where you started" and make amends for past wrongdoing.

Clay's "Crying Won't Help" is the album's opening track and its most direct challenge to the listener, throwing down the gauntlet on drug use and community apathy.

> Get off your corner, stop using dope
> For the user there's no real hope
> Look at yourself,
> And tell me what you see
> Do you see a real man
> Or something that'll never be
>
> Crying won't help you none, you got to do something . . .
> You know what you got to do
>
> Stop going around with your head up in the air
> Pretending you're a millionaire
> Smile at the people, please, and turn on your lovelight
> You know what?
> You may encourage some boy or girl
> To stand up for what's right

The message was topical, timely, and compelling. But it did nothing to help sell the album. **Clay**: "Those kind of songs don't go anywhere. We never made one yet that hit, one that people like to hear you sing. Church people don't want to hear anything negative. When that album came out, we were riding in the car listening to the radio, and a man came on and said, 'Pilgrim Jubilees, I know y'all supposed to be here tomorrow. If you're in town anywhere and listening to me . . . Don't! Please don't.' When we got to the program, I said, 'Man, what was that DJ saying on the radio?' It was 'please don't sing rock and roll.' He thought we were going to go rock and roll. And because we tried to change a little bit, the DJs wouldn't play it. That was the worst album we ever put out. And it was the best album we ever put out. But it didn't go anywhere. DJs turned round and put it in the garbage can—'Ain't the Jubes, man.' "

Clay sees the "message" songs as reflections of their times. "Trouble in the Streets," he says, was written from his observations of life for black people in Chicago. "People killing each other, and it's worse now than ever. So that's what the song was—trying to get somebody to see the light. There have been so many incidents where the police go in . . . instead of asking questions, they just kick people's doors in and start shooting. People have been shot while they were sleeping in bed. You'd be surprised at the abuses police commit on certain neighborhoods. They just don't care."

Ben Chandler sees the songs as a response to loss of religious and social values. "We went to church and Sunday school. We were taught at an early age about the works of God. But they're not doing what they're supposed to do for kids today. They've even taken prayer out of school. You can't tell a young child now to cut out that cursing or whatever like we used to do. He might have a gun. Or he might get you later. So there's no respect any more for the older people. There's no respect for the home. You've even got people sticking up churches."

Most of the songs the Pilgrim Jubilees perform are their own, something Cleave sees as a major contribution to their ability to maintain their own sound. "We don't have to go out and get somebody to write something for us. We have the writers right here." The main writers are Clay and Major. Of the two, Major has the more traditional style, often taking an old line or theme and creating a new song from it—although he is adamant in saying this is not something he does consciously. Clay has a more modern ear and is more inclined to try something new, either in melodic structure or lyric concept.

Clay: "Major's writing is somewhat anointed writing. And his punch line is always interesting. He's just a good writer, a very good writer. I've sold more records than he has, but I know who's the best writer. I can come up with fantastic things, soulful things that bust the peoples' hearts and everybody runs to the store to get it. But just to lay back and pat that foot, you listen to Major. And everything he writes has got a good meaning in it. My beat got a little more fancy than Major because I was a little younger than Major and had a different feeling on the beat. I get ideas . . . I got 'Don't Let Him Down' from the sound of a truck passing by. We were going through Tennessee, in the mountains. It was raining. I was driving that big bus going around those curves and that truck went by. I said, 'Whoo! Lord, how could anybody let you down when you're as good as you are to us.' And when I got out of there, I started writing on that sound of the truck. I'll write a song from . . . any sound can trigger off something. I write songs about my feelings. You'll just be walking along and something hits you, bang! There it is. The whole song is sitting there—you just have to sit down and put it together."

Major: "Mine's a more traditional style than his. He writes all kinds of stuff. But the musicians can grab my stuff faster than they can his. I don't have a lot of [*chord*] changes in my songs. I'm a gifted songwriter—I'm ordained through the Spirit to write. I don't write anything on my own. If I had to . . . 'let me see if I can think of a song to write' . . . I would never write a song. I get my songs from all kinds of things. I listen to people talk, or events—I can write about things. The song just automatically comes to me. Sometimes I have so many songs that pile up in me I have to get up in the night and write and I get tired. Then I pray to God to stop these songs, stop these songs, I need some rest. And after a while the songs will vanish from me. And while they're away, no use me trying to write songs. When my songs come to me, the song and the way the music goes come at the same time—it's just something the Lord gave me."

The use of a modern-sounding session guitarist on the *Crying Won't Help* album was not an accident, and it was not something imposed on the Pilgrim Jubilees. While the group regards the "homemade" traditional feel as the core of its style, it also wants to stay abreast of musical trends. One or two groups, notably the Dixie Hummingbirds and the Sensational Nightingales, sustain themselves by re-creating the sound for which they were famous forty and more years ago. It's an option that holds no allure for the Pilgrim Jubilees. They were trendsetters when they burst on to the national scene in 1960; today, they are at least going to keep up with the trends. Influences from soul, reggae, funk, and rap have appeared in the Jubes' repertoire, and in recording they seek to make as much use as they can of modern techniques and sounds. In 1975 the quartet wanting to stay up-to-date had to have a keyboard player.

Clay: "The first keyboard player we had was Larry Moten, from Houston, Texas. He stayed with us about ten years, then he went back home and started playing for his mother's church. They called him 'Ironfingers.' Because he wasn't fast—he would leave his hands on the chords, but he kept a full sound on the bottom for Mike and Bobby to play against. He'd set that sound, and the Jubes would just get up on that sound and ride." [*Moten was with the group for longer than the ten years Clay estimates. He left around 1985 but was back for recording sessions in 1989 and 1990.*] **Cleave**: "It was about '75 when we got the keyboard. Larry left us for some personal reason, then he came back. Then he left again. He was thinking about getting married. And it's kinda hard when the group's stationed in Chicago and you're living in Houston, Texas." **Michael**: "He came from Texas, and he was playing with a group there, George Hines and the Four Winds. We were down there working. We heard him and he heard us and we talked to him. We were trying to expand the music to come up-to-date with the sound. Because at that time, a lot of keyboards were coming in to quartet style."

Major: "You can't upgrade your material and bring new songs and keep that old music. You have to stay with what's going on now. You've got to keep yourself upgraded and your music upgraded so nobody can just come in and step on you. And we're able to change, so people don't get bored. In the writing and the music, we're just as current as you can get. And then we can be just as far back as you want to go." **Bobby**: "It has a lot to do with the young artists who are into it now. It's becoming their thing—like when we were young, coming in. They're young, bringing their sound in now. So the other groups have to upgrade their sound—keep the flavor but upgrade the music. It's in the instruments you use and the style of the arrangements."

Clay: "These young groups are coming out with these new sounds, and I don't want to get behind. I don't want to be like the Dixie Hummingbirds, going up on the stage with that one guitar. No, no! I want to bust the house. I want to go there with that full sound. We might be old as grass, but I want the Jubilees' sound to be there."

15. Cleave Graham: "Back Then"

Cleave Graham sits at his dining-room table, his mind on the days of nearly fifty years ago, when the Jubes first started traveling. "Back then, the groups sat on the stage when the other groups performed. Everyone who was on a program sat on the stage. They didn't stay in their dressing rooms—they didn't run it like show business. I used to admire that. They would call the first professional group, and the other groups would come out and sit. They would become like part of the audience, enjoying the groups just like the audience. But they're onstage where the people can see them. And I think that was a very good thing to do. But it started to cut out soon after we came on the road. We did it for a little while, then we found we'd be the only group sitting on the stage. The other groups would be in the dressing room. They made it like a show instead of a singing program. A gospel program. They made it more like a show. Some of the fellows still come out and sit in the audience [*to listen to other groups*]. I do it. But some of the groups say, 'Hey, you're through. Now you go.' They don't want you attracting people's attention. They want the people's attention centered on them while they're onstage. And you cannot blame them for that. But that old way, when the groups all came out and sat on the stage, to me that was the way. And I feel that we should really go back to that."

The tendency toward a more show-business atmosphere at professional programs was one reason for the demise of the everyone-on-stage era. Another was the extra equipment and personnel required as amplification and instrumental accompaniment became a part of quartet performance. Instead of having four or five performers, groups had eight or nine; instead of just one amplifier for the guitarist, each group had banks of sound gear and a drum kit. Few stages were big enough to hold everyone at once. But the old way demonstrated solidarity and a unity of purpose among the quartets; it also gave a grandstand view of the program—and an insider's view when something went awry. Cleave remembers one of the Pilgrim Jubilees' early away-from-home engagements, around the mid-1950s, in Tallahassee, Florida. Also on the bill were the Soul Stirrers and Morgan Babb—later the Reverend Doctor Morgan Babb—who had recently given up singing with his family group, the Radio Four, in favor of a solo career. At the time, he had no hit record of his own but was well known for his work with the Radio Four, especially "An Earnest Prayer," which starts with a prayerful invocation from Babb before going into an up-tempo variant of the traditional "Come By Here."[1] It was largely on the strength of this record that he was in Florida. Cleave tells the story amid chuckles of mirth.

"We had just come out on the road—that was our first time there. And Morgan Babb, had come out with that song. He'd start it off saying, 'This evening, dear Jesus, this is yours truly Morgan Babb calling upon you . . .' And it was a hit. So they had him on this show in Florida. We were all sitting out onstage and Morgan, he was a very proud man. He had his legs crossed, sitting right up the front. He had long socks on with garters, and he pulled his pants up so high you could see his garter. Had one record. He had gotten to Florida on this particular record. And they called a local group. This group said, 'Ladies and gentlemen, we're gonna come to you in a song that we know y'all done heard. But we're gonna do it our way.' Then they said, 'This evening, dear Jesus, this is yours truly Morgan Babb. . . .' And Morgan Babb is sitting there onstage. When they said, 'Good evening, dear Jesus,' he jumped, and when they said, 'This is your servant Morgan Babb,' Morgan Babb had his legs crossed real high. They used his name and everything. But he had to do that song. That was what made it so bad. Because they really did it! They put a hurtin' on it. I mean, they *sung* that song, man, they sung it good. And Morgan Babb . . . he got up and said, 'Well, my song's been sung already.' So he sang some other songs. But people said, 'Oh, sing the record, man, sing your record.' So he sang it. But that really got him."

Having one of your songs sung before you get to the stage is one of the hazards of singing on programs with other groups. Michael Atkins recalls a more unusual one. "We were in Louisiana one night. I was standing outside and I heard the emcee saying, 'Now, ladies and gentlemen, the Pilgrim Jubilees.' And I didn't have my uniform on or anything. I ran in . . . I'll just have to play in what I'm wearing. And I looked, and they had a female bass player. 'This isn't my Pilgrim Jubilees. . . .' It was a different group with the same name."

An accident-prone area of a gospel performance is the walk into the audience. Most lead singers will at some point in their program leave the stage and walk into the audience; experienced promoters know they need to make sure one of the microphones has a long enough cord to allow this. Singers have been going out into the audience at least since the 1940s; pioneer floor-walkers include bass singer Jimmy Bryant of the Heavenly Gospel Singers, Ira Tucker of the Dixie Hummingbirds, and Silas Steele of the Famous Blue Jays and later the Spirit of Memphis. In the Pilgrim Jubilees, Cleave, Clay, and Ben all have songs during which they leave the stage. To Cleave, it's a matter of "personal communication."

"The closer you are to people, the closer they are to you. It's a thing of feelings. They feel you better, and you get more personal with them. That's where that comes from. Some people [*singers*] do it when the Spirit moves them, for some it's part of their act. Sometimes you can run out there and get in trouble. People jump on you . . . they can trample you. You have to be mindful of people when you're singing and they're in the Spirit. You want them to enjoy. You want communication with them. You want them to feel what you feeling, what you're doing. But you can get problems. One time in Louisiana, I was singing a song and we were wearing regular neckties. I was in the audience, in the aisle, and this lady, she got so excited she ran out and grabbed at me. She missed me—I ducked—but she got the tie. She got the draw end, and she almost hung me. She was so excited, I couldn't even get the tie in my hand. I just had to put my hand in between it and my neck and hold it up until I could pull the tie over my head and let her have it.

"In Nashville one time—we weren't singing on the show, I just happened to be in the area and I went to the program. They had the Spirit of Memphis, they had the Pilgrim Travelers, and the Five Blind Boys of Alabama. They were all sitting up on the stage, and they called the Spirit of Memphis. They had Silas Steele—he was one of the first to jump off the stage. When he would get the song going and the people going, Steele would . . . he was very respectful. He would turn around, look at his fellows and say, 'Excuse me' or 'Pardon me, Spirit of Memphis.' Then he'd jump off the stage. But what happened this day . . . he got it going good and everybody was halellujahing. He turned around and looked at the rest of his fellow, said, 'Pardon me, Spirit of Memphis' and ran up to the edge of that stage—and it was high! So he changed his mind. To get to the audience, he had to go out the door off the stage, down the steps, and out through another door, and that way he's down in the audience. He turned round and went through the first door and closed it behind him. He got to the other door and it was locked. His fellows were on the stage; they've got the music going and the harmony going, waiting for him to come out. So he decided to come back to the stage. He came back up to the first door—and that one had locked when he shut it. Now his fellows are out there singing and waiting for him to come out, and he's locked in there. So he starts knocking. 'Open the door, I'm locked in.' And they act like they can't hear. Clarence Fountain and Percell Perkins [*of the Blind Boys of Alabama*] were sitting there together. Clarence says, 'What's wrong?' Perkins says, 'Steele got locked in that dressing room and he can't get out.' Clarence says, 'He's locked in? Can't get out?' Perkins says, 'He can't go to the audience and he can't get back to the stage.' Clarence says, 'You gonna open the door?' Perkins says, 'No!' Then Clarence says to Percell Perkins, 'Take me offstage, take me offstage!' Because Clarence is blind, and he wanted to get off because he didn't want the folks to see him laugh.

"And when they called the Five Blind Boys of Alabama . . . back then, they liked to go with getting the sympathy of audience. Him being blind, he had folks' sympathy already. But Clarence says [*Cleave goes into a remarkably accurate mimicry of Fountain's stage delivery*], 'Look-a-here, boy. Let me tell you one thing. The folks want to know, people want to know, how come I'm blind. Let me tell y'all what happened to me. You know they sent me overseas in the war.' The background singers said, 'Whoa!' Said, 'I was on the ship, I'm gonna tell you how I got blind.' 'Whoa!' 'I was on the ship . . .' 'Whoa-oh-oh!' '. . . and the ship got bombed. And I got killed! No. I mean I got . . .' Man! There a lot of funny things. . . . Same thing happened to me one night in Newton, Georgia. We and the Violinaires were there. I got up, and I was singing 'Too Close.' The Spirit was high and I was going and going, and I made a statement . . . I told 'em, I said, 'Lord, you know I'm your father, and you're my child.' Said it backwards. Meant to say, 'You're my father, and I'm your child.' Boy, my spirit left! I couldn't wait to finish that song."

16. Blazing in the Blizzard

Crying Won't Help was the last album the Pilgrim Jubilees made for Peacock. ABC-Dunhill wound the label down, and by 1976 it had ceased recording. Nashboro had shown interest in having the group back during the Don Robey years; now the Jubes were prepared to reciprocate the interest. Nashboro had changed extensively since they left it in 1959. Ernie Young, in his seventies, had sold the label to the Crescent Investment Company around 1966. The following year, a Crescent-owned theater in Nashville was converted into the Woodland Recording Studios, replacing Young's handkerchief-wrapped microphone with a multitrack recording facility. In charge was Shannon Williams, who joined the company as an eighteen-year-old in 1960. Although he was not a gospel music devotee when he joined Nashboro, exposure to the music—allied with his own white Holiness church background—converted him, and as well as running the company, he was its main gospel producer.[1] Nashboro still had a number of its older artists, including the Swanee Quintet; it had also acquired a number of new artists, among them some well-established names from other labels. Its marketing had improved, and it was a much more significant gospel force than it had been in the 1950s.

Although Major recalls Shannon Williams approaching the group during its Peacock drought, the Pilgrim Jubilees' return to Nashboro had its origins in discussions aimed at entering into a management contract with Alex Bradford's manager, Richard Becker. "We did a Broadway show in New York with Alex Bradford, and Richard Becker was there," says Clay. "So we started talking to him." Despite some misgivings, the Jubes decided that outside management might be good for them. **Clay**: "We went along with him—he and Major were arranging it. When they got everything hooked together, Major showed us the contract, and I said, 'Give it to me.' Because I had my lawyer then. Gene Shapiro. How that happened, I knew I wasn't brilliant enough to keep people off me with these contracts. And a lady called Irene Ware [*radio DJ and promoter Irene Johnson Ware*] told me, 'Clay, why don't you try Gene Shapiro in Chicago? He's a lawyer—he's got Albertina Walker and Mahalia Jackson.' " [*Eugene Shapiro was a young white lawyer in Chicago when Jackson abruptly shifted her business from a well-established black law firm to him; the world-famous client helped him establish himself as an entertainment lawyer.*[2]]

Shapiro advised against signing the contract—today Clay recalls that it contracted the group for twenty years and gave Becker half the group's earnings. The Jubes returned it unsigned and severed relations with Becker. But during their discussions, the manager had been in contact with Shannon Williams—Alex Bradford recorded extensively for Nashboro—about the possibility of the Pilgrim Jubilees joining the label. So when the group then went ahead on its own and signed a contract with Nashboro, Becker responded with lawsuits—Clay recalls that he, Cleave, and Major were each sued for a million dollars; Major remembers the figure as one hundred thousand dollars and says every member of the group was sued. Clay went back to Eugene Shapiro. "He called his secretary in and said, 'Write [Becker] a letter, please.' And we haven't heard from Richard Becker since. But we did sign up with Nashboro for two years and a two-year option."

Today, Major recalls Richard Becker with no more affection than does Clay—"He wound us up so tight in that contract till we would have been singing for him." One of the attractions for Major in signing with Nashboro was that he would retain publishing rights to his songs. While the Pilgrim Jubilees were recording for Don Robey, these rights were assigned to his Lion Publishing, meaning that Robey, rather than Major or Clay, received this portion of the song's revenue. "He took it all," says Major. "We got nothing." Appropriating the publishing rights—and sometimes even the songwriter credit—was once a common practice in sacred and secular recording; label owners considered it a levy artists should be willing to pay to be recorded.[3] But when the Jubes started recording for ABC-Dunhill, Major and Clay set up their own publishing companies. Clay's company is Clay Graham Associates; Major has Chi-Town Music and Wolfe City Music. Cleave also saw attractions in moving back to Nashboro. "Shannon was giving the groups good attention, and his distribution was better. To me, recordings are one of your biggest ways of advertising the group. So when they promise they're going to do good things for publicity for your group, that catches my ear."

The signing of the Nashboro contract was the point at which Clay became the group's manager. A quarter of a century on, the background to the change is hazy. Major recalls that he gave up being manager some time earlier, handing the position over to Cleave. From there, he says, several group members, including Larry Moten, held it before Clay. Cleave remembers succeeding Major as manager, probably when only he, Clay, and Bobby were on the road. But Major conducted the group's business during its time at Peacock, and he was in charge of negotiating with Becker. At that point, Clay stepped in, and when the group's first Nashboro album appeared in 1976, the notes listed him as manager. "I was very nosey and always wanted to know," he says. "There were things that weren't looking right to me, and I did a lot of grumbling. So the group made me the manager." It appears the change was accompanied by some acrimony, which would at least partially account for today's dim memories. Clay tells of heated discussions with Major over Becker's management contract and the decision to reject it but adds: "If somebody has been your leader for a while and then someone else comes in with different ideas, there will be some controversy. But we dealt with it. I stuck to what I believed and what I thought was right and what was good for the group. And Major . . . Major's a good man. He made a lot of obvious mistakes. But he's still a good guy. And he was a good manager. If it had not been for Major, we probably wouldn't have made it. We'd probably still be singing around on the North Side."

The sleeve notes to the first Nashboro album, *Don't Close In on Me* (Nashboro 7169), proclaim it as the "return of the Pilgrim Jubilee Singers to the Nashboro Records family," and the recordings show a group with renewed confidence in itself and its abilities. All the songs were written by group members, and they cover the full range of styles, from inspirational to core God-and-Jesus gospel. Admonition—for not spending enough time in church—is delivered in Clay's "Christians, What You Used to Do (You Don't Do Now)"; unequivocal Christian faith is in Major's "He Brought Joy to My Soul" and "I'm Coming Home" and in Clay's "We Need Prayer" and "Only God Can Help Us." Clay has a new sermonette, "Three Trees," which tells of "a large oak tree, a large pine tree . . . and a small cedar tree" growing on a hillside. A storm destroys the oak and the pine, but the cedar survives. When people dig down to find out why the smallest tree had defied the storm, they find its roots wrapped around a large rock. "My soul is kinda like this tree . . . wrapped up and tied up all in my Father," comes the denouement as the group eases into the traditional song, "I'm So Glad Trouble Don't Last Always." "Don't Close In on Me," the title track of the album, is a pensive reflection on aging, written by Clay.

> Life don't close in on me
> Life, please don't close in on me
> Life, oh life, don't close in on me
> Things I wanted to do, things I want to say
> So much needs to be done before my race is run

Clay was barely forty when he recorded this song. But, he says, "I looked at my friends around me, getting to where they couldn't bend over to pick things up, couldn't walk fast any more, couldn't climb the steps. The idea came from that. And it worked pretty good." Of the ten songs on the album, four were written by Major and five by Clay; for the first time, no traditional material was used apart from "Trouble Don't Last Always" at the end of "Three Trees." The last track was guitarist Bobby McDougle's first—and so far, only—songwriter credit. In fact, Bobby wrote the music for "Hand In Hand," but most of the lyrics came from Major. "He helped me a lot on it—he just didn't take any credit for it," says Bobby. "Just like I help on his. So he was showing he appreciated it by helping me with mine. That's the way it works." Major's recollection is similar but more succinct: "He had the music; I wrote the words, and I gave it to him."

Larry Moten's organ playing had not been fully integrated into the repertoire, and he plays on only three songs. If any instrument dominates the album, it is Michael Atkins's bass guitar. At the age of twenty and after five years with the group, he was well on the way to the full development of his distinctive style, combining driving rhythm with melodic ornamentation. Ben Chandler's top-heavy Afro hairstyle in the cover photograph gives notice that the group is moving with the times; the music on the disc confirms it. The choppy, propulsive push of the opening track, "Step Out," sets the pattern, and the bass guitar–driven impetus is sustained throughout the album, even on the slower numbers. One track, "He'll Step Right In," recaptures the "Stretch Out" beginnings, with a walking bass part underpinning Cleave's exuberant lead vocal and a guitar part from Bobby that ranges from Nashville country licks through blues tinges to jazzy ninth chords. The overall feel is of a group enjoying its work, and the album is a welcome return to form after the edgy pessimism of the last two Peacock LPs.

Clay: "With Nashboro, we always did an album in two days, three at the most. That was a long time. In the beginning [*the 1950s*] we were doing nothing but singles, so we'd do that in half a day and we were gone. But when you're doing eight, nine, ten, or twelve songs, and you're doing them in pieces, you consume a lot of time. The background sings it once, then when you've finished, we'd do that background over that again. Sometimes we'd do it three times. That's to bring that big sound in there. Then you do your instruments, then your lead [*singer*] has got to come in. So on one song, you could spend . . . sometimes we spent an hour and a half, two hours, three hours on one song. Today, sometimes we go for seven or eight days and they're still not finished. Go on home and go back later and finish 'em."

Don't Close In on Me was issued in 1976. The following year the Pilgrim Jubilees returned to the Woodland Studios to make *Now and Forever* (Nashboro 7181). Larry Moten played a full part in this session, and the instrumentation was augmented for some tracks by an electronic keyboard. But the overall feel is more subdued than on the first album; a somber mood is set by the first track, Clay's "We're the People," a statement of protest, pain, pride, and defiance. For the first two choruses, the group mirrors his "We're the people" line; on the third and fourth, the response changes with each line.

We're the people, we're the people
We're the people, we're the people

We've worked so hard, we don't even have a flag
We're the lonely people, don't even know our name

We're the people . . .

We give all we have, and that wasn't enough
You're trying to destroy my pride, you know you can't do that

Something within me that holdeth the reins
Something within me, helps me to bear the pain[4]

We're the people (Just keep on walking)
We're the people (Just hold your head up high)
We're the people (You should have a lot of pride)
We're the people (Just keep on walking)

After giving all I have, I'm willing to give more
You see, I'm a thoroughbred and I've got just what it takes
A whole lot of loving
And understanding
I've got compassion
For my sisters and my brothers

Clay: "The black man doesn't have a flag here. We just share the white man's flag. We don't know where we come from. We were captured in Africa and brought here. We were treated like horses. And we're the people that worked so hard. We didn't have anything to call our own. So you say it sometimes to let people know that you know exactly where you stand."

Four of the nine songs on the album are Clay's, although "Stop By Here," credited to him, is heavily based on the spiritual "Come By Here." Major also has four and is credited with a remake of "Wonderful" from 1963. Major provides the social commentary, with the fatalistic observation that "the world is in a bad condition, and we can't do nothing about it but pray." On the album sleeve and on a Nashboro single, the song is called "The World Is In a Bad Condition." On the record label and a subsequent reissue, it has the more neutral title "Changing World." On another of Major's songs, "He Went That Way," Cleave does an extended narration, delivering an emotional and passionate description of the life of Jesus, focusing on His ascension into heaven.

Maintaining the one-a-year schedule, the third Nashboro album, *Singing in the Street* (Nashboro 7198), went on sale in 1978. Of the eight tracks, all but two—Major's "Love Everybody" and Clay's "Like He Said"—were making their second appearance on record. The surprise among them is a new version of "We're the People." Lyrically, it is almost identical to the version on the previous album, but the backing is beefed up and after the last chorus goes into an extended instrumental groove, with solos from Bobby, Michael, and Larry. Says Cleave: "Shannon Williams wanted us to redo it. He wanted to put more to it. He felt like it was a good time for that song." A remake of "A Child's Blood" restores parts of the sermonette used in the Peacock single version but cut from the album version; a new "Exit 100" also has its narration extended. The other repeats are "Are You Ready (To Serve the Lord)" from the final Peacock album, Major's "My Soul" from the mid-1960s, and "Let Me Come Home," which had stayed in the group's repertoire since its first appearance in 1970. "People want to hear them again," says Cleave of the remakes. "Once a record gets a certain amount of age, the company doesn't put too much to it—it puts its interest in newer stuff. But when you got a bunch of people steadily asking for it, then the company says, 'Why don't you re-record it?' So you go back and redo it."

This policy reached its apogee with the next Nashboro recording. The aim for this session was twofold—to make the group's first live concert recordings and to create new versions of its older hits. The project was Clay's idea; it ran into almost immediate difficulties. Major was still the group's main organizer, but he had decided he needed to learn more about the business of music and had taken a temporary job with Subrena Artists, a New York agency that handled a lot of the Pilgrim Jubilees' bookings. "I was learning the principles of booking," he says. "It was very educational for me." He didn't sing on all the group's shows during his six months in New York but continued handling its bookings. Meanwhile, in Chicago, Clay was trying to organize the live session. He had decided the program to record was the Jubes' 1979 homecoming at the Dunbar High School on Martin Luther King Drive on the inner South Side.[5] His main obstacle was that Shannon Williams wasn't keen on the idea and didn't want to spend much money on it. As well, the project was plagued by technical problems—even the weather was against it.

Clay: "The day of the program there was just that much snow! It was banked up eight feet. They had to get salt and cut through the snow and ice so when the people got out of their cars, there were tracks they could walk through to the school on the other side of the snowbank. And when they were taking the recording equipment out of the truck, it fell and went down under the snow. So when we finished the recording, there weren't but two voices in the background—the other channels had cut out because the machine was wet. I had to go into that studio and stay sometimes till four o'clock in the morning re-recording the different parts. Because we didn't need for it to fail. It was our project. I meant for the album to be right."

Shannon Williams overcame his misgivings about the project and issued it as a double album, packaging two vinyl discs inside a single sleeve. The live session produced enough material to fill three sides; the set was completed with four tracks from previous Nashboro albums. The album (Nashboro 27212) was titled *Homecoming*, but the Pilgrim Jubilees refer to it as "Blazing in the Blizzard," the heading on a dedication Clay wrote for the sleeve notes. Although only one of its songs had not been recorded before, it was the group's most successful Nashboro issue, selling more than twenty-two thousand copies. "That's a good album for gospel," says Clay.

Gospel music is particularly suited to live concert recordings, as the interaction between performer and audience fuels the excitement, often producing better performances than could be done in the studio. "I enjoy doing them and then listening to them," says Michael Atkins. "And when you're doing it . . . to me, it makes me more aware. Because once it's on that tape, it's there. It keeps you on your toes." In fact, it was possible even in the 1970s to do studio overdubs to patch up mistakes—or insert vocal parts not taped by a soggy recording machine—although the practice was not as widespread and blatant as it is now, when concert recordings are routinely augmented with extra singers and musicians.

If the sequence on the *Homecoming* album is the same as that of the concert—and it appears likely most of it is—the Jubes came out firing, opening with an aggressive rendition of "We're the People." Strongly displayed is an addition to the instrumental lineup, the lead guitar of Chris Johnson, a young Chicago musician whose playing has many of the hallmarks of "Barringer," the session guitarist used on the final Peacock album. **Bobby**: "That cat was awesome. He used to have his own group, Little Chris and the Righteous Singers. He'd been around us, opening shows and things like that, but he wasn't actually with us at that time. He rehearsed with us for it, but we just had him as a second guitar player for the session." Unlike record buyers four years earlier, the audience obviously had no qualms about the rock-influenced guitar sound, and the reception for the opening song is enthusiastic. But Clay is still feeling his way as he introduces "Life's Evening Sun," concluding with the applause-milking line, "If you remember this song, I want you to give us a great big hand." The applause duly comes, then the group sings only one verse of the song, setting a pattern for much of the early part of the program—"Stretch Out" is rattled through in just over two minutes, "No Time to Lose" takes a minute and a half, "He Brought Joy to My Soul" comes and goes in two minutes. The only song making its first appearance on record is "I've Got Jesus (That's Enough)," a reworking of the Dorothy Love Coates song "That's Enough," recorded by the Original Gospel Harmonettes in 1956.[6] The sermonette "True Story" gets a longer run—and an enthusiastic reception—and the group finally hits top gear on the eleven-minute open-throttle "Don't Let Jesus Down."

Cleave's introduction to this song encapsulates the differences in the onstage personas of the Graham brothers. Clay works assiduously to the audience, building rapport, seeking involvement and approval. "Did you like that one? If you liked it, please give us another hand." Cleave's focus is on the message he wants to convey, and his stern declamations leave no doubt it is a message the audience needs to hear. "I want to tell you again, the same thing I told you last time. Those of you that's under the sound of my voice that know you've been born again, I beg of you as one Christian to another to lift the name Jesus." The 1979 concert version of "Don't Let Jesus Down" has evolved considerably from the Peacock version of six years earlier. Cleave starts it, singing the verses over a driving beat. After working through the verses, he moves the song into its drive, singing single lines to the backing vocal response of "Don't let Jesus down." The backing line shortens to "Hold on," and Ben Chandler steps forward to take over the lead. The song is now a free-form chant during which Ben prowls into the audience, going as far as his microphone cable will let him, delivering a series of repeated lines—"Have you been born again?," "He sanctified my life," "Anybody got the Holy Ghost?," "Can I get one witness?"—a stream-of-consciousness torrent in which each thought is related only to the overall theme of the conversion experience. The audience is on its feet, shouting encouragement and clapping in time. The end is signaled when Cleave picks up the vocal again from the stage. He and Ben duet as Ben moves back to the stage, and an accentuated percussive bass riff from Michael Atkins cues singers and musicians that the end is nigh.

"Don't Let Jesus Down" in this form is a tour de force that has stayed in the Pilgrim Jubilees' repertoire. On that winter night in 1979, it paved the way for another guaranteed showstopper, Clay's "Old Ship of Zion." This, too, had evolved from the 1964 Peacock version, gaining a spoken introduction that Clay still uses today. His delivery then and now is that of a preacher reaching the peroration of a sermon, including use of the collective noun "church" to refer to the audience, repetition of words and phrases for emphasis, and the leaving of long gaps to increase the tension. He speaks in short, sharp phrases, punctuated by audience calls and shouts. His 1979 speech is a classic gospel introduction, linking the song just sung to the one about to be sung, then bringing in a personal element to establish a link between singer, song, and audience.

> You see, He's been too good to me, church, to ever think about letting Him down. God brought me from a mighty long way. And I'm so glad, church, that I can stand here and tell you what side I'm on. That is Jesus. Jesus! I wonder do you ever call Him sometimes when things are not going too well? I wonder, do you go down on your knees, tell God Almighty? One thing I want to know from you, church, that is, has God been good to you? Has He been good to you, church? You see, I remember down at a little place that they call Houston, Mississippi. Jesus! He untied my hands. I never will forget that day, church. One Wednesday, oh yeah! One Wednesday, He got all in my hands, church, He got all in my feet, He got all in my eyes. Every, every, every time I think about it, Jesus, Jesus, Jesus all over me. I never will forget the song they sung. The preacher walked up in front of the mourners' bench [*a long pause*] said, "You've been here for three long days now. If you believe, come up here and take this seat." Oh Lord! "If you don't believe, stay there. Stay there." I never will forget what the preacher said. Walked down in front of us, looked up towards Heaven and said these words: " 'T-i-i-i-s-s . . ." Seems like it was just yesterday . . . " 'Tis the old ship of Zion . . ."

The extended " 'Tis" before "Seems like . . ." is a false start to the song. Today, Clay will repeat this false start three or four times, each time turning the screw a little tighter on the tension. When he finally carries on with "the old ship of Zion," the shout from the audience is as much release of that tension as it is enthusiasm for the song.

* * *

A gospel group deciding which songs to sing in a program has to consider a number of factors—and in the end, for the Pilgrim Jubilees, the usual process is to start with nothing planned apart from the first number. But even if the planning is abandoned, the factors still exist. One is the conservatism of gospel audiences. They know many of the songs, and the ones they want to hear are the ones they know. Then there are the request lists. Before any program, the group will receive audience requests—sometimes more than it could sing in a six-hour performance. The length of the program has to be considered. A twenty-minute set has to have maximum impact with little lead-in; an extended performance has to be paced so audience interest is maintained without peaking too early. The group's place in the program is a factor—driving too hard near the start of a program can push the audience more than it wants to be pushed. The performance of the group immediately before may force modification to a planned list, either to create a contrast in styles or because someone earlier on the program has done one of "your" songs—although this problem is sometimes ignored by a following group with confidence in its version of the already-performed song. A group with a new recording has to make sure it performs some of the new material to publicize the recording. And finally—as happened to Cleave Graham the first time he sang "Too Close"—the Holy Spirit may intervene and completely change any predetermined plans.

When the Pilgrim Jubilees performed their Chicago homecoming at Mercy Seat on Mother's Day in 1999, Clay wanted to start the set with some newer songs the group had never sung in Chicago. It wasn't a resounding success. The group was uneasy about singing the songs—"We mumbled our way through them," Clay said afterward—and the audience didn't know the material and reacted coolly. An exception was one woman in the second row. She wasn't hearing what she wanted to hear and maintained a barrage of comments—"You're not singing yet" and "When are you going to sing?" were the mainstays—which easily carried to the crowded stage area. The Jubes battled her for five songs, then gave in and rocked into "Don't Let Jesus Down." The effect on the second row critic was immediate. "Now you're singing," she crowed triumphantly, "now you're singing!"

Major: "They'll let you know where they stand. They want you to hurry up and get to what they want. You can't do all the requests. Time won't permit that. But sometimes, you might have a good hot song and you'll get ten or fifteen requests that people bring up to you for the same song. So that's an advantage. Two songs, I can hardly remember doing a program without them. 'The Old Ship' and 'Don't Let Him Down.' 'Stretch Out' was like that, too, twenty years ago. It took us a long time to get away from 'Stretch Out.' When we got ready to sing a fast song, it had to be 'Stretch Out.' But it wore out—other things took its place. It has an old sound now. If you played it, it wouldn't sound like the nowadays music."

Cleave: "I believe in building your own fire. If a group's been on the stage performing and they call you after that group, you have to come in a different way than they left. If they left the stage with a beat, with a hallelujah song, you don't come up with a hallelujah song. They just left—now you have to get the people attracted to you. So you have to do something different."

Clay: "Sometimes we decide ahead what we're going to do. Like at Mercy Seat I put in four songs we had never sung in Chicago. Do a little of them to let them know we can do it. But we were kinda tippy-toeing. And the audience starts grumbling that you're not singing enough of the right songs. 'Old Ship,' 'Too Close,' 'Don't Let Him Down,' and 'Won't It Be Wonderful.' Those four we just cannot take out of the lineup. Because when the request lists come up, you're gonna see those songs. Then when you sing them, other folk say, 'Y'all singing those same songs all the time.' When you have a new album, you've got to sing those songs. You'll sell 50 percent more records singing a song than you would if you just put the record out without singing the songs from it.

"Usually we don't decide before a program what we're going to sing. I go up there with an open mind and feel my way. I can tell the atmosphere of the audience, what kind of spirit they've got, from that first song. When you see them laying back in their seats, you've got a problem. But if they're sitting up in those seats when you come out, they're waiting on you, they're ready for you. And if they're responding when you're out there and then they start leaning back in those seats again, they're getting comfortable on you so you have to come up with something, a gimmick, to arouse them again. So you go to your gimmick things [*amusing songs or songs with choreography are examples of "gimmick things"*] and loosen them back up. Then you go on and sing to them. Sing to them in the Spirit. Let the Lord . . . you're singing for the Lord, not for them. Go on and praise him. Once you've started praising Him, they've received it already."

Another important element for groups performing in multi-artist programs is their place on the bill. The Pilgrim Jubilees are sufficiently well known and well regarded that they are unlikely to be ever asked to open the show. But they also very seldom close a program, even at their own homecomings. This is also an indication of their status, as the closing spot on a gospel program—unlike a secular show—is not keenly sought. It seems to be almost a rule that programs will start late, then overrun their time. The group that comes on last often has to sing to an audience that is tired, restless, and ready to go home. But being on too early also has drawbacks.

Clay: "If you're at the start of a program, by the time five or six more groups come on after you, what you did is forgotten. If you're down there where the timber is falling, you can put a tree in the road and they can't move that tree. You've starred. You can put a tree in the road at the start, but somebody's gonna dig it up. So you get about two before the tail end, or next to the tail end, and those last two can't get that tree out of the road, and your name is ringing! Right at the end, that's the wrong spot again. I like to be at, say, number three or number two from the end. Because then you've got the minds of the people. If you're last and your stuff isn't knocking them out of their seats straightaway, you'll see them putting on their coats and going home. But if you've got somebody behind you, they'll sit there because they want to get a taste of the other group, so you've got a chance to get your point over. I like to be in that last three. I don't want that tail end, and I don't want the front. I want to be where you can be thought of after you're gone."

17. "We'd Have Been Up There . . ."

Although the "Blazing in the Blizzard" album sold well, Clay Graham says: "We didn't get a quarter out of it. The company went out of business. Well, they sold it to another company, then they sold it to some bank, then that bank did something else with it. It moved around so much that it was hard to keep up with what was going on." Nashboro was not, in fact, sold until 1981, but the Pilgrim Jubilees' contract expired around the time of the double album, and lawyer Gene Shapiro found them a more lucrative opportunity. At the same time, they signed a professional management deal—then changed their minds.

Clay: "There was a DJ in Nashville called Hossman. [*Bill "Hossman" Allen, a white DJ on Nashville's WLAC who played blues, R&B, and gospel. Like many DJs of the time, he also promoted concerts.*] We did a lot of things for him, including some free things. In return he hooked us up with Buddy Lee. He was the manager of Sammy Davis Jr. . . . all the biggies.[1] Him and Hoss Allen were buddies. [*Buddy Lee, a New Yorker who started his entertainment career as a professional wrestler, died in 1998, but the Nashville-based Buddy Lee Attractions is still active, handling mainly country music acts.*] We went to Buddy Lee's office and talked to him. He said, 'Well, I don't know that much about gospel, but I'll listen to your group.' He drove to Atlanta, Georgia, to hear us. Then he booked a big show in Nashville. He was used to getting thirty thousand people at his shows. This one got about twelve hundred. And when he walked in to that gospel show with all that talent and saw about twelve hundred people, he said, 'Wow! I've got a lot of work to do.' But he kept searching out things, working for us. Then Gene Shapiro called me, said, 'Hey, I've got you a contract. Savoy.' His daughter was married to the son of the man that owned Savoy. He said, 'They need a good group. They want the Pilgrim Jubilees. I can get you a $144,000 contract over a period of years.' I said, 'Go after it.' I mean, that was big money!"

Savoy, founded by Herman Lubinsky and based in Newark, New Jersey, was by the 1980s gospel's leading label and the only one still active from the big four—Peacock, Specialty, Nashboro, and Savoy—of the 1950s and 1960s. Its catalog included some of gospel music's biggest names, led by James Cleveland, who recorded more than fifty Savoy albums. The new contract put the Pilgrim Jubilees on a label that was still actively recording and promoting gospel music. It also led to a decision Clay now acutely regrets.

Clay: "We had a nice contract coming up with Savoy. Buddy Lee was supposed to get 15 percent of us. But we got afraid and starting to talking. 'If he finds out that we're getting this much money. . . .' So we got our little change and put it in our pockets. Then we called Buddy Lee and canceled his contract. What we should have done, we should have turned that Savoy contract over to him. Then he would have seen some real money coming in from the Pilgrim Jubilees, and he wouldn't have minded spending some thousands to put us where we're supposed to be. But we didn't have sense enough to know. We got a little piece, and we tried to stick it under the table. We'd have been gone! We'd have been up there. Shows with Sammy Davis Jr. and all. Because that's where he was heading—booking us with those people as an opening gospel act. It would have been nothing to get ten or fifteen thousand dollars a night. But we ran right away from that money."

After the success of "Blazing in the Blizzard," the Pilgrim Jubilees decided their first Savoy record should be another live album, but one containing all new material. This meant appearing at the New Refuge Deliverance Church in Baltimore with a program mainly of songs no one had heard. "It was dangerous for us to do that," says Major. "Because when you sing a lot of stuff people aren't familiar with, you don't know if they'll like it. You're taking a big chance. You could get booed off." That didn't happen—the group was in good form, and the presence of the recording equipment would have smoothed the new material's path—and *Keep On Climbing* (Savoy SL-14584) was issued in 1980.

The Jubes' lineup had expanded to eight with the addition of drummer Wayne "Puddin' " Davis from Rocky Mount, North Carolina. He became the group's longest-serving drummer, staying for about five years before ill health forced him to leave. Augmenting the accompaniment for the Baltimore program was Savoy session pianist James Perry, who played on all the group's recordings for the label. The album produced two popular successes, one from each of the writers—and neither in the hard-driving style for which the Jubes were noted. One was another Clay Graham sermonette, "Rich Man, Poor Man," about a wealthy man contemplating suicide. "He was standing in an open window on the eighth floor. But before he jumped, he looked down and saw an old ragged man singing and eating out of a garbage can. It was amazing to him; he said, 'Well, before I take my life, I've just got to talk to that man.' " The song the poor man is singing is the reflective "I'm Happy with Jesus Alone"; predictably it saves the rich man's life and soul. "I'm Happy . . ." is the only song on the album not written by Major or Clay; it is by Charles Price Jones, cofounder with Charles Harrison Mason of the Church of God In Christ. The other success was Major's gentle "Don't Let Me Drift Away," led by Clay—a departure, as Cleave sings lead on almost all of Major's songs—but with the harmony of Cleave, Ben, and Major prominent.

When they joined Savoy, the Pilgrim Jubilees were in effect consorting with the enemy. Savoy's roster included quartets, but its focus was mainly on soloists and choirs, and by the 1980s, choirs were seriously eroding the quartets' popularity and status. Radio stations were playing choirs rather than quartets, the number of choirs performing outside churches was increasing, choir recordings were proliferating, and the gospel music audience's loyalties were shifting. Choirs that appear in public concerts, or "services"—quartets have "programs," choirs have "services"—are a long step from the traditional church choir. Vocal harmonies are elaborately and carefully arranged behind strong soloists; accompaniments use a wide range of electric and electronic instruments and often mirror developments in secular pop music. Some church-based choirs have achieved wider fame, but since the 1970s the best-known choirs have mainly been "community" choirs—ensembles established by one or two people and not affiliated with any single church. Choirs can be as small as fifteen or twenty voices, or they can have more than a hundred. The larger ensembles are known as "mass choirs," and these are the ones that have dominated—the Mississippi Mass Choir, the Southern California Community Choir, the Georgia Mass Choir, and a number of others, including various ensembles fronted by James Cleveland.

Cleveland's influence in the rise of choirs is huge. Initially it came through "Peace Be Still" and his other recordings with choirs. But his biggest contribution came in 1967 when he set up the Gospel Music Workshop of America as a more modern alternative to the National Convention of Gospel Choirs and Choruses, founded in 1932 by Thomas A. Dorsey. (The two organizations hold their annual conventions in successive weeks, enabling the truly dedicated to attend both in one vacation.) The GMWA's convention draws around twenty thousand people, the vast majority of them involved in choirs—most as singers, others as musicians or directors. In recent years, it has made an effort to include quartets, but choirs are still in the ascendancy, and relations between the two branches of gospel music are chilly. To many in the choirs, the quartet men are worldly womanizers of dubious religious integrity; to many in the quartets, choirs are ostentatious showpieces, overly populated by male homosexuals and far too influenced by secular music. The Pilgrim Jubilees see the GMWA as the birthplace of the choirs' ascendancy, not only because it brought them to widespread public attention but also because of the influence of its Gospel Announcers' Guild, an organization for gospel music DJs from all over the United States.

Major: "Choirs don't like quartets. I don't know why. Some quartets don't like choirs. But the choirs are dominating the country. There's so many of them. And it's just got ridiculous. They're not even trying to save anybody or give them a message. They're out there trying to do rap and they've got . . . I don't know what kind of choreography they call it. But they're not feeding your soul. It's just a show. And it's ugly. They're talking about reaching out to grab the young folks. Get 'em and do what? They're not telling them anything about the Lord. They're not talking about Jesus—some of them, the Lord's name, God's name, isn't mentioned in the song. They're showing them how to do other stuff and sound like some of these rap people. But, like that old song said years ago—'Everybody talking about Heaven ain't going there.' They just want to make some money, and they're leading everybody down a one-way street."

Clay: "James Cleveland was a smart man. He organized the choirs and put 'em all together. Then he came up with a DJ school. All the guys you hear on the radio now playing nothing but choirs, that came from James Cleveland. There's probably about a thousand DJs that belong to James Cleveland's Workshop that wouldn't put a needle on a quartet record if you shot 'em."

Michael: "Quartets came into radio first, and you very seldom heard a choir. But the whole thing has done a turnaround, and now stations that used to be quartet orientated play choirs all the time. If we had the same chance of being played as the choirs, it would be better. You have people that like choirs and don't like quartet singing. And vice versa. It's sad, because we're all serving the same God. But if a choir is on a program with a quartet, the majority of them, once they sing, they'll leave. They won't even stay and listen to the quartet."

Cleave: "Quartet is like the Mississippi River. It's just like Old Man River. In some places, the Mississippi River is no wider than that street out there. But it's still there. That's the way the quartets are. They're there, and I feel like they're the format of gospel singing. The roots are in quartet. It goes right back to that barbershop quartet."

Major: "You can't do anything but wait for the change. It's going to come back to basics again. Then you'll hear the quartet. Quartet's about one of the oldest voices in the business. You're not going to exterminate that. There's still good quartets around. And they will be around. And they'll always have their audience."

Clay: "I tried to organize a quartet union in 1975. I called together the Soul Stirrers, Slim and the Supreme Angels, the Highway QCs, and the Williams Brothers. We met and talked about it. Then at our next meeting, one guy got up and said that if any officers were going to be selected, he'd be the one to do it. That was Slim [*Howard Hunt*] from the Supreme Angels. I told them, 'Gentlemen, it doesn't work like that. No one man is going to call the shots here.' Then Slim went to James Cleveland with the idea of organizing the quartets. Everybody was supposed to meet at the Workshop, and Slim set up a meeting with James Cleveland. All the quartets were invited, but nobody was there but Slim. James Cleveland got up at the meeting and told everybody, 'The quartets are unable to organize themselves—they don't have the education to do it.' So Slim walked out. But I was so anxious for it to happen, I said, 'Well, we're going [*to the convention*] anyway.' Wasn't anybody there but the Pilgrim Jubilees and the Williams Brothers. No other quartets. So this is what James Cleveland did to us. That quartet night, they had about eighteen hundred people. In Washington, D.C. We sang until we were wet in our shoes. And because there were no other quartets there, we had to come back and do another show. James Cleveland gave us two hundred dollars. It didn't even pay our rent. And that wasn't just one night. We sang twice that night. And we sang three more nights to the same type of audience. Tickets were seven or eight dollars. What kind of money did he make out of that? Then he gave us two hundred dollars. After that, I just didn't have the desire to go back."

Clay eventually returned to the convention in 1998. "I started going back because I know that if your face ain't in the place, you're going to die out. My record company wanted us to go. It was just me and Ben. I didn't really care to be there—I was there because I was best to be there. But I'm not going to miss any more. Because there's a lot of business around the Workshop that ordinarily I wouldn't know anything about. We made at least twelve or thirteen thousand dollars from different promoters that saw us there and called for a date. Just by going to the Workshop."

On Savoy, the Pilgrim Jubilees were working with another leading producer, Milton Biggham. Biggham was also a singer, best known for his work with choirs, including the Georgia Mass Choir, which he established from his home state in 1983. But he knew how to produce quartets. **Michael**: "He was just fun to work with. He showed me what it was like to not be tense in the studio." **Clay**: "Milton was good to work with. Milton feels what you feel. Milton is a singer. He's a soul singer. And you'd rather work with a man who knows singing than one who is just a producer." One of the things Biggham knew was that gospel sounds were changing, even for the quartets. Hard drives were being supplanted by a softer melodic approach that often went outside traditional gospel for its melodies and lyrics. So when Clay suggested that the second Savoy album should use this more contemporary sound, Biggham was amenable. The group recorded its songs in Savoy's New Jersey studio, after which Biggham augmented them with a horn section that included flugelhorn and flute as well as trumpet, saxophones, and trombone. A few tracks also employ another innovation in quartet recordings—the use of choral-styled backing vocals augmenting the group's voices in an effort to bridge the record-buying gap between quartets and choirs. These voices were supplied by a group that Clay recalls as the Alvin Dovon Ensemble—four singers of whom at least two, possibly three, were female. Says Clay: "I always wanted to try horns and all that stuff. It was a good album. The man really did a good job."

The album, *Come Together* (Savoy SL-14626), was the Pilgrim Jubilee's closest step so far to "inspirational," with pop-styled melodies and lush harmonies. But the religious message remains strong. Major's "You Are My Life" sounds like a middle-of-the-road pop song in its arrangement and melody. It would be possible to sing at least part of it in the camouflaged style used by gospel artists seeking a crossover hit—a style in which "God" and Jesus" are not mentioned, so the song's sentiments could be addressed to a deity or a lover. But Clay's interjected references to "you, Lord" make it clear this is a religious song, and his driving off-the-back-of-the-throat finale makes it equally clear that the old Pilgrim Jubilees style is still around. The album also opens with a steadfast declaration of belief in Major's "Me, My God and I" (titled on the album "Me, My Lord and I"). This was one song that the Jubes retained in their repertoire from this session; the other was "I Love You," which they now use as an audience loosener, getting people to hold hands and say "I love you" to each other before the song is performed.

Savoy's contract required an album a year, so in 1982 the Jubes returned to New Jersey to record *Whensoever I Pray* (Savoy SL-14646). Milton Biggham was again in the producer's chair, but the album takes a big step back from the lush approach of a year earlier. That had pleased producer and group, but record buyers weren't so sure. **Clay**: "It's hard to stray away from what you're noted for. If a new group had put it out, they would have accepted it. But they wouldn't accept it from the Pilgrim Jubilees." The lesson was learned, and the new album played safe—no extra voices, no brass, and a mixture of new songs and proven material. Of the four repeats, three—"At the End of the Line," "Put Forth the Effort," and "Two Sides of Life"—were from Peacock's *Don't Let Him Down* album; the fourth was "Step Out" from the Nashboro *Don't Close In on Me* album. The back-to-basics approach is strongest on "Church Song," written by Major and sung by Cleave, who opens it with a brief narration:

> When I was a little boy, I grew up in a home where our mother and father would never leave us alone. . . . And I never shall forget the words my father used to say. He said, "Son, one day you're gonna grow up to be a man. And you're going out on your own." But he said, "Where ever you go, whatever you do . . ."

and the group sings, "Please don't forget to sing a church song." Cleave sings verses from two staples of church music, "There Is a Fountain Filled with Blood" and "I Want to See Him," then brings Clay in for a verse of "Amazing Grace," after which Cleave returns with "I Want to Go Where Jesus Is." The various verses are all shoehorned into the same tune, and each is followed by the chorus "That's a church song. / Oh I like to hear a church song." The song struck a chord with the Pilgrim Jubilees' audience and has remained one of their more popular pieces. The album's most overt departure from the traditional is Clay's "Standing." The song is an expression of sorrow over racial discrimination—"Wondering how long, how long / Will our troubles last?"—and its lyrics are at incongruous odds with its soul-ballad arrangement and Clay's torch-singer delivery, which builds to a full-throated finale worthy of a Las Vegas nightclub. **Clay**: "I was trying to make it a little classy. A lot of people liked it. But it's hard to get the kind of folks that we're marketed to to understand that kind of record. They listen and say, 'Oh, that's cute,' but they want somebody telling them some sad stories and they want the drive."

The album's last song is one of Clay's more dramatic sermonettes, built on his own song, "(Lord) You Are There." One Sunday afternoon he is walking to a neighborhood restaurant when a friend pulls up in his car. They go for a ride, and when the friend takes him back to the restaurant, it has been destroyed by a bomb that killed nine people. The story is based on fact, although the number of fatalities is given poetic license and, for obvious reasons, a neighborhood bar becomes a restaurant. "It happened back in the '60s. I was on my way to the bar. It was on the ten hundred block on Wells, and I lived at 1111 North Wells. Our bass singer, Mack Robertson, pulled up and said, 'Come up to the Cotton Club and we'll come back down there later.' We went to the Cotton Club and sat around for a little while, then he said, 'Let's go back down on Wells.' When we got within two blocks, we could see all the traffic and the smoke. The Mafia had set a bomb in there. It was supposed to blow up after the bar closed that night. But something went wrong and it went off that evening. It was set in the basement, right under the seat where I used to always sit. Two guys lost their legs, and one boy was killed. I would have been sitting on that bomb. The Lord always saw me through . . ."

The 1983 album, *Put On Your Shoes* (Savoy SL-14701), was recorded before an enthusiastic audience at DuSable High School in Chicago, although the album sleeve and label give no indication it is a concert recording and the spoken introductions are omitted. The songs are a mixture of proven and progressive. "Exit 100" makes its third appearance on record, as does "Wonderful"—retitled "Won't It Be Wonderful" and, for the first time, credited to Ruth Davis. On Nashboro it was credited to Major; on Peacock it was credited to "V. McCollough," who also received the Peacock credit for the very traditional "Wicked Race"—none of the Pilgrim Jubilees know anything about V. McCollough. The fact that the Davis Sisters recorded for Savoy may have had some bearing on the amended credit and title. "Church Song" appears again, with applause greeting each song excerpt as it appears. The progressive side of the album is reflected in "Peace of Mind," "Longing to Meet You," and "Looking for a Miracle," all firmly in contemporary mode, with soft-edged harmonies and pop-flavored melodies. The first two were written by Clay, displaying the gentler side of his writing and the way he has absorbed modern trends in gospel and secular music, although old habits assert themselves on "Peace of Mind," which has a short narration, after which the vocal impetus hardens as Clay moves into the drive. "Looking for a Miracle" was written by Elbernita "Twinkie" Clark, of the Clark Sisters, from Detroit. Lyrically, it lauds the beneficence of God; melodically, it sounds like a showpiece from a Broadway musical. Says Clay: "Milton wanted us to do that song. That was the best song on that album. It did real good for us. We got a lot of requests for it." Despite this, the song did not stay in the Jubes' repertoire, although Clay says he is considering reviving it.

A year later, the Pilgrim Jubilees made their last album for Savoy. *Put Your Trust in Jesus* (Savoy SL-14728) was supposed to have been the second to last, but the company was sold. "They lived up to the contract until the last session," says Major. "We didn't get the last session." The 1984 album continues the pattern set the year before, mixing traditional and contemporary, with a couple of repeats from earlier records—"Take Your Burdens to Jesus" from Peacock and "Life, Don't Close In on Me" from Nashboro. The opening track, Major's "Put Your Trust In Jesus," is unequivocal mainstream gospel as Cleave warns "don't trust no man, because men will fail you every time." The final track, Clay's "Little Boy," is unequivocally contemporary and inspirational—a syrupy first-person evocation of a little boy's all-American Christmas. "It was done for the Christmas market," says Clay. "But Savoy didn't know what to do with it. They stuck it on the regular album instead of on a Christmas album, so it wasn't played at the right time."

Although the permanency of recordings makes it easy to focus on them as signposts of musical progress and development, creating them is a secondary part of a group's life—a break from the stream of one-nighters that takes up most of the time and provides most of the money. Outside the studio, the Pilgrim Jubilees continued driving countless freeway miles to towns and cities all across the United States.

Michael: "We were at it wide open. We would sometimes leave on the first of the month, get home on the last of the month. In the mid-1970s on well up into the '80s, it was nothing for us to do a month tour. After a time, guys didn't want to stay away that long, and we started breaking it down. Instead of four weeks, we'd do three weeks. Then we started doing two weeks at a time. That was really good. So we stayed with the two-week thing for quite a while. And then we'd do a week. Then we started the weekends. Now we do the weekends—we've got so used to doing the weekends and coming home that now if you take the guys out for a week straight . . . oh man, after four days, everybody's lip will be stuck out. Want to come home."

Clay: "Expenses and everything went up so high that we had to start doing weekend shows. Friday, Saturday, and Sunday, when everybody's free to come out to the show. Monday, Tuesday, and Wednesday are just about a no-no unless you've got a special spot you are going to—there are some towns you can work in on Monday nights. But not many. So we try to work on weekends and come back home. You work on the weekend, you make a little money. But if you try to stay out and work Monday, Tuesday, and

Wednesday, you don't get anything. So we figure it's best to do that Sunday night program and come on home. Then you've got your payday in your pocket, and you aren't laying around in a motel, spending it and hoping you've got something else coming.

"Carolinas and Mississippi are our best areas. And New York. Georgia and Alabama we don't work in that often. And Florida. We go there, but not as often as Mississippi, North Carolina, South Carolina, Ohio, New York, Connecticut—all through there is Jubes' territory. You can sing in North and South Carolina for two years and never sing in the same place. That's two states that haven't gone all choirs yet. It's quartet—they love quartets. We used to go out to California often, but it's so hectic. And so long a ride. It's twenty-four hundred miles from Chicago to Los Angeles. We used to go out there and try to stay a couple of weeks, and it didn't work. You end up during the week spending the money you make at weekends. So now, if a promoter wants us, we'll go out there and do, say Friday, Saturday, and Sunday. Fly out, fly back. We can get tickets for seven men for around eighteen hundred dollars. So you ask for seven thousand, spend two thousand, you've got five thousand dollars to split up with the men. And you get back on the plane and come on home with no hassles."

In the early 1970s the group changed its mode of travel. The last car was a blue 1968 Cadillac; in 1970 it was traded in on a van that, while not as fast as the car, had more room. The next step was to buy a bus, the favored transport for many American entertainers, as it enables them to travel in relaxed, spacious comfort, with room for equipment and luggage. Some affluent artists have their buses custom built as traveling homes, others just remove seats to give more luggage space and bring the number of seats below the legal maximum for noncommercial use. "We took seats out, then we turned the other ones around face to face," says Clay. "And if I put a board across between them, I can put my feet up—and I'm in bed." The first bus the Pilgrim Jubilees bought was about fifteen years old; they kept it for a short time, then traded it on a 1969 Eagle—the Eagle bus is a gospel industry standard. Around 1979 they bought a 1974 Eagle that they found in Los Angeles. They still have this bus, although it has not been used since it broke down in Arizona in the early 1990s. "We had so much trouble trying to get things straightened out there that once we got it going, we just brought it back and parked it up," says Clay. "The parts are so hard to get now." The demise of the bus more or less coincided with the decision to reduce the touring schedule, so the Jubes returned to riding in cars. But Clay wants them back on the bus. It would give the older members a more comfortable ride he says—and, as well, a bus is a status symbol.

Clay: "You just can't ride up to a program as a legendary group that's been out here all these years, and pull up in a van or somebody's little car. And there's all these young ones sitting up with those big pretty buses looking down on your car. I ain't going that route. When I go out, I want to go out as the Jubes—were somebody and are somebody. You can't be somebody when you're not properly equipped. We were at the Stellar [*gospel recording*] awards. John P. Kee, Shirley Caesar, Kirk Franklin, and all those were there. There were five Eagle buses sitting there. And there we go with a little blue van sitting up between all that prestige. I can't stand that. And you get tired, riding to a program with all those big guys in the van. So I want to get that bus so I can get up there and go to sleep. And when I get to the program, I'm rested."

As well as giving comfort, space, and status, traveling by bus is safer because of the protection afforded by the extra bulk and height. Road accidents are a constant risk for people who travel as much as the gospel quartets—pleas for divine guardianship "as we travel up and down the dangerous highways" are a staple of quartet prayers—but the Jubes have had remarkably few.

Cleave: "In all the years we've been out there, we've had three serious wrecks. And none of us got hurt. The Lord just blessed us to come out of them. The first one, we were doing eighty-five miles an hour. We went into a low place in the highway, where it was shady, and it wasn't nothing but black ice. The minute we hit that ice, the car swerved. We were going so fast it was going sideways. And when it switched back around, it came up on the dry pavement, and that flipped it. But God blessed us. The shoulder of the highway was soft. The car didn't hit anything that would cause it to flip again. It just went down the highway bottom upwards—I don't know how far we slid. And just before it stopped, it turned over on its side and just laid there. There was five or six of us in there, one man had a little scratch on his leg."

Major: "That was back in the '50s. Everybody shook themselves and we opened up that door—the car was on its side, so we had to reach up to open the door—and just like little bugs, we came out. That was a car I had just bought, a Mercury. I hadn't even put the license on it. We went to Anderson, Indiana, to sing. On the way back, we had the accident. Then we were on our way to Houston, Texas [*around 1961 or 1962*]. Head-on collision. All of us stepped out of the car. And the other guy got his head cut off. And the next time was in our bus, the one we have now. The driver [*one of the group*] went to sleep. And we went off . . . the road ended [*at a T-intersection*]. You had to turn. He went to sleep, and when he woke up, he was right at the stop sign where he's supposed to turn. Too late. We went right on across. And a truck came along and ran into the bus. But nobody got a scratch. You've got to thank God for these things."

Ben: "A couple of years ago, three of us were on our way to New York. Eddie [*Graham*] and Fred [*Rice*] were in my van. Fred was driving, and I was sitting in the passenger seat with the seatbelt on. Around Greensboro, North Carolina, about four o'clock in the morning, a young lady went off the highway and hit the van. The van flipped on top of the car, the big window broke out, and Eddie fell out on to the highway. We went across the highway and we were going down the road meeting cars coming the other way. I was sleeping, and when I woke, all I knew was all this tumbling. 'Lord, save us, you got to save us.' Fred was lying on the floor, so I got the wheel and stopped the van. Then Fred said, 'Eddie was thrown out on the highway.' I got out and I said, 'Lord have mercy.' I looked and I saw him coming, walking towards me. I ran and grabbed him, said 'Man are you all right?' He said, 'Yeah,' but his little finger was bent back [*dislocated*]. I just caught it and pulled it back in."

18. Houston, Mississippi: Eddie Graham

Houston, Mississippi, seat of Chickasaw County, was founded in 1836 on an eighty-acre block given for the purpose by local landowner Joel Pinson. A memorial stone in the town square tells how Pinson requested that the town be named after his friend Sam Houston, "previous Governor of Tennessee and only president of the Republic of Texas," who also gave his name to a much better known city in Texas. Chickasaw County's Houston has outgrown Pinson's eighty acres and now straggles along State Highway 8 from the gas station and barbecue shop at one end to the local hospital and the Holiday Terrace Motel—the town's only motel—at the other. Its heart, as in small towns throughout the South, is the square. Around three sides of Pinson Square are the downtown shops, not as busy as they were before the shopping center opened on the eastern outskirts of town. The fourth side is the two-lane Highway 8, the main route in and out of town. In the center is a large grassed area surrounding the county courthouse, a classically styled concrete building disproportionately larger than the mainly single-story buildings around it and crowned by a large cupola. Although Cleave and Clay's family left in 1952, Grahams still live around Houston. Uncle T. J. Graham lived on the outskirts of town and until the late 1970s rode in on a wagon pulled by mules to do his shopping. Second cousin Robert Graham still lives a few miles out of town. One of Robert's sons is Eddie, second guitarist since 1987 for the Pilgrim Jubilees. Born on March 19, 1961, he has always lived in Houston, apart from a time in infancy when his father took a construction job in Newport, Tennessee.

"We moved back in 1964, and I've been here ever since. When I was small, my mom bought me a play guitar for Christmas. Then after I got bigger, I went to a gospel concert—the Pilgrim Jubilees were singing. It seemed like the lifestyle was so nice. I'm seeing these guys perform, then after they can go back and lay in the hotel and sleep. As late as they like. And I was thinking 'I want to do that one day.' I prayed about it. I wanted to get on the road. It didn't have to be a gospel quartet—I just wanted to get blessed in the fact of going on the road, period. I started playing with a couple of local groups. My first quartet was a group called the Heavenly Jubilees out of Okolona, Mississippi [*about twenty miles from Houston, at the eastern end of Chickasaw County*]. That was the first time somebody gave me a chance to play—I was about sixteen or seventeen. I started on bass guitar. But my brother and I were rehearsing at home; he was playing bass, and I was playing lead. He doesn't play for a quartet, but he plays for our church choir. When we're not on the road, I play for the choir, too. I was brought up in church. When Sunday came round, I knew where I was going. There was nothing about 'I don't feel like it.' And I think from being raised that way, it's still in me today. I was eleven when I was baptized. Nowdays, they have the pool inside, and everybody gets baptized in church. But then, we were baptized outside. We had to wade out in the water and at the same time there were cows in the water.

"In 1983 one of the musicians working with Leomia Boyd asked me if I was interested in going on the road with them. I had known him from childhood, and he had thought about me. I did a couple of trips with them—I didn't play, I went to just sit around and listen. I felt as though I wasn't ready within myself at the time. Around two or three months went by, then I gave it a shot. It was real nice. I stayed with her about two years. We recorded for the AIR label, which is Atlanta International Records. While I was playing for Leomia, we did concerts together several times with the Jubes. And by me being kin to Cleave and Clay, the influence was there. I was at home one day and there was an announcement about the group was coming to Starkville, Mississippi [*about forty-five miles from Houston*]. I decided to go out to the concert that night. And at that time, the keyboard player, Larry Moten, had just left. So I went to the concert and they said to me, 'Larry's not here. Do you want to play for us?' I always take my guitar with me when I go to a concert, so I played and it just went from there."

Leomia Boyd, Eddie's first professional employer, is a solo singer from Aberdeen, Mississippi, about thirty miles southeast of Houston. Although she is not one of the top names, she has carved a secure niche for herself and has recorded extensively. Her 1988 LP That's the Way the Lord Works *(AIR 10122) was nominated for a Grammy; Eddie played on her first AIR album,* I Am Ready *(AIR 10105). Her music is traditionally based, although many of her recordings have a contemporary styling, and her singing has a bluesy edge—she has rejected several offers to record blues but accepts the billing "The Queen of Soul Gospel."*[1]

"Leomia is known as more like a blues gospel singer. When I got with the Jubes, it was a whole different thing. I had to learn how to play the beat and make it mean something. It was like learning how to play again. The two styles are like day and night. The Jubes have an old soul sound that sounds so easy when you listen to it. But once you start playing . . . you've really got to put yourself into what the [*lead*] singer is saying to get to where he's feeling. Bobby McDougle is my mentor. He was the inspiration in getting me into the group. He spoke up for me . . . he liked what I did. The rest of the guys really didn't understand, because I was playing with Leomia and it was two different styles. But he understood what I was doing. He said, 'I think he'll work.' And he and I have just jelled. It took a while. But what really made the difference was in about 1991 or '92, when he had hip replacements, and I had to play guitar by myself with the group. That's really when I learned how to play Pilgrim Jubilee music. But Bobby sat down with me and showed me a lot of things. And he said, 'Just think and relax. It'll come to you.' He showed me things I thought I already knew. But I was far from it. Once he showed me the easy way . . . it was simple, but I hadn't come up with it. Bobby is the soul of the group. Without Bobby McDougle . . . I wouldn't say we're lost, but we search. He's been an inspiration for so long, and everything works around his guitar playing. So whenever he comes up with a pattern, I have to find a way to go around what he's doing and make it jell. At first it was really difficult. I thought I had it, but we were playing against each other because I had patterned myself on trying to play like Bobby. So when we got on stage, I was playing so much like him that it was pulling apart. I had to figure out how to play around what he was doing. Michael is an inspiration, too. I don't really think anybody else could play bass and make it fit the Pilgrim Jubilees like Michael Atkins. It just seems like those two guys were cut and fitted for the group. Without them, we've got a really big problem.

"I think the sound that makes the Jubes different is the down-home feeling that comes from the heart. You have the contemporary sound, then you have a traditional sound—then you have the Jubes. From the start, they created a style that everybody copied. But the thing about the Jubes is that we play a lagging beat, and people [*who copy*] don't understand it. Our songs sound fast, but they're not really that fast. We lag back. And that's what makes the Jubes. Anybody can give you a drive. But can you drive me and pull me back? It took me three years to understand this. The drive sounds like a regular drive that you hear every day. But it's not. It's different. It's pulled back. We keep the music up to date. But the singing—you put that old traditional feeling into this new drive that's going on today, that's what makes you stay on top."

Eddie is the only Jube who works a job as well as performing with the group. He's not married—"I was close a couple of times"—but has three children, two daughters, aged seventeen and fourteen, and a two-year-old son. He's been living with his parents but is about to move into his own home—"I'm just in the process of getting the paperwork done."

"I work in a foam factory. We cut foam for living-room furniture. And at the same place where I work, they build furniture on the other side. I've been there for thirteen years. Part time. It was just an anointing and a blessing. I was at home and the guy called me and asked if I was interested in a job. I had known him from a previous job, and I guess he was satisfied with my work. I told him I was interested, but I was on the road playing music. He said, 'Well come on and talk to me, and we'll see what we can work out.'

So I went up and we talked. He said, 'OK, I can understand what you're doing. We'll just try to work it out. If you can let me know at least a couple of weeks in advance what you've got to do, I'll try to work with you.' And everything has worked out pretty good.

"But the traveling with the group can be very hard when you work part-time like I do. Last Saturday, we sang at Monticello [*in southern Mississippi, more than 220 miles from Houston*]. I worked from seven till twelve, and I drove to Monticello and we sang. Then we got in the car and drove to South Carolina. [*The Jubes left Monticello at about one o'clock in the morning for the 650-mile journey to South Carolina, arriving only a short time before they were due to sing on an afternoon program.*] Only dedicated people can do these things. People say they want to do it, but when they get out here and experience what we have to go though . . . if it's not in your heart, you can't do it. You've got to be really committed. And the Lord's got to be on your side. You take the average person that has a girlfriend or wife, children. It's OK if you're gone a day or two. But sometimes we'll be gone two weeks, three weeks. Staying away from home and having to go through the trauma of dealing with a female and little children—it causes great problems. You've got to figure out what you really want to do and go from there. For me . . . I had prayed about it. I wanted to do this all my life, and I got the opportunity and that was my commitment. Regardless of whatever it cost me, that's what I wanted to do. And I'm enjoying every moment of it."

The quartets' days of dominance were well passed when Eddie joined the Jubes, and choirs were entrenched as gospel music's frontrunners. But he's been a quartet man for long enough to know the history and to see himself as a participant in it.

"For a long time, quartets were on top. And you had so many of them. Some were for real, some weren't. So people pointed fingers at the ones that weren't real and painted this ugly picture of all the quartets. Then once the choirs got in and started doing something different . . . James Cleveland's movement paved the way—he did a whole lot of things for church choirs. It used to be that choirs were laid back, quartets were out front. Now, the choirs are out there right beside the quartets. So choirs and quartets really have to learn how to work together. We're working in the same vineyard and trying to come up with the same solutions. The future for the quartet is that everybody's got to keep their heads up, and we've got to stick together. Because it's almost getting obsolete, quartet music. But you've gotta hang in there with that traditional feeling, because you really can't get away from that. I love choir singing. But the quartet is what we were raised on. Now you've got a whole new generation—that's the difference. We didn't have all the music they have today. We'd go to church and there'd be the old foot stomping and the amen corner with the sisters and brothers singing—we don't have it any more. This generation's coming up with all the new music and all the different moves in the singing. But we [*quartets*] have to stick together.

"Quartets are still very, very competitive. But we've learned to try to get along with each other. And it helps us minister to the people when we're dealing together. Because your group has this song and people want to hear it, and my group has that song. . . . We're trying to get a concept that we go onstage and you do it this way and we do it that way and then everything meets up to do the same thing. We're trying to reach out and touch souls. And the groups become friends. We get along, we laugh and talk and go out and eat together. That means a whole lot. I know they used to do things like . . . go behind the curtain and pull the plug and all that kind of stuff. But it's not so much like that now, because everybody's out here for the same purpose—we're trying to bring a message. And maybe some song you sing or even a word you say might lift up a bowed-down head or bring a soul to Christ. And that's what you really want to do, that's what your singing's all about. And you really want to try to live the life you sing about and make it mean something. Then you've fulfilled what you're trying to do."

Although Eddie started full-time with the Pilgrim Jubilees in 1987, he left for about a year in 1988 when keyboard player Larry Moten returned. When Moten left again, Eddie rejoined. But his absence and the timing of the group's recording sessions means he did not play on a Pilgrim Jubilees recording until 1991. Unlike the older group members, Eddie has always worked with the "layering" method of making recordings piece by piece.

"Usually when we go in the studio, we lay the music tracks first. Then the guys come in and start singing. Then you come in and listen to them singing to your music track. And an idea might pop into your head that you want to do something different. So you go back in there and do it over. Something that's going to add to the song and make it work. When we're learning new material . . . if it's Major's song, he just comes in with a set of lyrics. Usually, he depends on us to help. He comes up with the words. And he'll read them or sing 'em and we go from there. Sometimes when we start out it sounds good, but he says, 'No, that's not what I want.' We don't ever do anything to mess with what he feels. We want to do something that's going to complement what he feels. But before a day is gone, we'll have something to match what he wants. Clay is a little different. When he comes up with the song, he usually has an idea about what he wants with the tune. Most of the time he has an intro for it. He plays a little guitar, so I think that gives him a little more insight. Major doesn't play a guitar. He can blow harmonica. And he's very talented in movements, the dance steps. At one time, the Jubes were called 'the gospel Temptations' on the road because of their movements. They don't do it do much now, but everybody knows the movements."

The Jubes have now largely abandoned their choreography, partly because some members aren't as agile as they once were but also because synchronized dance routines are not as fashionable or remarkable as they once were. But traces remain. In the sermonette "Three Trees," the excavation to find out why the small cedar tree survived the storm is accompanied by digging actions; in "Too Close," the words "to turn around" are sung as the backing singers swing through 180 degrees. One enduringly popular routine comes in "Wonderful"; on the line "I'm gonna sit down, yes I am" the singers sit in unison on chairs placed on the stage for the purpose while the musicians vamp on one chord until the maneuver is completed. Says Eddie: "It sells the song."

19. Meridian, Mississippi: Fred Rice

Advertising and political wisdom has it that if something is said often enough, it will become the truth. The Super Inn motel, next to the I-20 in Meridian, Mississippi, defies this belief. No amount of repetition is going to make the Super Inn super. Its blocks of units are separated by pitted asphalt that hurls the summer heat against the walls, helping the sun's direct rays peel paint and split timber. Someone has smashed a bottle against the base of the tall sign proclaiming to passing freeway traffic the motel's superiority. But the Super Inn's rooms are comfortable enough, the air-conditioning works, and it's cheap. So it is ideal for a traveling gospel group needing a base away from home for an on-the-road rehearsal or a place to stay between programs when it's cheaper to do so than return home. The motel's owners know the Jubes as regulars and can always find them quiet rooms and somewhere to rehearse. But Fred Rice, the group's youngest member, doesn't stay at the Super Inn. He lives in Meridian with his partner and their daughter. Fred can sing tenor and baritone—and bass, if the Jubes ever want to reverse history and reinstate the part—and plays guitar, bass guitar, and drums. He's also teaching himself to play keyboards but says, "I don't think I'm ready for the stage yet." Because of his versatility, he has no defined role in the group but is what he calls "a spare" and what the old quartets called a "utility." In conversation, his manner is guarded, and he thinks carefully about each question before delivering a slow-spoken, precise answer.

"I was living in Starkville, Mississippi, when I joined the group. That was in May of '93. I just got laid off my job—I was working at a steel plant. Got laid off on Wednesday, and the Jubes came to town on Thursday. I knew Eddie—we were from the same part of Mississippi—so I talked to him and asked where Mike was. He said, 'Mike's not here.' And I said, 'Well, can I play?' He said, 'Yeah. Talk to Clay.' I played that night—and been playing ever since. I was born [*on October 5, 1972*] and raised in Starkville—I moved to Meridian after I got with the group. I had a daughter born there, started a family. We're not married. Not yet. I've been living with her about four years. I want to marry, but I want to take my time. I was previously married—I was eighteen. It lasted about four years. We didn't have any children. So I've got the one daughter—she turned three years old last month.

"I was singing at an early age. I didn't have a choice. I had to sing in the choir and . . . my father was a singer. He sang in groups, and he started me singing with a group. He showed me how to sing all the parts of the background, and I took it from there. So I was singing with the choir on Sunday morning, then I'd leave there and go to the program. That was with the Southernaires of Starkville. Drums was the first instrument I played. I was really young, about five or six years old. My father and his group would be rehearsing, and when they finished, I would go in there and mess around. He bought me a guitar when I was about eight years old and showed me two keys. And I went from there to listening to records and learning, and when groups played I would be there watching, trying to see what they were doing. I just worked on it until the Lord blessed me. One of the guys I listened to was Bobby. I always wanted to play like Bobby. There were some guys in the area who played, but the only one I wanted to play like was Bobby. Bobby put a sound on the road, and his sound went across this country.

"The Violinaires, the Mighty Clouds of Joy, the Canton Spirituals, I listened to them all. The Jackson Southernaires, the Bright Stars of Michigan—quite a few groups. But my favorite groups now, I would say, would be the Violinaires and the Jubes. The more modern styles, I listen at them. But some of the material they do, I'm still trying to grasp on to. I see where they're coming from—trying to attract the younger generation. But I just . . . I'm young, but I grew up in the old thing. I'm not trying to cut down what they're doing, because they're working for the Lord—it's what they feel. But it's kind of slow setting in to me. I listen to all types of music, not just gospel. I'm trying to learn all I can. When I'm at home, my fiancée tells me, 'I don't know what kind of person you are—you never watch TV, all you want to do is listen to music.' And I have my guitar around the house and half a set of drums. And I have a keyboard—I'm still learning. So I'm always keeping up noise around the house. I have to stay upgraded on my music. I don't play often, but when I do play, I have to be able to produce.

"I started out with the Starkville Southernaires. I sang there until I was about ten or eleven years old. I don't have a lot of brothers and sisters—I'm the oldest and I have two sisters. But my mom has a lot of sisters and brothers and they've got a lot of kids, so I do come from a big family. I've got cousins that sing and play, so we formed a family group called the Rice Brothers. I didn't stay with them very long—about a year. I was about thirteen when I joined a group called the Melody Kings in Starkville, and I played with them up until I got with the Jubes. We did a couple of recordings, cassette tapes, during the time I was with them.

"Joining the Jubes happened at a crucial time. I lost my job and I picked up this job the next day. And I was young, I was nineteen. It was a big move in my life. I toughed it out—it was what I wanted to do. When I started, I wasn't making a lot of money. But it was the determination—I always wanted to be successful in music. One thing I think helped steer me in a direction to where I am now was that when I was coming up, my mother . . . I would have other things I wanted to do, but she made me go to choir practice. I didn't have it like other guys. I'd be playing ball with my friends, she'd call me, 'Time to go.' And that kept me motivated in this path.

"I've learned a lot, a whole lot with the Jubes. On and off the stage. All my life I've been around older guys. A lot of the kids call me old-fashioned. But seeing them [*older people*] and the way they conducted themselves, it rubbed off on me. So I try to keep myself in that positive path. The older guys have a lot more wisdom, and they can tell me when I'm wrong—which they do. Kind of like father figures. You've got to learn how to fit in, you've got to learn. . . . I had to learn steps and moves, although we haven't come up with any new movements lately. But when I came, there were some songs they were doing that had certain steps. And sometimes we still do them

"And I had to learn the singing—the thing about the group is that you can hear something but it doesn't actually go the way it sounds. Like some of the tricks in the background. One man might do something, and it sounds like the whole background is doing it. But it's just one man. I had to learn that. Sometimes Cleave's voice in the background is doing some tricks when Clay's singing. He'll do one little thing, and it'll turn the whole background. Sometimes Major does a little slide up or under the key at certain times to make it fit that Jube flavor. It's just one man. But it sounds like everybody. It's something they do that distinguishes the real thing from anything else. Because I hear the Jubilees' sound and flavor in a lot of other groups that are singing today. The Cantons are one. The Supreme Angels are trying to steal our background singing sound. That little sound they've got? That's the Jubes background."

Living in Meridian, Mississippi, and working with a group based in Chicago means a lot of traveling. It's not so bad if the program is in the South. Then Fred—and Ben in Atlanta and Eddie in Houston—can drive directly to the venue and join the Chicago contingent. But if the engagement or the rehearsal is in Chicago, it's a long haul.

"It takes me about fourteen hours to drive to Chicago. About 820 miles. It's a lot of highway. But I have to do whatever it takes for me to get to the group. When you first start, it's tough. You've got to want to do it to stay. You've got to love it. We got a lot of guys come in and play for two or three, six months. Then they're gone. Too tough. It's tough, but it's a way of life for me and I wouldn't take anything for it. We're together so much it's like family. I've got some times to remember in my few years, even if I don't have the amazing stories like the other guys. We usually sing in places like auditoriums and civic centers, gyms. In the South, it's very seldom we go into a church and sing. In the South, people don't like to sell tickets at the church and pay an admission to get in. In the northern states and on the East Coast we sing at churches. Big churches. But in the South we'll usually be in an auditorium or a civic center, somewhere like that.

"When we're working with other groups . . . if a group is short of a man, I can fill in for a guy on a program. I've done that. But the only time I've been off with another group was with Clarence Fountain and the Blind Boys of Alabama. Bobby introduced me to Clarence. They're good friends from way back. Clarence was in Chicago, and he needed a bass player for the weekend. Bobby called me and asked would I do it? I told him, 'Yeah, I'll do it.' So Clarence called, and I played with him down in Lafayette, Louisiana, and in San Antonio, Texas. Then about a month later, they were getting ready to go overseas and there was an opening, a bass-playing job. We went to Amsterdam and we went to Scotland. I had to change my sound and fit in with them. But it was interesting for me, and I felt good doing it. And it let me know I can do more than one thing if I need to. It was real nice working with the Blind Boys. That was my first time going overseas, and I look forward to going back."

At the beginning of 2000 Fred Rice left the Pilgrim Jubilees to work with Fountain and the Blind Boys. In late 1999 he effectively started working as a member of both groups, playing bass with Fountain and continuing his utility role with the Pilgrim Jubilees. Inevitably, a clash of dates arose, and Fred's "resignation" came with his decision to give the Blind Boys priority. But he has not completely severed his connections with the Jubes and will appear with them if they need a stand-in and he is available. He says the parting was amicable, that he left with the blessing of the rest of the group. But the Pilgrim Jubilees is an organization built on long-serving loyalty. A number of men have come and gone, but the core of the group is committed to being Pilgrim Jubilees. Although he had been with the group for "only" seven years, Fred was viewed as part of this core. And committed Jubes do not quit and go to work for the opposition.

Fred: "It was a business transaction. Nothing personal. Strictly business. Clarence had a lot of work at the time, and I needed it. It just fell in place. I talked to the guys about it and everybody understood. Everybody gave me their blessing so I went ahead and did it. So I work with Clarence now, and on my off time I work with the Jubes. We've still got a steady relationship, we still talk. I haven't quit. Just kind of moved. It was a positive move for me. There was a dry spell and I had to keep working. I'm still an honorary member. No bridges burned."

Cleave: "He jumped. He's kinda bouncy. So we've just about cut him loose. We like him, and he's a good guy to have, but you have to have somebody that's faithful. He's not too faithful. So we have to put him on the back burner. I think we had voted him in as a member. I'm not sure. Because we generally work a guy a good while before we vote him in as a member. You don't just come in and bam bam, you're a member. I think we did vote Fred in as a member. But he's been a little bouncy, and now he's jumping to whatever."

Major: "Fred wanted a solid job. So every time we were off, he would work for Clarence. And now he's over there with Clarence. We talked, and he said that when he's off, whenever we needed him, he'd be there. But he's more with Clarence than with us."

Clay: "He went overseas with Clarence and did two shows and got fourteen hundred dollars. He thought that was it. He was going to try to play with both groups—go with the Blind Boys when they want him and go with us. I told him, 'No. I've had you seven years, and I can't share. I need you when I need you.' "

20. "That's the Way We Run It"

"Strictly business" . . . "fourteen hundred for two shows" . . . "a solid job"—it's the worldly side of a spiritual business. A gospel group is a vehicle of religious expression that through its singing gives praise and thanks to God and messages of hope and joy to its audiences. As long as it stays an amateur group—one in which members earn their daily bread at other occupations and sing together essentially for the pleasure it brings them and others—it can function primarily on this spiritual level. But black American gospel music has two tiers. On one, it is a community-owned religious expression. On the other, it is a multimillion-dollar business, creating income for record companies, promoters, broadcasters—and artists. Groups that make the move to this level by turning professional will keep delivering their spiritual message. But now they are singing heavenly praises for earthly reward.

Clay: "When we first went on the road, a group was getting top money if it made a five hundred–dollar guarantee. So when Edna Gallmon Cooke got us a two hundred–dollar guarantee, I figured we were doing pretty good. Today, our price is no less than twenty-five hundred on Sunday. And up. It depends on what kind of show it is and where it is. Some places I know we don't draw so well. So I don't press the promoter for it. But I try to go to those areas where we can do well. There are places where we get seven thousand, ten thousand dollars a show. But they come so scattery. We'd maybe get three or four of this kind of show a year. A group of our standing gets twenty-five hundred to five thousand, and you're lucky to get up to five thousand. But for a group of eight or nine people . . . that's why we stay broke all the time."

Even twenty-five hundred dollars seems handsome reward for an hour or two on stage. But a Pilgrim Jubilees performance involves usually eight men. So the twenty-five hundred–dollar pie is cut into eight slices. All expenses—gas, meals, accommodations—are deducted. Longer-term costs, such as taxes, uniforms, equipment, and vehicle maintenance, also have to be paid. If the booking came through an agency, it takes a fee. The glamour of twenty-five hundred dollars in one day quickly disappears into the reality of around two hundred a man. Sometimes the group will have three or four bookings in a week; sometimes it will have none. Recordings provide some extra income—through royalties and from sales at programs—although their main purpose is to keep the group's name "out there" and maintain the flow of concert bookings. But a successful record can boost a group's earning power.

Clay: "I've booked some dates for next year. But I've said the price is subject to go up. A guy in Ohio, I've given him a date in February for twenty-five hundred. I told him, 'Our record is coming out. And if it gets hot, you won't get us for twenty-five in February.' He said, 'How much will it be?' I said, 'No less than four thousand.' We could have made money at the time of 'Stretch Out.' But we didn't have sense enough to know what to do. People like the Soul Stirrers, the Harmonizing Four, and the Pilgrim Travelers, they made our money. We were hot. And the top price we were getting was about four hundred dollars for a program."

Cleave: "The older [*quartet*] people that were out there, they knew how to manage it so you come in and still don't make nothing. You're young and don't know, and you're really just in it for the joy of singing. It's very easily done, and that's the way it went down."

Clay: "Today, the choirs and stuff like that are making money. Because they're in a different vein. Kirk Franklin, John P. Kee, all these guys make money. But the quartets . . . nobody's making any money. You make enough to go back home and pay your rent and your tax, buy some clothes and stuff like that. The Cantons make money. They came back with our style—new, different, and bigger, on the rock style, and bang! Now they're getting five, eight, and ten thousand dollars a night. The Clouds make money. They've got a white guy [*California-based Zack Glickman*] who's had them under management for thirty years. That's how the Clouds make money. 'Cause he puts them in everything he can."

When a promoter wants to book the Pilgrim Jubilees, the call goes almost always directly to the group's booking manager—for years Major, now mainly Clay. Sometimes he asks for a deposit. "I'll ask them to send a hundred dollars or so," says Clay. "Then you know they're serious." In some groups, the booking manager is regarded as an agent and charges a fee for obtaining the engagement. In the Pilgrim Jubilees, all the money belongs to all in the group. "If a booking agency gets a deposit, it takes care of its percentage from that deposit," Cleave explains. "But if it's booked within the group, the booking manager doesn't charge extra because that's just his job in the group." The Jubes' egalitarianism also extends to the way fees are split. In some groups, the leader takes a larger share than anyone else. Others operate a seniority scale, under which long-serving members are paid more than recent recruits. In the Pilgrim Jubilees, everyone gets the same.

Clay: "Whatever money comes in belongs to the organization. That's the way we run it. Other groups are run differently. But we look at all our members as somebody that's equal. That's why we don't change members. We've had the same fellows for years. So you can't say, 'Well, I'm superior over you,' when you're walking down the same road, taking the same bumps."

Major: "I figure Cleave, Clay, and myself should really get more than the other guys. But we give everyone the same thing. And all the other artists we talk to, they don't understand how we do this. They don't do it. Most of the guys here now [*in the group*], when they came in they would make at least a hundred dollars a show. It was five years before I made a hundred dollars. But we started out that way, and we can't change it now."

Being booked is the first step. Traveling to the venue and doing the performance is the second. The third is being paid. But not all promoters accept that the laborer is worthy of the hire, and the Pilgrim Jubilees have many memories and many stories of times when they sang, then went home with empty pockets. Occasionally, the promoter's claims of impoverishment are genuine—such as when a program fails to attract an audience and artists and promoter are confronted by rows of empty seats. But the Jubes—like many other gospel performers—have sung to packed rooms and gone away empty-handed.

Bobby: "You look around and there's no promoter. Or they say somebody stuck 'em up, stole the money. Or there's no money to pay you because the expenses have taken it. And you should see the people there! We've had all that happen. I remember when we working with James Cleveland. We were in High Point, North Carolina, and his booking manager, Allan Clark went to collect—he didn't wait until the end; when the show began, he'd go and collect. And this man told him he didn't have all the money. We were singing. We were doing 'Wonderful,' and man, people were just praising and shouting. And Allan Clark came up to the stage and told us to cut it. In the middle of the song. He said, 'You must stop; we haven't been paid.' And he told the people what happened. Then he went back out there, and the man paid him. Then we started back to singing."

Eddie: "We were in Miami, Florida, at the war memorial auditorium. The room was packed out. Then the guy claimed somebody stole the money. And my group, the Jackson Southernaires, the Williams Brothers . . . nobody got paid. It hurts. But there's nothing you can do. They were charging seventeen dollars and twenty dollars. And this place was almost capacity. I'd say four thousand people. And he claimed somebody came in, held up the position [*ticket-selling office*], and stole the money."

Major: "Sometimes we go to places and don't get paid. We have the contract, but they say, 'Well, it wasn't there. The people weren't there. So you've got to take a cut.' We say, 'Hey, we brought all these guys all the way from home.' 'Well this is all we've got.' We have to take that to survive and get back home. Because sometimes we weren't able to check in to the hotel, go to the restaurant and eat, then sing on the concert. We had to go to the concert and sing. After we sang, we could go find a hotel and some food. Because before, we didn't have any money. So when you get there and the man doesn't pay you, you're in terrible shape. I remember going to a place in Alabama. When we drove up in the yard at the promoter's house, we ran out of gas right there. And didn't have another dime. He heard the car, so he opened the door, says, 'Who is this?' I said, 'It's Major. Pilgrim Jubilees.' 'Oh yeah? Where y'all going?' Boom! I said, 'We're supposed to be coming here to sing for you.' 'I called your agent over a month ago and told him I had canceled that program.' Lord have mercy. We don't even have gas money. What are we going to do now? So we call back home, and somebody sends us fifty bucks. Fill up, take off for the next program. You've got fifty dollars and rooms then were eight dollars. You find an eight-dollar hotel, get a room, and all of you pile up in that one room."

Michael: "Some of them, you tell 'em you need to get paid and they'll try to put this guilt thing on you. 'You're supposed to be singing for Lord and not for the money.' And to me, it's just . . . 'If you know the Lord like you say you do, why are you doing this to me?' Those people hollerin' about you're working for the Lord . . . if they got a job in the steel mill and on Fridays when they went to get their check they were told, 'Well, since you know the Lord, I'm not going to pay you,' what do you think they're going to say? OK, same thing here. It's a business. I have a product. The Pilgrim Jubilees is a product."

The operation of the Pilgrim Jubilees as a business extends to the way the group is organized. Unlike many modern groups, they retain the traditional structure of officeholders. Clay is the manager; he also now handles most of the work of the booking manager. Cleave is the road manager, dealing with the mechanics of getting the group organized for engagements. Michael is the secretary/treasurer and shares the role of musical director with Bobby. Group business is discussed at meetings, usually held in conjunction with performances or rehearsals so the out-of-town members can attend. Within this structure is the senior triumvirate of Cleave, Clay, and Major; everybody is equal in Pilgrim Jubilees, but these three are a little more equal—with Cleave as the éminence grise. However, decisions are seldom made trilaterally. "We all have an input," says Michael. "That's what I like about this group. It's not just one man saying, 'This is the way it's gonna be done,' even though we have a leader of the organization. But he says, 'Let me go to the whole group and discuss it.' " In another throwback to earlier times, the Jubes also have defined rules, with fines for breaches.

Ben: "We have rules about dressing, conduct, how you're supposed to be to the other guys. If we get fined, the money goes into the expenses—buying gas or something. If you're caught doing the wrong things, a hundred dollars. If you are, say, smoking in the wrong place or drinking alcohol at the wrong time or cursing or stuff like that. You've got to be right in front of your audience. I know nobody's perfect, but what you do, be discreet with it, don't let folks see you."

Fred: "You've got to be straight [*not affected by alcohol or drugs*] onstage. Offstage, too, in public. Some of the other rules are being on time, being in uniform . . . just the basic things that are understood between everybody. If someone is fined, that comes down from the management—Clay, Cleave. It doesn't happen very often. I've been fined for missing rehearsal—$250. It's real tough."

Fred didn't specify why he missed rehearsal, but it must have been deemed a serious breach to incur a $250 fine. Being under the influence of alcohol or drugs on stage is a $150 fine for the first offence and $200 for a repeat offence. A third offence brings suspension from the group, a fourth dismissal. Fines have been imposed for being onstage while affected by alcohol, although not in recent years. No one has ever been suspended or dismissed.

The Pilgrim Jubilees' strict rules on uniforms are in keeping with the quartet practice that began in the early years and continues to this day. While gospel dress standards have followed those of other musical genres in becoming more casual over the years, quartets almost universally appear in matching suits—the "uniform." The Pilgrim Jubilees have a number of uniforms, ranging from an almost casual look with open-neck shirts to a black tuxedo and white dress shirt with black bow ties.

Cleave: "It doesn't seem to be as important as it used to be. Sometimes you see groups where everybody's wearing something different. Or they might come up in a pair of blue jeans. But we've always had uniforms. Michael and Clay are our uniform people. They decide—it might be every two or three months or whatever. There's no certain time. But when you come in [*to a clothing shop*] wanting seven or eight suits at a time, they're glad to see you. Shirts and shoes, too, even the socks. We have about five uniforms that we're using now. The old ones . . . I gave some away to people that needed clothes. And I've got some more to give."

Michael: "Clay and I normally pick the uniforms. We know all the guys' sizes, shoes and everything. And both of us will agree on it. It's hard to say how often we get new ones, because sometimes we must just pop up and say, 'Let's get a suit.' Then sometimes there's a special occasion. We have some uniforms we don't use any more that we could still wear. I'd say we have maybe ten we could still use. The only time we're supposed to wear them is when we're using them for group purposes. I wore a uniform once . . . I was going to church and it was the only thing I had to wear. I was in Columbus, Mississippi. A friend of mine pastors a church there. So I said, 'Well, I guess the guys won't mind,' because I was going to church. But then I hurried back home and took that thing right off. None of the guys were even in Mississippi at the time, but it's just the respect I have for the organization."

Of the core Pilgrim Jubilees, only one—Eddie Graham—has been with the group less than thirty-five years. It is a relationship that has endured longer than many marriages, and it raises the same questions as those directed at aged couples who achieve their brief moments of local fame by staying together for a notable number of years. How do you continue to get along? Do you ever fight? The Jubes don't talk much about their disagreements, but they have occurred. The relationship between the Grahams and Major Roberson has not always been harmonious—Major was the older, more experienced singer who guided and shaped the younger ones when they came to Chicago in 1952; as the Grahams gained in experience and confidence, they sought to reclaim what they saw as their family heritage. As recently as November 1998, Ben Chandler withdrew for three months. The reasons are not clear—Ben does not acknowledge ever being away from the group—but one afternoon, he simply arrived at a program and resumed his place. "It was just . . . sometimes you get frustrated and things are not clicking like you want to, so you rebel," says Clay. "So we let him work it out himself. And when he came back, we all welcomed him and hugged him." Having a defined leadership structure and rules gives the Jubes a basis for stability, but high on the list of reasons for their longevity is a sense of loyalty to the organization. Being in the Pilgrim Jubilees is more than a job. And those such as Fred Rice who leave find it very hard to get back in—their departure establishes them as, in Cleave's term, "bouncy," and "bounciness" is not a trait of a true Pilgrim Jubilee.

Cleave: "If you have five people in step and you get out of line, your head is popping up. So you've got to get everyone back in step and keep on pushing. And do the right thing. You have a line and you stick to that line. When you've got an organization, you're going to have people with different opinions. But when people have been here as long as these fellows have, their minds and decisions have got to mean something. Because those fellows, they're talented enough—anybody would want them. They could get with whoever they wanted. But they won't leave because they love each other. This group is a loving group. I used to get upset when disagreements came. After a while I said to myself, 'What do you get upset for? You know they're all here.' They might run their mouths, but when push comes to shove and the Jubilees say, 'let's move,' the Jubilees move. It's just that simple."

Bobby: "We argue sometimes, but that's as far as it goes. We can talk to each other. We have disagreements. But we can iron it out without fighting. Because we are gospel singers and we are Christian people. So we keep everything in harmony. We might talk loud to one another, but that's about it."

Clay: "It's not always Sunday morning in any organization. There have been a lot of disagreements, a lot of arguing, a lot of cussing, a lot of fussing. But we always stuck together, I don't care what happened. We fought like dogs at times, we thought we hated each other. But we never moved. . . . I can look back and come up with some things about why I would be able to tell Major to go to hell. But they don't outweigh the part of 'that's my brother' and that's the one I been with all of my life and I love him."

Major: "You have arguments and disagreements. Sometimes we can't stand each other. But we've managed to stay together despite all that—I guess we don't know how to do anything else. When you dedicate yourself to something, and you've done it for so long—Cleave, Clay, and myself are the three organizers of this Pilgrim Jubilee thing and we're standing there. Sometimes we fall out, but we keep going."

Michael: "Everybody can't be a Pilgrim Jubilee. The organization's not just for anybody. You have to have a certain standard to be a part of the Pilgrim Jubilees. You can't just let anybody come up and say, 'I want to be a Pilgrim Jubilee.' He might have all the talent in the world, but if he hasn't got the right standards, then he can't be a Pilgrim Jubilee. We worked to build this, and we can't afford to let just anybody come in and tear down what we've worked all these years to build."

Major: "The rule is that you come here [*with the group*] and you be here at least a year. That way, everybody gets a chance to look at each other and we can find out not only your talent but other things about you. If the group likes you and you like the group, then we have no problem. In a year's time, we will vote you in. There haven't been that many voted in."

Secular pop music has lured many artists from gospel, and most of the Jubes have heard the call in some form. In the early 1970s the entire group briefly considered defecting to the secular as a way of escaping Don Robey. They decided against it, and individual members have also rejected moves away from gospel. But they don't condemn those who do cross the line. For Clay Graham in particular, the contrast between the earthly rewards of pop and gospel is close to home. Soul and R&B singer Miki Howard, who had six top-ten hits in the mid to late 1980s, is his daughter from a liaison with Caravans singer Josephine Howard.

Clay: "My daughter made three million in one year. Three million dollars in one year! And had two records out on the street. Here I am, got a volume of records and can't make it. But back in the '60s, Chess Records . . . they liked my voice. They said I had soul in my voice. They told me they'd pay me five thousand dollars if I'd do a blues song. And I turned it down. But blues and gospel are real close together. You sit and listen to a blues record and sing it, put the lyrics to it, and you got a gospel, straight up. They're heartbreaking songs. Tired. Trouble. That's what it is. That's what both of them are about."

Major: "No, nobody ever offered me anything like that. But the group agreed to do rock and roll at one time to get away from Peacock records. Don Robey wouldn't give us a record, and he wouldn't release the group. So we were trying to figure out how could we still operate. We were going to try to find another name and do some rock and roll. We brought it up at a meeting, and everybody agreed this was one way out. We thought of just calling ourselves The Jubes. . . . But by the time we made up our minds to start rehearsing that stuff, Don Robey released that record [*"Let Me Come Home"*/*"Too Close"*]. That started getting real hot, so we didn't think about rock and roll no more. But I started writing that stuff—I've got a lot of R&B songs that I wrote. It's easier to write than gospel. But I've never given it to anybody. I just have it at home."

Cleave: "I've been offered. I just never talked about it. Rhythm and blues is my thing. But I can sing the blues, too. Oh yeah. I know I can sing 'em. I'm a lover of music. I can relate to most any kind of music. I've even been to places that I really didn't have any business [*blues and other secular music clubs*]. . . . The church folks didn't know anything about it, but God did. I prayed to the Lord as a little boy to sing. And He gave it to me. Now what am I going to do? Turn around and give it to the Devil? I'd be a little bit afraid to do that. But I love music. Because music is music, regardless of what you're saying—'Oh Lord' or 'Oh baby.' To me, the only difference in it is the different messages for different purposes. But God blessed me to sing, and I'm going to sing for Him."

Michael: "I probably could have been playing rock and roll and stuff like that; I can handle that type of music. And I have nothing against the guys that do it, but I just thank God that I'm in this particular field. In school, I played in the jazz band, and I play some jazz now when I'm sitting around the house. Because you can learn different moves, different chords or whatever from listening to it. I love jazz. But I listen to my gospel a lot of times when I'm traveling. If I'm riding alone and they're playing blues or whatever on the radio, I have a tendency to get tired. So I take some tapes out and put that gospel on and I stay awake."

Ben: "When I was very young, about fourteen or fifteen . . . when I won the talent quest. Some DJs from WDIA in Memphis came down, and they wanted me to do some rock and roll. But my mom, she didn't believe in that. She said, 'No way. He's going to sing gospel.' I could have sung rock and roll, but I probably wouldn't have been happy doing it. I'd probably have been doing it for the money. There's a lot of money to be made in rock and roll, and I could sing anything. But I don't know how long I'd have lasted. Because I wouldn't have been doing what I wanted to do. Most rock and roll singers, I think, came up in the church. They sang gospel. But they want to sing rock and roll. Fine. I don't think entertaining and singing is taking anything from you being a Christian and serving God. You don't have to be a sinner to sing rock and roll. It's your calling, and you still can go to church. As long as you're doing it from your heart. And God knows every man's heart."

Bobby: "One time back in the '70s . . . we were staying at a motel with the Mighty Clouds, and Wilson Pickett was there. He was talking to Elmo Franklin and Johnny Martin of the Mighty Clouds about getting a musician.

They said, 'Thumper knows how to play.' Bobby Womack was playing for Pickett at this time, and they told him I sounded as close to Bobby Womack. . . . Pickett asked them to bring me, so they came and took me over to Pickett's room. And we sat around with an acoustic guitar he had in the room and he loved me, so he wanted me to go to the show that night with him. I went, stayed backstage, and listened at him. He wanted me—he offered me a certain price and everything, but I told him I was into gospel. I told him this was just my raising and my insight in my soul. It wasn't about the job, it was just that I just want to stay in gospel. I listen to rock and roll—I like the music. Some rock and rollers, I believe, are just doing it for the money and some of them are still active in their churches. That's why I don't knock 'em. I just like quartets. I'm a quartet man."

Eddie: "I went on stage on three occasions with Mr Johnny Taylor. I played three concerts with him around 1993. And also one time with Mr. Bobby Rush, about a year later. [*Johnny Taylor and Bobby Rush sing in the "soul blues" style especially popular in the South. Taylor, who died on May 31, 2000, was a former gospel singer who sang with the Highway QCs and the Soul Stirrers. Bobby Rush was born Emmit Ellis Jr., son of a preacher with churches in Houma, Louisiana, and Pine Bluff, Arkansas; although he went to church as a child, he has never been involved in gospel music.*[1]] I was very tempted to go to the secular world. I was offered a contract with Mr. Johnny Taylor, and I was almost up for signing it . . . well, I was up for signing it. But I wanted my parents to check it out, and they talked me out of it. In fact, they went as far as calling my church, and my pastor talked to me about it. So I didn't pursue it. At the time, I hated that I didn't go. Now, I'm happy that I didn't. I'd make more money. But I asked myself, would I be happier?"

21. Burying the Goat

The second half of the 1980s was not a good time for the Pilgrim Jubilees to be without a recording deal. The old labels were gone; the new ones were more interested in choirs and crossover gospel. But in Jackson, Mississippi, one company was having success supplying a mainly southern African American market with two staples largely neglected by competitors—soul-oriented blues and traditional-based gospel. The Malaco label grew from a band booking business started by Alabama-born pharmacy student Tommy Couch at the University of Mississippi in Oxford. In September 1967 Couch and his brother-in-law, Mitch Malouf, opened their Malaco studio—the name is derived from their surnames—in the single-story warehouse on West Northside Drive in Jackson, Mississippi, that still houses the company.[1] (Coincidentally for the Pilgrim Jubilees, the I-55 freeway turnoff to Northside Drive is Exit 100.)

Tommy Couch: "In '75 we signed the Jackson Southernaires. That was really our big leap into gospel music. [*Group member*] Frank Williams was the guy really responsible for it. At the time, they recorded for Peacock, and this was right after Peacock sold to ABC. Ironically, after we signed them, the next group we went after was the Pilgrim Jubilees. This would have been in '75 or '76. They were doing a show, I think at Jackson State. I made this big pitch to sign them, and they turned me down. We were just a little company in Mississippi, and we weren't held in very high regard. But I talked to Cleave. . . . I haven't ever reminded him of this—he probably doesn't remember."[2]

Cleave does remember. "Malaco was on our case when they first got started. We were friends with the Jackson Southernaires, and they were always on our case about coming where they were. Because Malaco was doing good for them." But the Pilgrim Jubilees didn't consider it until 1986, after talking to Frank Williams, by now the company's director of gospel and its main gospel producer. The initial discussions weren't promising. Clay recalls that the company was paying an advance of five thousand dollars an album; with Savoy, the advance had been twenty-four thousand. But even that was academic, as Tommy Couch wasn't seeking new artists at the time. During a discussion with Couch and other Malaco executives, Clay relates, someone raised the subject of a sermonette called "The Goat," recently recorded for Malaco by the Williams Brothers—a group made up mainly of the younger brothers of Frank Williams. A parable of perseverance, it tells of a goat that falls into a disused well; the farmer is unable to haul it back up and decides to bury it. But as he throws dirt down the well, the goat tramples it beneath his feet and is eventually able to clamber to freedom.[3] In a burst of self-promotion, Clay told Couch: "I preach. And if I ever get a chance to record, I'm going to bury that goat." Clay recalls that the comment was heard by a visiting radio announcer, who later said on air that Malaco and the Jubes were talking. "People started ringing the station asking when the Jubes were going to record for Malaco. Soon after, Frank Williams called and said, 'How would you like to bury the goat?' "

When the Pilgrim Jubilees joined Malaco, its gospel catalog was well established, partly due to the efforts of former Peacock publicist and jack-of-all-trades Dave Clark, who started working for it in 1979. "He had a lot of weight and a lot of influence, and a lot of people trusted him in the music business," says Tommy Couch. "So he was responsible for us getting a lot of artists." Around 1985 Malaco widened its gospel involvement by buying the dormant Savoy label, gaining access to its large back-catalog—including the Pilgrim Jubilees' recordings. Tommy Couch: "It was the hidden crown jewel. It just had a little dust on it. And nobody recognized it."

The Pilgrim Jubilees' first Malaco album was *Gospel Roots* (Malaco MAL-

4419). Although it uses synthesized string and horn sounds, the soft contemporary sound present in varying degrees on every Jubes album since the mid-1970s is set aside, giving full rein to the bass-driven push on which the group's reputation has rested since "Stretch Out." Only one song is a repeat—an impassioned version of "Old Ship of Zion." Clay has a new sermonette, "Barnyard," telling of a young farm worker who, whenever he felt the need to pray, would fall to his knees. His overseer tells him to "pray on your own time" and whips him when he is again found praying at work. The young man responds by singing a stanza of "Every Time I Feel the Spirit (I Pray)"; the nearly ten-minute story ends with the barnyard conversion of the overseer. Of the eight songs on the album, Clay wrote three and Major four. Two of Major's songs, in completely different ways, draw on the same common gospel theme, the idea of a telephone to heaven, which is almost as old as the telephone itself. "Illusion" tells Christians that "if you have an illusion, from so much confusion" you can "call Jesus . . . He's always on the line, anywhere, any time." "Stay On the Line" reverses the charge, enjoining the faithful to "Stay on the line . . . God will give you a blessing if you stay on the line." The eighth song, "Tell the World," is Ben Chandler's first songwriting contribution. Musically and lyrically, it is firmly in mainstream Pilgrim Jubilees style, an up-tempo romp with a propulsive beat and an extended drive section as it delivers its message—"Tell the world that Jesus is coming back." Ben takes the lead in a strong, open-throated tenor, lighter than Clay's or Cleave's lead voice but covering just as wide a vocal range.

Gospel Roots is still the Jubes' best-selling Malaco album. "Barnyard" was one of its most popular tracks, and the album's title, suggesting the group was returning to its beginnings, obviously appealed to record buyers. Malaco's marketers heeded the lessons, and the next Pilgrim Jubilees album, issued in 1989, was *Back to Basics* (Malaco MAL-4431). Despite its title, it mixes traditional and modern stylings. Clay has another sermonette, "Little Willie," a rather tangled story of a young man brought back from heaven by the prayers of those left behind; its song is the quartet favorite "Pray for Me." Ben Chandler returns as writer and lead singer with "God's Child," a solid drive built around the traditional line "Talk about a child of God that do love the Lord, here is one." Cleave Graham makes his first appearance as a songwriter since 1961's "Helping Hand" on the first Peacock album with "I've Got a Mind (To Work for Jesus)." "That one, Cleave came up with it in the studio, and we recorded it. Instantly," recalls Bobby McDougle. "He said, 'I have a song I'd like us to try. Bobby, you and Mike come up with some sounds for this.' So we jumped right on top of it." The spontaneous composition is a rolling chug over which Cleave sings a collection of familiar lines, melded into a new song. At the other end of the spectrum, Clay revives "Standing" from the 1982 *Whensoever I Pray* record. The torch-singer delivery of the Savoy album is replaced by a sound transplanted from 1970s soul music, with a horn section that, although created on a synthesizer keyboard, sounds straight from the glory days of Muscle Shoals, Alabama. The result is a strikingly effective vocal and musical powerhouse; it is also—once again—quite at odds with the rest of the album.

During the late 1980s and early 1990s the peripheral personnel of the group kept changing. Around the time of the last Savoy album, Harold Jefferson from Oklahoma City became the first full-time second guitarist. He left after about a year and was replaced by Chris Johnson, who had played on the "Blazing in the Blizzard" album. Johnson stayed only months before leaving to join soloist Shirley Caesar's band. On the first Malaco album, the second guitar was played by session player Joey Wolfolk, but for the second, Chicagoan Rev. Earl Moore was part of the group. The drummer on the first Malaco album was a group member, Timothy "Man" Burgess, from New Jersey. By the time of the second album he was gone, replaced by Gregory "Bobo" Harris from the Violinaires. Earl Moore, who now pastors a church in Chicago, stayed with the group for around three years and was voted in as a member. Although Bobo Harris stayed longer, he did not pass the bounce test and never became an official Pilgrim Jubilee.

The group's third Malaco recording session produced not a record but a videotape, *Live from Jackson, Mississippi* (Malaco MALV-9008). It was filmed in 1990 at Jackson's City Auditorium during a marathon "Night of the Gospel Legends," which also yielded videotapes of the Angelic Gospel Singers and the Sensational Nightingales. The Jubes were the last group to perform, and by the time they appeared, the audience was flagging. "They were tired, and a lot of them had gone home by the time they got to us," says Major. Probably because of this, the start of the set is low key as the group works its way through "We're the People," "I Love You," "Standing," and "Any Other Way" (retitled from the *Back to Basics* CD as "We've Got to Move

Along") before moving up a gear with "Church Song." Two sermonettes are included, "Three Trees" and "Barnyard," which closes the show. The group worked hard, and the performances are crisp and polished. But the lack of a large audience and the fact that the sound track does not capture the responses from those who did stay mean the excitement and interaction that characterize a gospel program are noticeably missing.

For their next album, issued in 1991, the Pilgrim Jubilees took full advantage of all Malaco's resources. Frank Williams again produced it; he also wrote a song for it and sang on it. His brother, Melvin, of the Williams Brothers, sang and helped with the production, and the Mississippi Mass Choir—then and now Malaco's biggest-selling gospel artists—sang backings on three tracks. Eddie Graham made his first appearance on record with the group, and Dwayne Watkins of the Canton Spirituals contributed some guitar playing. Fittingly, the album's title is *Family Affair* (Malaco MAL-4442). Its accompaniments make heavy use of keyboards and synthesizer brass and have a "contemporary" sound. But mainstream gospel songs dominate, from the opening "Doors of the Church," Major's invitation to worship—"The doors of the church are open, come on in"—through remakes of "True Story" and "Life's Evening Sun" to an ebullient reworking of the traditional "When We All Get to Heaven," on which Ben Chandler sings the lead, spanking the song along under the impetus of a bass- and drums-driven beat.

When Larry Moten left the Jubes for the second time, they initially didn't replace him, using stand-in keyboard players instead. Around 1992 Mississippi keyboardist Darrell Johnson became a regular part of the lineup. **Cleave**: "He was with us about two and a half years. Then he left and went to the Jackson Southernaires. His home was right out from Canton, near Jackson, so it was better for him." **Clay**: "He went with the Jackson Southernaires. Then he went with the Lumzy Sisters. He left them and went with the Keynotes. Now he's left the Keynotes and is back with the Southernaires. I told him, 'You ain't coming back here, son.' " Although Johnson is far too bouncy to be ever considered again as a permanent member of the Pilgrim Jubilees, they often make use of him on programs when their paths cross.

In 1992 the Jubes recorded their first CD, *I'm Getting Better All the Time* (Malaco MCD-4456). The title track, with its reflective message of religious self-improvement—"I'm not what I ought to be, but I'm better than I used to be, and I'm getting better all the time"—was popular with gospel listeners and has entered the repertoires of other singers, including the Blind Boys of Alabama, who recorded it in 1995.[4] Clay revives "Are You Ready (To Serve the Lord)" from 1975's *Crying Won't Help* Peacock album, and "The Good Lord"—narrated and sung by Cleave—is a more polished version of Major's 1978 resurrection narration "He Went That Way." One track, "Have You Seen Him," features members of the Mississippi Mass Choir, earning liner-note praise from Tupelo, Mississippi, gospel radio announcer Dexter Witherspoon, who lauds the Jubes as "one of the first gospel groups to bridge the gap between choirs and quartets." The song, however, is a bridge in a different direction—it is Clay's reworking of the 1971 secular hit "Have You Seen Her" by Chicago soul group the Chi-Lites.

I'm Getting Better All the Time is a solid, professional album but not a landmark in the Jubes' recording career. Their next issue did hit the heights. *In Revival* (Malaco MCD-6016) is a recording of the 1993 Mississippi homecoming at Houston High School. The auditorium was packed, and the Jubes were fired and in top form. Recalls Bobby McDougle: "Houston hadn't had anything like that happen before. The whole town was excited about it. We had a wonderful time." Clay is the dominant personality on stage, soliciting reaction ("Are we doing all right?"), exhorting ("Hallelujah! Praise God!") and involving the audience ("Could you be a witness to that today?"). Cleave's main lead is on "Church Song," which he extends by making the group repeat the chorus line because "they can say it better than that. . . . Do you mind if I make 'em say it again?" Predictably, the audience is vociferously in favor of 'em saying it again—and again and again. An eight-minute version of "Old Ship of Zion" receives a warm welcome, fuelled by Clay's local-interest introduction: "My testimony is about when I found Jesus. Right down the highway, a little place that they call Horse Nation, a little old church that's set back in the woods, they call it New Zion Baptist Church. . . ." The high point is the sermonette "Child's Blood," which on disc fades out after fourteen minutes obviously still some way from its conclusion. The narrative is basically the same as the recorded versions, but the song, "Precious Lord," is a firestorm of gospel technique and passion, climaxing with a searing twin lead from the Graham brothers.

In Revival revived the Jubes' record-store popularity, ranking close to their first two Malaco albums in sales. When the time came to record again,

Malaco followed a basic dictum of the record business—"if it worked one time, it'll work again"—and the new release was another live CD, this time coupled with a videotape of the performance. They were recorded at the Alabama Theater for the Performing Arts in Birmingham in 1995. It was a repeat of the 1990 "Night of the Gospel Legends" session—again with the Angelic Gospel Singers and the Sensational Nightingales and the Jubes performing last. The band had changed since the Houston recordings. Darrell Johnson was with the Jackson Southernaires; his place was taken for the program by session player Derrick Nation. Greg Harris was back with the Violinaires. His replacement, Marco Atkins, was joining the family business—as Cleave Graham's son from a relationship with Michael Atkins's sister, he was working with his cousin, his father, and his uncle. Although it was late when the Jubes took the stage and many seats in the auditorium were empty, those who stayed were more resilient than their Jackson counterparts. The result is that while the excitement and tension of the program don't match that of the Houston homecoming, the performances have a vibrancy and drive missing from much of the Jackson performance. On the final song of the program, the Jubes are joined by Charles Green, who sang with them in the 1960s. His appearance was prearranged—he even has the uniform of green collarless jacket and black shirt—but no acknowledgment is made on CD or videotape of his presence. The group has maintained contact with Green, and he has occasionally stepped in to help when a stand-in singer is needed. His appearance in Birmingham was, in effect, a reward for years of service. "I pick up that phone and call Charles, he doesn't even wait," says Clay. "Charles is a good guy. And just being able to come back to the stage and say something meant a lot to him."

The first four Pilgrim Jubilees albums on Malaco were produced by Frank Williams, whose quartet background enabled him to work well with the Jubes. But in the early 1990s Williams was afflicted with the lung disease blastomycosis, and on March 22, 1993, he collapsed at the Atlanta airport on his way home to Jackson after a Mississippi Mass Choir concert and died soon after of acute cardiorespiratory arrest at the age of forty-five.[5] Without Williams, Clay Graham took on another role, as producer of the Houston and Birmingham discs. It is not a job he entirely enjoys. "I know I can produce a little bit," he says, "but I don't know what these producers know today. The machines and stuff they have—I don't know that." When the

Jubes returned to Jackson in 1997 to make new recordings, the producer credit was shared by Clay, Cleave, and Major. The title track of the new album (Malaco MCD-4491) was "Trouble in the Street" from the Peacock album *Don't Let Him Down* (with a title trim from "Streets" to "Street"). Clay had always felt the song should have done better than it had and believed it might be more acceptable in the 1990s than it was in the 1970s. The 1997 version is the album's first track and is even bleaker and more uncompromising than the 1974 original. It opens with the sound effects of gunfire, sirens, and a gruff voice saying, "Get on the ground, boy, get over here. You're in big trouble." And it gains an extra verse, accompanied by machine gun sound effects:

> Killing, and fighting in the streets y'all
> The blood; frightened boys and girls
> Running down the street,
> Just like war

The rest of the disc is a more conventional Pilgrim Jubilees mix, with a couple of surprises. After forty-five years with the group, Major Roberson makes his debut as a lead singer on his own composition, the bluesy "The Train." **Major**: "I never thought I was good enough. I'm not a lead singer. I write for other people. Cleave talked me into 'The Train.' It scared me to death when he told me to do it. But now, if I can find something else, I might try it again." **Cleave**: "He writes, but he doesn't try to lead. I was the one that made him sing lead on that one. I said, 'You sound good with it, it fits your voice.' I've been with him a long time, I know how far he can go. The songs he writes, he writes them beyond his ability to sing. He's not thinking about doing them himself. But I made him do that one. And he was so proud." The song uses the long-established gospel image of the heaven-bound train—"I got news today, my train is on its way. I ain't going nowhere, 'cause Jesus is going to meet me there"—and is sung to a relaxed shuffle, punctuated by guitar-created whistle effects.

Ben Chandler's lead outing comes on his own song, "My Christian Journey," although he shares the vocals around, inviting a verse each from Cleave, Clay, and studio visitor Roger Bryant of the Jackson Southernaires. The last track is a version of Charles Albert Tindley's 1905 composition "We'll Understand It Better By and By." Accompanied only by the piano playing of Mississippi Mass Choir musical codirector Jerry Smith, the Jubes create an old-style quartet harmony under the lead singing of Rev. James Moore, a popular Malaco recording artist who usually performed and recorded with choirs. For the first time since Mack Robertson left the group in the early 1960s, the Pilgrim Jubilees have a bass vocal line, sung with not quite unerring accuracy by Cleave. The combination of Moore's florid choral singing, Smith's churchy piano, and the Jubes' old-style harmonies doesn't seem a recipe for success, but the song overcomes the disparate nature of its parts and emerges as an unusual and effective whole.

Unfortunately for the record, the group, and Malaco, Clay's faith in "Trouble in the Street" was misplaced—something he now acknowledges, while remaining optimistic the song's time will come. "People wouldn't play it on the radio," he says. "A DJ told me it turned the audience off. You hear enough about violence and people killing each other anyway—then you listen to gospel and here comes a siren. He said it turns them off. I don't know if it really does or not, because lately we've been getting a lot of requests for it. Looks like everything I write turns out to be too far ahead." "Trouble in the Street" was only one song on the album, but it was the opening track and the title track. When it failed to gain an audience, so did the other nine songs, and the disc was the least successful of the Jubes' Malaco recordings.

Jerry Mannery was Frank Williams's deputy at Malaco and in 1993 took over as director of gospel. A slender, elegant man, he speaks fluently and eloquently about his three passions—his work for Malaco, his managerial role with the Mississippi Mass Choir, and his Christian faith. The walls of his large but windowless office buried within Malaco's sprawling building are decorated with pictures and posters of Malaco gospel stars, including the Pilgrim Jubilees. He uses the jargon of the record industry—recordings are "projects"; sales are measured in "units"—but is forthright about the failure of *Trouble in the Street*.[6] "Clay was trying to do something a little bit different to try to attract a larger audience. But I think if they concentrate on what they do well they'll always be very good. The Jubes need to be true to their form. Add in the little elements of the new technology, but still be true to your roots. Clay and I had discussions about the project [*Trouble in the Street*], and . . . they've been self-produced. Sometimes you need an outside person, someone who can be a little bit more objective and show you another way of doing this.

"Their first two releases for Malaco, *Gospel Roots* and *Back to Basics*, did very well. And also *In Revival*, the live project. Video sales . . . it has just been phenomenal. They probably sold fifteen to twenty thousand videos [*of Live In Birmingham*]. That's a very substantial number for any musical genre. In record sales, the Jubes are right there with the average seller. Because when you look at gospel today, quartets are really only a small portion of the sales. Other than the Canton Spirituals, the Williams Brothers, maybe the Jackson Southernaires, most groups are going to sell twenty-five to fifty thousand units. The Jubes would fit in there. If they have an exceptional song, they could sell more than that. But the norm would be between twenty-five and fifty thousand.

"I think the quartet market has really shrunk over the last five years. The buying market is getting younger, and I don't think that market is buying quartet. I think it's the moms and pops, the aunts and uncles. But quartets are not dying out. Every day I'm getting projects from young quartets who are looking for a deal. And when you have quartets whose members are fifteen, sixteen years old, that's very encouraging. One thing that's happening is that quartets are getting organized. It used to be a thing where everybody had their own little island. But then they started looking around and they found they weren't in the mainstream. So the guys formed the American Gospel Quartet Convention. It's based in Birmingham, Alabama. It gives them a forum where they can talk about issues and why quartet music is not as popular as it was. So what's happening now, I think, is that the guys are really starting to turn their attention to improving their product. Not just the product but the image, the ministry . . . more of the groups are talking about ministry, and that's where the people today want to hear—you can't get by with just entertaining them.

"But it's a tough lifestyle. People look at the artists onstage and see the glamour. But when you go behind the scenes and see the wear and tear and the separation from your families. . . . I don't care what artist it is, it's still rough being out there on that road. And even more so for the gospel artists, because a lot of times the returns are not there. So it has to be more than just a business. I think the guys are all committed to the gospel. So often, groups are accused of being in this for the money. Most of the time when you're out there, you're not making the money you would if you just had an eight-to-five job. So I've got to take my hat off to the Jubes. To be sixty and seventy years old and get in an automobile and drive twelve hours then get up and sing, give it everything you've got—then get back on the road and drive ten more hours? That's some kind of commitment."

Through the 1990s the Jubes maintained their close relationship with the freeways of America, although they had by now settled into a routine of going out at weekends and staying mainly on the East Coast. Occasionally, they ventured beyond the local auditoriums and civic centers that provided the bulk of their income; one such booking, around 1991, took them to an American shrine of popular entertainment. **Major**: "We did Disneyland, out in California. That was the most exciting thing I've done in my life. The stage was surrounded by water, and they had a boat to transport you across to the stage. You'd do your forty-five minutes, and when your time was up, this ship would be coming back with someone else. We were singing on the water, and you could see the ducks swimming all around. The people were on the banks on the other side, and after nightfall they had all kinds of lights. It was beautiful."

The group also started obtaining festival bookings; they are regulars at the annual Chicago Gospel Festival and in 1999 sang at one of America's largest music festivals, the New Orleans Jazz and Heritage Festival. In April 2000 they went outside the United States, performing at the Umbria Jazz, Gospel, and Soul Festival in Perugia, Italy, in a booking arranged by Chicago Gospel Festival organizer Pam Harris.

Such bookings are part of a small but growing interest in gospel music from outside its community. A similar interest, mainly from young whites, developed for blues in the 1960s; by the 1990s it was a lifeline sustaining a music largely discarded by the culture that created it. Some of the new interest in gospel comes from people who discovered it as an offshoot of blues, but unlike its secular relative, gospel is still very much a living and developing part of its culture, and even the older forms—such as quartet—do not have to rely on an external life-support system. However, bookings at primarily secular events, such as the New Orleans festival, do provide new opportunities. One problem is that the audiences are likely to have no great interest in religion and may not even speak the language in which the songs are sung. At Perugia, the Pilgrim Jubilees went onstage for their first concert armed with their surefire successes—"Old Ship of Zion," "Won't It Be Wonderful," "Don't Let Him Down"—and found the rules had changed. "We weren't getting anywhere," says Clay. "Nowhere at all. On the way back in the bus, I told them, 'The Lord told me we're singing the wrong songs.' But he didn't have to tell me. The audience told me that. That stomp thing wasn't going to get it. The next night we did some old songs they all knew." These included chestnuts such as "Oh Happy Day" and even "When the Saints Go Marching In"; Clay also obtained the services of an American woman living in Italy, who interpreted his onstage comments and explanations. But even when those listening understand the words, they may not want to hear them. "You've got to keep those hard heavy beats going," says Major. "The less slow stuff you do, the better off you are. If you start doing these sacred songs, slow stuff, you'll lose them. They don't care about the religious-type stuff you're singing. That takes away from it a little, because you're there to try and give a message." Michael Atkins and Eddie Graham are less pessimistic. "We get a chance to spread the word to the unsaved people," says Michael. "Those people wouldn't go to church, so we bring the church to them." Eddie observes: "You might have some that go to church, and some that have never been to church in their lives. But they enjoy themselves. You have to be able to entertain. But at the same time, you can't forget the spiritual side, because there might be somebody there that you can lift their bowed-down head."

With the increased attention from outside the Jubes' core market came recognition from within it. In 1988 their *Back to Basics* album was nominated for a Stellar award—the gospel industry's Grammy. The 1996 CD *Don't You Let Nobody Turn You Around* was also nominated, as was *Trouble in the Street* two years later. They haven't won yet, but Jerry Mannery believes their chances are improving. "The more your name is mentioned, the better the odds are that you will eventually win. So I think the next release will stand a better chance." Early in 2000 the Jubes were inducted into the American Gospel Quartet Convention's Hall of Fame. Clay was skeptical when he first heard of the award—"I thought halls of fame were for baseball players, football players"—but changed his mind when he went to Birmingham for the ceremony. "I didn't think it would mean that much to me. But to be recognized like that by the other quartets . . ."

The "next release" that Jerry Mannery predicted as a Stellar winner (it wasn't) had a rocky road to completion. The logic behind it was straightforward—if the live CD of the Houston homecoming and the video of the Birmingham concert had sold, a combined CD and video project of another Houston homecoming must surely sell. "I think Malaco always regretted not doing a video of *In Revival*," says Bobby McDougle. On June 6, 1998, the oversight was rectified, and the program was filmed and recorded for a joint CD/video release. Anxious to redeem themselves after *Trouble in the Street*, the Jubes worked hard on the new project. Its centerpiece was a dramatic re-creation of the crucifixion, starring Clay as Jesus Christ and narrated by the Reverend Benjamin Cone, a Jackson-based Malaco artist who specializes in narrations and sermonettes delivered in a rich, sonorous bass voice. Clay has vivid memories of the filming. "What made it look so true was that the cross I was carrying was heavy! I had a big cut in my shoulder from it, and when I would pick it up, I had to sure enough put some strength in it." The success of their passion play at Houston encouraged the Jubes to consider taking it on the road. Spiritually, it would be a dramatic and moving reminder to audiences of what and who their religion was about. And it had worldly advantages, too. "It's gonna be a mess for another artist to follow," said Clay, only half-jokingly. The plan to simultaneously uplift audiences and stymie rival groups was derailed by Malaco's decision to remake the CD. At the homecoming concert, the Jubes had followed normal practice and performed a mixture of old songs and new. But four of the songs—including the thrice-recorded "I Love You"—were from the *Trouble in the Street* disc, and Malaco balked at the duplication. The group had to come up with new songs and record them in the studio, and this and other delays pushed the release date back to August 2000. The video's release date was pushed back even farther—it was eventually released in January 2001—almost certainly to avoid having two new and different Pilgrim Jubilee offerings going on sale at the same time.

The CD is called *Were You There* (Malaco MCD-4508). It's the wrong title. *Were You There* was supposed to be the title of the video, taken from the gospel classic sung by the Jubes during their passion play. The CD was to have been called *Reach Up*, after one of the four Major Roberson compositions on the nine-track disc. But the video's title was transplanted to the CD—the song "Were You There" is not on the disc—and the video was issued as *A Night to Remember*. Although Clay and the Jubes did the initial production work on the CD, the finishing touches were overseen by Savoy's Milton Biggham, and he and Clay are listed as producers. Back too from the Savoy days is keyboard player James Perry, who also did the synthesized horn and string arrangements.

The recipe Biggham, Perry, and the Jubes worked from was a familiar one, and the disc contains all the usual elements of a Pilgrim Jubilees release. "Reach Up" is the opening track and the only one to survive from the Houston concert. After a somber introduction of descending bass runs, it quickly settles into a solid up-tempo Jubes one-two groove over which Clay tells his audience that "God's got a blessing" for everyone prepared to "reach up" and claim it. "You Can't Change My Mind" is written by Shadrach Robinson, son of one of the leading gospel soloists, Rev. Cleophus Robinson. **Clay**: "It's more the Pilgrim Jubilees than I thought it was. It's the Pilgrim Jubilees, period. He said, 'Mr. Graham, I grew up on your stuff, being around my dad and all. I know how y'all sing.' And when we started singing this song, and we started looking back through our past material, that's where he's coming from. Because if you notice, on all the fast songs, the background's talking almost just as much as the lead singer, instead of pausing and the lead singing something then the background coming up. And he got it in this song, it's right."

One of Clay's own compositions on the album is "Dying Testimony," a seven-minute narration in which he relates the story of his father's deathbed conversion. In words similar to those he used to describe the event during our first interview session, he tells of how Columbus Graham would prepare the wagon to take his wife to the New Zion Baptist Church, then comes forward in time to the hospital room scene; the song accompanying the story is "Everything Will Be All Right." Until not long before the final decision on the CD's contents was made, Clay and Jerry Mannery had been planning to leave "Dying Testimony" "on the shelf," as Clay felt it needed more work. But the delay in issuing the disc gave him time to polish it, and despite its stark title and subject matter, it was one of the record's successes with listeners.

Gospel music's traditions make their appearance in a song with the unlikely title of "Fireball"—explained by Cleave in his spoken introduction. "I like the new songs and the way they sing them," he says. "[But] there's something about the old songs that kinda puts chill-bumps on your arms, you know what I'm talking about? My auntie, a long time ago, she loved those old songs. . . . Her name was Elvira Smith. But in church they called her Fireball. Fireball got up and she walked towards the pulpit and everybody would stand up and they'd begin to gather round Fireball because they knew they had a treat coming. You see, Fireball had a special song she would sing and she would say words like this. . . ." The song is one of gospel music's best-known pieces, "Give Me That Old Time Religion." It's often performed at a fast tempo, but the Jubes slow it to a solemn and deliberate beat with a rich, smooth, group harmony underpinning Cleave's lead. The only song on the record not new to disc and the Jubes' repertoire is "That's Enough," writer-credited to Major Roberson but a repeat of the Dorothy Love Coates song that made its first appearance on the Nashboro *Homecoming* album in 1979.

22. "I'm Not Perfect . . ."

Cleave Graham's statement is elegant in its simplicity. "I'm not perfect," he says, "but the one I sing about is." In that one sentence is encapsulated his abiding Christian faith, his desire to spread a message in song about that faith, and his recognition of human frailty, including his own. As veterans of nigh on fifty years on the road, the Pilgrim Jubilees have met all the pitfalls and temptations that await the traveling performer—and learned from their experiences.

Major: "We had to learn. It's a hard way out there. When you get in the lights, they'll all be pulling at you. And you end up messing around until you get used to the lights. But you know they only want this because you are in the lights. You figure out what you're going through and what you're doing to yourself. Then you start slowing down. You say, 'Do I want a girlfriend or do I want a fan? Do I want somebody who'll stay with me forever as my fan, or do I want somebody who's going to get mad and then there won't be no fan and no girlfriend?' Time will teach you, and you'll get some of that stuff out of your system. But when you first go out there, you think 'Oh my God. They're carrying on over me, I must be . . .' No, it's only because they're looking at you on the stage. Then they can go back and tell their friends, 'Oh, I go with one of the Pilgrim Jubilees.' They can tear your name up real good. So . . . you can't stop it from happening, but you try to keep it discreet. I'll admit that when we first went out, we weren't used to it, and sometimes it would end up in a little mess that it shouldn't have. But that will wear off. Once you learn . . . they're doing you like this, and when the next set of guys comes through, they'll do the same thing to them. They go from one group to the next.

"And you find out that if you start messing around with your fans, you get a bad name. Because if something goes wrong with the relationship, they'll start putting the bad mouth out there, and it'll ugly you up. So you learn. When they're sitting on the front row in the auditorium with their dresses all the way up, legs so you can see everything, you know what it's all about. And you learn how to live with yourself. At first, it's exciting—"Whoo, look at this!" But you learn after so long and you're careful. But when you're young . . . you don't have to be young in age to be young; it's being inexperienced and running into an environment so different from the one at home. Everything's swarming around you. 'We want your autograph.' 'We want you over for dinner.' And when you get there, you find out it's not only for dinner. Down the line you learn if there's a hook under that bait. You don't know until you get caught a couple of times. And then . . . you have to do a lot of praying. If you cease to pray out there, everything will grab you."

Clay: "When women go crazy over you, you go crazy over them, too. Then you go on about your business. When I say go crazy over them, you love 'em at the auditorium, you talk to them, you kiss them on the jaw—and when you leave there, you leave by yourself. Ain't nobody perfect. But if I try to stretch myself out across this country with every woman that comes to me, I would have been dead a long time ago. And when you're singing the gospel and praising the Lord every night, you've got to have some right somewhere. You don't go to bed with women just because they are there. That just isn't what it's supposed to be. Everybody does a little something, but you don't go and lay down and wallow. You've got to back up and go on about your business. And you got to pray. When you stop praying and asking the Lord for your direction and strength, you've got a problem. When you get hung up to where your mind is focused on one or two things—it's making me a buck so I can do what I want—and you forget where it's coming from, then you're not going to last long. You can be an adulterer and be sleeping from bed to bed, but that's just not it. And we're well away from that now."

Bobby: "You've got to be real strong. Because you're only human. The best way to deal with it is to talk to them about 'Thus saith the Lord. . . .' Try to show them the way that Christ . . . try to lead them to Christ, change their conversation and talk to them about the goodness of God. But it's difficult. Because the Devil is always busy. You can get weak sometimes—I'm not going to say I've been perfect, but . . . you have to be strong. See, most people look at you as being a celebrity, women are gonna be women and men gonna be men, so that brings temptation. You can easily get on the wrong track if you aren't steadfast about what you're doing."

Ben: "As you get your years, you get common sense. And you can't hide. I remember a long time ago, I used to take a drink of gin. I was coming through North Carolina, around Durham or Raleigh, and I stopped . . . 'way outside of town I saw a liquor store and I was by myself, so I'll go in and get a little bottle. I bought my package and paid the man, and he said, 'Hey Ben, where you guys singing at tonight?' So what you do in the dark will come to light. Somebody will see you and know you. But the Jubes, we have our rules, and we try to stick by those rules. We've been singing together a long time. And nobody's perfect. We all make mistakes. And when one needs some help, we talk, we pull each other's coattails. Because it's just the nature of a human being. He'll step out of bounds some time."

Michael: "It comes back to being professional offstage as well as onstage. When these temptations come, whatever they may be, you've got to realize that's all it is and know how to turn it off and be professional about doing it. You've got to know it when you see it. Because if you're not aware, anything could happen. I've been here for so long, I know it right away. The women will come at you sometimes and . . . I don't want a woman that wants me because I'm a Pilgrim Jubilee. You like me for who I am, for being Michael Atkins. I really enjoy meeting people, talking to them . . . every woman doesn't want to be hit on, and every man doesn't want that either. You can meet a nice one—we're not blind. Some of them look exceptionally well. And that is noticed. But what is more noticed is what I am out there for. Because I might say something or do something to make this person come closer to Christ. And that's what I'm about."

* * *

An oft-laid accusation against quartets is of insincerity in performance, of allowing entertainment techniques—"putting on a show"—to take precedence over the religious message. As has already been discussed (chapter 9), quartets walk a narrow line between show business and ministry, a balancing act made more difficult by the fact that their calling requires them to be entertainers and ministers. Their songs are religious, spreading the gospel and praising God. But they must present their message with skill, panache, and flair, because as well as being uplifted, quartet audiences expect to be entertained. A group's success as entertainers and religious instructors is often measured by how effectively it can "shout" its audience, moving it into a jubilant state of religious ecstasy. A "shouting" audience is evidence that the Holy Spirit is present and the program is succeeding as a religious event. (The term "shout" is misleading, implying as it does a loud vocal expression. Any expression of religious joy, ranging from hand clapping and rhythmic swaying to full-blown shrieks, is part of the shout.) Singing also affects group members, and lead singers often appear to be in a state of trance as a performance reaches its climax. But no matter how "in the Spirit" singers may become, they must remain aware of their surroundings and of the dynamics of the performance. If they "fall out," entering the semiunconscious state of complete surrender to the Holy Spirit that sometimes overcomes audience members, they can no longer perform. However, singers—usually the leads—often display less extreme manifestations of being in the Spirit, ranging from changes in singing style through delivery of emotion-charged "testimony" to running apparently out of control through the audience, sometimes singing without a microphone.

It is generally acknowledged in the quartet world that not all such displays are genuine, that some singers will fake being under the influence of the Spirit in an effort to increase the excitement level at a program and shout the audience. Clay Graham admits than in his young days, he would sometimes select a female in the audience and use his performing skills—rather than the religious power of his song—to push her into a shout. "I'd look over there, say, 'That one. I'm gonna shout her.' And I'd ease over close. . . . But you don't do that! You let the Lord take control." Many in the quartet world believe onstage fakery is not as common as it once was. As Eddie Graham and Jerry Mannery suggest, groups are now more aware of the spiritual side of their work; as a corollary, audiences are more aware and less tolerant of "clowning." And quartets are no longer gospel music's leaders, reducing their appeal as a career option for those more focused on stardom than salvation.

In *Fire in My Bones*, Glenn Hinson quotes singer John Landis, of the North Carolina quartet the Golden Echoes, criticizing quartet singers—especially the leads—for using "the same little gimmicks" every time they perform.[1] Hinson is discussing artists who pretend to be touched by the Holy Spirit, but the supporting quote from Landis paints with a broader brush. He believes that even rehearsing what one is going to say to an audience is evidence of "putting on a show." The Pilgrim Jubilees, like almost every quartet and certainly every professional quartet, are "guilty" of having standard lines and actions—usually evolved in performance rather than as a part of the rehearsal process. A seasoned performer, sacred or secular, recognizes these as proven ways of winning over audiences. The hardline critic would view them as evidence of hypocritical "show." To the Pilgrim Jubilees, they are a necessary part of imparting the Christian message.

Cleave: "The main thing is, we're trying to make it effective as much as we can. I want to have something for everybody. To me, you need to be able to reach people. Not just certain categories, or certain minds—you're supposed to be able to entertain people. We've got songs that can make people laugh. And we've got message songs and novelty songs . . . different songs that we do for people that like that. But the bottom line is to say something to help somebody or make somebody have a different outlook on life. Everybody doesn't come there to shout. Sometimes you get people there to find something to laugh about and joke about. And you can give them a message that will put them on Straight Street. And that's my prayer. To say something to help somebody."

Major: "You're doing religious stuff, but you're entertaining, too. If it takes something else to sell your act, you do what you have to do to sell your act. Because people come into the concert for all kinds of reasons. All of them aren't there to see how serious you can be. Some of them come to see your choreography or to see if you have anything special. Are you going to do something different to the rest of them? Like that thing in 'Wonderful' where we get chairs and sit down. Before you get there, that's often top priority on the request list. And when you get on the stage and look around, somebody's got chairs and set them up there where you can get them. They look forward to it. That's what they paid for, and that's what they want."

Bobby: "When you go up to sing, you've got to put Jesus first. And you've got to go on with your mind on what it's all about—to sing the praises of God in song. You got to put your whole heart and soul and mind into it. You can't have your mind on something else—that's not going to work. You have to have your mind on what you're doing. You do have to entertain, too. Have good coordination on different songs. It's good—makes your format work out. Because people are paying to see you, you've got to look as neat as you possibly can. But the main thing is to be about what you're there about. And that is singing God's praises."

Ben: "You have to minister to people and tell them what to do. People love singing. They love preaching, they love praying. And the entertaining is still singing, because whatever God wants you to do, he'll bless you in it. The Bible says, 'Make a joyful noise unto the Lord, all ye lands.' So as long as you're telling the people the truth about 'thus said the Lord.' . . . And you've got to praise Him. People praise God in different ways. Some people cry, some shout, some run, some do this and some do that. Some laugh . . . you've got all different kinds of people. But as long as you're getting the message over to the people and they're enjoying it, I think you're doing a pretty good job. I think God is well pleased with you."

Cleave: "I've had so many people come to me and say that something I've said called their fathers to church or made their brothers accept Christ in their life. Then I just say, 'Thank you Lord,' because that was my prayer from the start—to do something or to say something to help somebody or call somebody to go to Christ. I want to help people to know Him. To inspire somebody to go to Him. To let people know that He is the answer for everything. Back in the '60s I had an ulcerated stomach. Sometimes when we were traveling, I'd be up in the back of the car on my knees, because if I sat down, it hurt. But I didn't stop because I always felt like He would deliver me. I just kept faith and kept going. And I was praying about it. But one day, that thing set in on me again and I said, 'Well, I just give up.' I said, 'Lord, I've prayed about this and I give up. I'm going to the doctor and if they want to operate, I'm going in for them to operate. Because I can't handle this.' So I went to the doctor, and he said, 'I'm going to send you to the radiologist.' Next morning I went downtown to the radiologist.

When I went back to the doctor . . . he had a pile of X rays about three inches thick. He threw them on the table and he looked at me, said, "I want you to tell me exactly what you've been doing.' I said to myself, 'Oh Lord, I guess I'm gonna die or something.' He said, 'X ray after X ray, we see no ulcer, nowhere. What did you do? We need to know this.' I said, 'Doc, I prayed.' He said, 'Oh.' That's all he could say. When I walked out of that doctor's office, I was light as a feather. And it came to me—'You gave it to the Lord and you gave up yourself and turned it loose—that left Him where He could work it for you. He wanted to show you He had answered your prayer, so He let you get sick where you could go back to the doctor and see for yourself.' And all of these things, that's what I want people to know. I want people to know the real deal. Christ. And prayer. And in our singing, we get to say these things. To me, that's the ministry of it. All these things you get to say to people. And I've dedicated my whole life to it."

Clay: "I don't go on the stage without praying. And I don't go on the stage with anything on my mind. I'm clean when I hit the stage. And I feel the Spirit. Sure I do. Years ago, I couldn't, and it worried me so. Until my mind said, 'Well, go back to praying like you used to pray.' And that's what I started doing, asking for that Spirit to come in. Because it feels terrible when you get onstage singing and other people are shouting off you and you're not feeling anything. I asked the Lord how could somebody else feel what I'm doing and I don't feel it? And the Man said, well, He doesn't dwell in unclean temples. So you got to clean yourself up, clean that mind up, have a positive mind, a positive attitude. And you've got to be anointed. You've got to know Him. When you ask Him to join you and you really mean that, you go on that stage and your heart is clean, your mind is relaxed. You go to work! You got to work for the Lord."

Cleave: "When I go on that stage, I go on there concentrating and meditating. In fact, I pray before I go on the stage. And when I go up, whatever's given to me, that's what I give the people. There are some certain routines you've just about got to do. But the words are what's given to you—I don't know what I'm going to say. I've listened back [*to tapes of performances*], said, 'Did I say that? Man! I was going, wasn't I?' When you're doing it in the Spirit, it's different."

Michael: "You pray and put God first and then it happens. I'm serving Him, and I feel that from the heart will reach the heart. And I just hope that I will do something to encourage someone to realize what we are about and what we are singing about—who we're singing about. Some people come for a show, and some come for the spiritual purpose. But when those that want to be entertained see the joy the saved people are experiencing, it'll rub off. Something that powerful, you just can't shun it. So they'll quit looking at the show part and see the real deal."

It seemed an obvious question to ask a group of performers, some in their sixties and seventies, who have dedicated their lives to singing God's praises. "What does being a gospel singer—or musician—mean to you?" Although the group members were asked the question individually, most answered in a similar way, singling out the opportunity to do good as a dominant area of job satisfaction and citing specific instances of how their music had helped somebody. But none of the answers came glibly or quickly. Each Pilgrim Jubilee had to stop and consider, seeking a way to put into words something he'd never enunciated, possibly never even really thought about. Gospel music has been their lives, and it's not something that has needed to be discussed since the hard times of the 1960s, when the decision was made to "stay out there." Clay Graham, Ben Chandler, Bobby McDougle, and Fred Rice have not had any other jobs since becoming professional gospel artists. Michael Atkins closed his father's grocery store to stay with the group. Major Roberson made his forays into security work in the 1960s and promotions in the late 1970s but remained a member and continued working as booking manager. Eddie Graham has his part-time job but continues working at it because it allows him to be a Pilgrim Jubilee. In the early 1990s Cleave Graham took a job as a limousine driver for a Chicago funeral company. It gave him something to do when he was at home, it brought in a little extra money, and it was another way in which he could minister.

Cleave: "I was picking up the families and carrying them there [*to the funeral home*]. I wasn't making a lot of money, but it was still pertaining to my ministry. I got to say things to help so many people in bereavement. So many times when I'd pick up bereaved families, they'd soon be wiping away those tears and singing about something. So it was still what I'm about. Because being a gospel singer is my life. It is my way of doing something that I promised to do when I was a little boy. We can't give God anything—He's got everything. It's what you do for your fellow man that counts. And if I can do something to help your mind or help your thoughts or something well and good, then I've done what I prayed to do. It's a fulfillment you get when you know you did something to help somebody. Help somebody find their way to Christ. Help somebody to say, 'I'm not gonna give up. I'm not gonna let the Devil defeat me.' That's what keeps me going. I've started to quit. I've said, 'I've been out there a long time, now it's time for me to pull in.' And every time I get that mind, something will happen. Maybe we'll have a good record come out that I know folks are looking for me to sing. I say, 'Well, I'll keep on going, I guess.' "

Clay: "Being a gospel singer means I'm in the field working for the Lord. That's number one—that I'm carrying his messages through song. Number two, it's been a livelihood for me. Number three, gospel came down through my family, and I'm a spiritual man. So being a gospel singer, that's what I want to be. It's my life. Working for the Lord. There are people . . . in New York, a woman got up out of a wheelchair after seven years. She hadn't walked in seven years and we did 'Old Ship of Zion.' She got up out of her wheelchair and walked to the table and stood there at the table, starting screaming. That's something to be thankful for. That's what singing gospel means to me. I'm able to touch people's souls. That's what it's all about. Saving souls. We see lots of incidents like that—people shouting and jumping out of the balconies without breaking their legs or busting their brains out. They fall out in the balcony, jump all the way down on to the first floor, fall on all those seats, get up and go on home. I just say, 'Brother, with the Lord Jesus, He ain't gonna let nothing happen to you.' Another thing that made me feel good. We were going to Columbia in South Carolina. This lady called the radio station and asked them to ask me to promise that I would sing 'The Child's Blood' when we came there in two weeks. The promoter got in touch with me, said, 'Clay, you got a serious problem down here. There's a lady prolonging her life so she can hear 'Child's Blood' before she dies.' Because she was very sick—she was supposed to have been dead. But she waited to hear 'Child's Blood.' I came onstage, I said, 'There's a lady here that wants to hear 'Child's Blood,' and I came here to sing it for her.' And she stood up—people helped her—and raised her hand. When I had sung that song, I saw them carrying her out. She died immediately after I finished the song. Closed her eyes and died. Man, I almost wanted to quit. After she died, I couldn't do that night's program. I couldn't sing. And I called my pastor long distance. He said, 'Clay, you should be shouting with joy. That was a blessing. You know you extended life for her. That's a blessing. She didn't die from your singing. She stayed to hear you sing.' And that brought me out of it. I didn't understand it until my pastor and a couple more preachers explained it to me. But that's what it means. That's what gospel means to me. It's a good feeling."

Major: "It's a ministry to me. It's inspiration. It's a message that you're sending out. I've had people come up to me and say they changed their ways—they found Christ through listening to one of my songs. That means I've done something for somebody. I put something out that changed a person's ways. Like the song I have, 'I'm Getting Better All the Time.' I had a lady call me, a white lady from down in North Carolina. She said that song has changed her son. She played that song and she didn't know he was listening. But he asked her to play it again. Then he got a copy of it and . . . he plays football. And when his team goes to play football, she said, they sit down and listen to this record. It gives them inspiration—it made a change in his whole organization. And when she told me that, it meant I had done something. What I'm doing is worth it. I'm doing something that somebody's listening to."

Ben: "What I get joy out of is seeing people come to Christ through your singing. That means your work is not in vain. I remember we were in Los Angeles. We had finished singing and were going back through the church, and a man stopped me. He said, 'I was lying in a hospital about a week ago. . . .' We had a song called 'Reach Out' which came on the radio. And he said that while he was lying in the bed, he was singing 'reach out.' His wife was there and when the song finished, he told her to call the radio station and play it again. They played it over again and he reached out his hands towards the sky. And he said that right then and there, he was healed. That meant to me that what we're doing is not in vain. We're reaching out to people that need to come to Christ."

Bobby: "It's my life. Being a minister, to sing about God's praises, sing about the goodness of God and sing about good times. Sometimes you sing about things that happen to you in life. But most, it's about giving God praise. It keeps you in touch with God. That's what it means to me. Keeping my mind on Jesus. I want to do some good for Him. It's a spiritual thing to me. It means doing something for Christ that will last. And what better way of doing it than singing His praise and playing those instruments? Let everything praise Him. That's what it means to me. To make someone happy."

Eddie: "It's a legacy for me. It's a dream come true. When I started out, I prayed for the opportunity to travel and play music. I never thought I would end up in the gospel field, but that was the way the Lord had it planned. And by me coming up in church and having love for the Lord and having been brought up in knowing Him, then it made me think, 'Well, hey, He chose me to do this.' So I guess I'm doing His work through music."

Michael: "I thank God that He gave me the mind to want to play for Him—He blessed me with the talent, and so I want to use the talent for Him. And it means a lot because I get the opportunity to spread this talent He has blessed me with. I meet young musicians who tell me 'I learned how to play by listening to you on the records.' That really makes me feel good—I'm doing something positive and it has been spread abroad. I have met young fellows . . . they were little-bitty guys when I first came on the road, and then when I go back years later, these guys are grown, some of them married with families, and they say, 'I used to listen to you when I was a little kid.' And there's so many young women I have met on the road. I talk to them, try to tell them what's right, and I have encouraged a lot of them because of what I do and who I am. One young girl, I met her when she was twelve years old, and her mother told me, 'My daughter has a crush on you.' So I told her, 'You go to school and you make sure you get your lessons.' And when we came back to the town, the first thing I see was pigtails, running straight to me. It was the little girl, with her report card. 'I got good grades. I passed.' Oh, what a joy!"

23. Today and Tomorrow

In Houlka, the sun has gone down. The temperature hasn't. In the high school gymnasium, the large fan by the back door is still shifting hot air, pushing it across the room until it meets the blast from the fan by the front door and is sent back again. On the stage, the Holy Visions have been followed by the Shining Stars—from Bruce, Mississippi, twenty-one miles west of Houlka—Houston's Spiritual Harmoneers, and the New Magnolia Jubilees. The late start has robbed the Friendly Brothers in Christ and the Aires of Joy of their chance to sing, and they have changed back out of their uniforms unheard. Now the main part of the program begins. Promoter Joann Reel's "baby sister," ShaLandor, opens it with a melisima- and grace note–laden national anthem; her dramatic ending draws murmurs and chuckles of admiration. Houlka's mayor, Betty McDaniel, makes a brief speech of welcome, followed by Joann Reel and Robin Mathis, long-time owner of Houston's local radio station, WCPC, who performs the ritual of welcoming the out-of-town visitors. Clay Graham's speech in reply is a mixture of response to the previous welcoming speeches and a welcome of his own to the audience. He speaks in conversational tones, but his words draw affirming responses—"Yes!" "All right," "That's right"—as though he were preaching. "Sometimes stumbling blocks get in your way," he says, referring to the change of venue. "But if you're strong enough and believe, everything will work out for you. Can I get a witness? . . . Everybody is talking about how hot the building is, but to see you all here . . . if nobody else comes here tonight, the Pilgrim Jubilees appreciate you being here."

So far, the contest between gospel music and stifling heat has been an even match, with almost as many people staying outside as have been inside to hear the local groups and the speeches. But now gospel is bringing in its heavyweights, and the room starts to fill. Most of the floor-level seats are occupied, although the bleachers on either side of the room hold only scattered listeners. The main undercard starts with the semiprofessional Gospel Warriors from Bruce, Mississippi; the Echoaires from Moscow, Tennessee; and the True Believers from Magnolia, Mississippi. These are local groups but ones that have made recordings and are gathering reputations outside their home areas. They'll be followed by the Victory Travelers, the veteran Chicago group that also sang on the Jubes' Chicago homecoming three weeks earlier. It doesn't take a finely tuned ear to pick similarities between the Travelers' sound and that of the Jubes; promoters often use the two groups on the same programs. The Violinaires were supposed to be here, but lead singer Robert Blair had a stroke last week. Their place is being taken by the Christianaires, who were also at Mercy Seat three weeks ago. Although the Pilgrim Jubilees are the stars, they will be performing before the Christianaires. Major Roberson explains: "They don't seem to be able to do a short program. They have a lot of testifying and things like that. So a group like that, you put at the end, and then if the people get tired they can put on their coats and go home."

Unfortunately, one of the people who doesn't know the Jubes are on before the Christianaires is Clay Graham. As the Victory Travelers start their second to last song, he is outside in his car, with the air-conditioning on "high." And as the emcee starts his introduction for the Jubes, he is in the Houlka gym coach's office, hurriedly changing into a black tuxedo and dress shirt. The rest of the Jubes are in the players' changing room at the other end of the gym. Clay doesn't know that, and they don't know where he is. And as the emcee's "How about it, Houlka, for the Pilgrim JUBILEES!" echoes around the cavernous room and the rest of the group walks out on to the stage, Clay is still missing. The musicians play the introduction for "Lonesome Road." No Clay. After fourteen bars of instrumental vamp-ing, the emcee steps back in. "All right, we're nearly ready," he extemporizes, making it quite obvious that we're not. The vamp passes the point of being able to pretend it is part of any plan. Cleave steps forward to sing, even though the song is not one he usually leads—and Clay discovers the rest of his group, stepping quickly through the audience on to the stage area and taking up his microphone. "Are y'all hot?" "Yeah!" "Are y'all hot hot?" "YEAH" "This is a lonesome road. . . ." It's a truncated version, just long enough to let the group settle, but when Clay asks at the end, "Was that all right?" the response is enthusiastic; over a wave of applause and cheers, a female voice exhorts approvingly, "Just sing!" The Pilgrim Jubilees are at home.

Viewed objectively, it's not one of their better nights. Bobby McDougle's absence means some of the guitar cues on which the singers rely are also absent, and Bobo Harris is pushing the pace more than it should be pushed—soon after, his application to become a Jube again will be definitively rejected. Major Roberson is not onstage. He'd planned to sing only a couple of songs and then "dismiss myself," but even this is beyond him. The hot, close, humid atmosphere is aggravating his emphysema—"I lost all my oxygen," he explains. Eddie Graham is filling in for Bobby, so Fred Rice is playing second guitar to fill in for Eddie and singing baritone to fill in for Major. A secondary problem is that a black tux with frill-fronted dress shirt and four-in-hand bow tie is not the most suitable uniform for performing in Mississippi's largest sauna. Cleave decided before going on to dispense with the tie, and Clay didn't have time to put his on; the rest of the group quickly follows the leaders' example, and by the end of the first song all are tieless. But the difficulties are just more stumbling blocks to be overcome, and the arrival of the headliners has given gospel music a clear points lead over the heat.

The quiet "I Love You" is a chance for some audience participation—"Put your hand in somebody's hand and hold on. . . . Look 'em straight in the eye . . . look at your friend and say these words . . ." (the song starts) "I love you, I really love you. . . ." When Cleave takes over the lead, Clay introduces him: "There's only two peas that's left in the pod. That's Cleave and I." It's a reference to the fact that they are the only surviving members of their immediate family, and Cleave's first song poignantly continues the theme. "This song came to me in a dream . . . how many of you have dreamed about your loved ones that have already gone on? . . . I believe that one day, I'll see Mama again." "Heavenly Reunion" is taken at a much slower pace than the recorded version, and even at the reduced pace, Cleave's first verse is interspersed with asides telling the band to "take your time." But the intensity with which he and Clay name the family members they see waiting for them—"my eldest brother, my brother C.B., my little sister"—fires the audience and the group. As Cleave introduces "Church Song," the cries of encouragement are rising, and many are standing in front of their seats, some waving arms in the air, others tapping, swaying, and almost dancing to the music.

"Getting Better" is a quieter song that initially damps the fires built by "Church Song." But as Cleave builds to the finale, sweat dripping from his face, leaning forward and tensed by the exertion of his delivery, the shouts rise again. He overrides the applause at the end with a sternly delivered statement: "I used to sing because I loved singing. Now I sing because I know what I'm singing about. I'm not here tonight to praise myself. I come tonight to praise the name of Jesus. . . ." The tempo of his speech lifts. "How many of you feel like that? Are you a witness? Are you a witness? Don't let Him down." The last four words are an instruction and the name of the next song. This is where the Jubes get down to business, lifting the pace, the energy, and the intensity; this is where gospel music lands its knockout blow on the heat. As Cleave hands over the song to Ben for the drive, it takes a conscious effort to realize that the singer standing on the side of the stage wiping sweat from his face and moving in time to the music is seventy-one years old; the one stalking through the audience as he demands, "Has God been good to you? Has he been good to you?" in rhythmically repetitive urgency is sixty.

Clay takes the lead again. "I came here to be a witness for him. I'm not going to let the Devil get in my way. He's here today. But we're going to ask him to leave the building." His voice rises and hardens into a preacher's chant. "G-oh-oh-oh-od! Is good to me! Something I want to ask you. Has God been good to you?" The assent erupts; amid the shouts, someone urges, "Come on, Clay!" He does. "I declare! That I've been born again. You ask, 'Clay, has God been good to you?' I would sa-ay-ay-ay-ay. Say yeeesss! Say yeeeesss!" Most people were standing after "Don't Let Him Down"; now everyone in the room is on their feet. The musicians punctuate Clay's staccato phrases with body blows of bass- and drum-driven chords as he works to his climax, body bent forward and sideways in a discus-thrower stance as he drives his words out. "Somebody. Somebody. Knows what I'm talking about. Wave your hand. Say yeeesss! Yeeaahh! Yeeaahh.! Has God been good? Has God been good? Yeeesss! Yeeesss! Yeeaahh!" A downward wave of the arm; band and sermon come to an abrupt halt, stranding a chorus of audience "Yeahs" and "All rights." The stop is momentary, and Clay moves into the sermonette for "Barnyard." Usually, the free-form introduction segues into the structured narrative; tonight the Spirit has risen too high to allow this, so the only way to get into the narrative is to stop completely and start again. Clay tells the story of the young farm worker whipped for praying during work time; when he comes to the song, he and the band make another dramatic halt, Michael Atkins plays a flurry of bass notes, and Clay teases out the first word. "I'mmmm . . ." The musicians, led by Michael Atkins, pick up the cue and ease into "I'm So Glad Trouble Don't Last Always." It's an adroit piece of improvisation—and it leaves Clay completely cast adrift. The song for "Barnyard" is "Every Time I Feel the Spirit." "I'm So Glad" belongs to the "Three Trees" sermonette. But by singing that first "I'm . . . ," Clay has signaled "I'm So Glad," so that's what the musicians are playing. He solves the dilemma by singing a verse of "Every Time" to the tune of "I'm So Glad," then handing off to Ben who switches back to a verse of "I'm So Glad." The lapse in concentration badly dents the dynamics of the song, but the audience—many of whom know "Barnyard" as well as they know "Happy Birthday"—responds with delighted calls and applause to Clay's slightly apprehensive phrasing of his usually pro forma "Was that all right?" Reassured that another stumbling block has been overcome, he tosses a brief prompt over his shoulder to the musicians, and everyone moves into "Every Time I Feel the Spirit" with its rightful tune; after the program he says this was "to let the people know I knew I made a mistake."

Cleave steps forward; the movement triggers a ripple of expectation. The group's time is nearly up, so many in the audience know what is likely to be coming. "We've been requested to sing a lot of songs," says Cleave, "but it's late and it's hot. But I got to say this to you because it's on my heart to say to you that I may not see you again. I want you to remember that I said these words." It's the introduction to "Too Close," but stripped to the bones.

Usually, Cleave stretches it, building to a climax that leads into the song. The bald announcement that "I may not see you again" is an icy dart that spears through the heat and enthusiasm; the audience noise mutes suddenly. Cleave cues the band, sings the declamatory opening words "Well, I'm . . ." then stops. "I ain't gonna holler this time. I just want to make myself plain. I want people to understand what I'm saying. Because I might not continue to get here." When he starts singing again, the stentorian beginning is abandoned, and he almost croons his way into the song, telling the musicians in a quick aside, "Not loud." The somber introduction, the low-key start, and the lyrics of the song change the feeling in the room. "Too Close" is usually a storming house-wrecker; tonight it is a reflective mixture of personal statement and farewell. The audience still calls, but now the voices offer encouragement and understanding. "All right!" "Take your time." The song usually finishes with the singers walking off while Bobby McDougle takes center stage to close with a fiery guitar solo. Bobby is not here tonight, and even if he were, the customary ending would be out of place. The band plays the final chord, and Clay takes the microphone. "Thank you so much. We hope you enjoyed the Pilgrim Jubilees. Now I'm going to ask the emcee to come up and bring the rest of the groups on." The "rest of the groups" is the Christianaires. They are one of the most popular of the younger quartets, but tonight they have been eclipsed. Their set—expanded by copious quantities of testimony—will last more than an hour, but the homecoming finished when the Jubes walked off the stage.

The next morning Clay is in a pensive mood. The homecoming has not been the success it usually is, mainly because of the venue. "We walked away with a hundred and twenty dollars a man. Two days rent out of that, forty dollars a day . . . that's why we've got to work hard two or three days to get back home and pay for what you need." This is another interview at which Clay knows what he wants to say; today's topic is the difficulties of making a living on the road, and the Jubes' mistake in turning down the chance to be managed by Buddy Lee. "You need that manager to put you in that right place and know what to do. Know how to make some money for you, put you with the right people Like the Blind Boys [*of Alabama*]. They work overseas and everywhere. They don't make great big money, but it's consistent. Every night they're making money. But it's not like that 'round here.

You're doing good if you can get three nights a week where you can make a little money—enough to pay your house note at home."

If the big break is going to come for the Pilgrim Jubilees, it will have to come soon. All the main singers are more than sixty, and the group's time in its present structure is limited—Major is already starting to restrict his onstage appearances. But the Grahams are determined to defy the advancing years for as long as they can. At the 1998 Gospel Music Workshop of America convention in Philadelphia, one of the features of the quartet division's main concert was an "Honoring the Pioneers" segment. As a child group—the Forte Brothers from Atlanta—sang, a procession of quartet veterans came one by one to the stage. They included performers from the Sensational Nightingales, the Swanee Quintet, the Mighty Clouds of Joy—a who's who of quartet singing. Clay Graham was present but did not join the lineup.

Clay: "I haven't crossed that 'old' bridge yet. When you start catering to it, that's where they'll put you. I let all the old guys go up there. Then people will say, 'Clay's not thinking he's old. . . .' I might be a pioneer, but I'm not going to walk up there for somebody to make an example of my being old. I accept it, I am a pioneer. But don't call me and put me in front of an audience as an old man. I'm not there yet. Blair [*Robert Blair of the Violinaires*] went up; I told him afterwards, 'I looked at you old people standing up there.' Blair said, 'I ain't going up there no more.' Maybe in the next five years, I might get a cane to walk up onstage. [*He laughs.*] But not now. I ain't getting in the background. Because you've got to go to beat me. You've got to go to get out from under the Jubilees."

Cleave: "My fellows call me 'the iron man.' Because I can get under that wheel, drive all night, make the interviews the next morning, and be ready to hit that stage tomorrow evening and wake that audience up. Then I'll be ready to move again the next day. And at my age, I know the Lord is blessing me. But I don't holler and shout, 'Oh I'm seventy years old.' There's some personal things of a man that aren't a secret but just aren't the public's business. It's better not to publicize it. Because folk believe in the young. They see a group come out and they say, 'They're good, and they're young.' Now if the Jubes have a show someplace and I start talking about how old I am, maybe some young person who needs to hear what I have to say . . . 'I ain't gonna listen to all them old folks.' So you leave it alone."

The Graham brothers agree on standing firm against the years, but their views diverge sharply on the subject of what will happen to the group in the longer term, when the older members—Cleave, Clay, Major, and Ben—are no longer able to get behind the wheel, drive all night, and be ready to hit the stage. Clay has given the matter considerable thought and has laid some plans. Cleave regards the question as almost blasphemous, because to him, the future is completely in God's hands.

Clay: "Hitting that stage out there, fighting those young boys . . . I figure I can hang in for the next ten years. Ten years is a long time once you get up to a certain age. If you're in your thirties and forties, ten years doesn't mean anything. But when you get to be sixty-five and seventy, ten years is a lot of years. And I've often thought about it. I have a son that's an excellent singer. Kevin Graham. He's thirty-four. He's in Washington—he's got a little group there. I've been thinking in terms of bringing him in. I want to keep the Pilgrim Jubilees moving. And Kevin is able to carry it. But I always wanted him to be himself. And I know he couldn't be in here. So I told him to pursue his own career instead of coming up here and walking behind me. That was one reason why I haven't brought him in. And the other reason is Kevin is very energetic. He pursues what he's doing highly and he totally controls. I know . . . it's hard for me to handle it. And I know Cleave wouldn't be able to handle it. And that would push Cleave further back. Cleave's last days and somebody gonna come in and just push him right out? Cleave's nowhere near ready to say, 'You go ahead.' And I wouldn't want anybody to come in here right now and push me in the back. But I've always told him, 'If something happens to me or Cleave, you know what you've got to do.' "

Cleave: "Well, I've always said it like this—I do what I got to do. I don't worry about what's going to happen when I can't go. How do we know what's gonna happen? If it's going to be like that, I should have been planning when I was ten years old. So I'm not gonna jump up and down. The Lord has carried me this far and now I'm gonna go 'Oh I better start getting somebody else 'cause I'm going to be . . . ?' Oh no, no, no. I don't bother with that. Because there'll always be someone. God's always got a ram in the bush for you. So whatever's needed will be. It might be a time for the Jubes to shut off, period. But if it isn't, it'll be somebody else that'll keep them moving. It'll be the right people. And it won't be somebody I chose.

I'll let the Lord work that out. If we need to keep going, it'll keep going. If we need . . . every road's got an end. If the Jubes need to end, let it end."

Major: "I don't want to retire. I don't want to sing any more, I don't want to get on the stage any more. But I want to stay in the industry. I want to deal around producing, promoting, and writing for the group. The older ones won't all drop out at the same time. They'll leave one at a time. And then . . . will this group be as well as it was or stronger? It all has to do with who takes over. If you move into having a new group of people, it really has to do with who can write. That keeps your flavor. And what kind of men they get to hold that certain standard. That's something you never can tell. If they change the group and make it sound like some other artist, you're going to kill it then. Because people want to hear a Pilgrim Jubilee sound."

Ben: "There's six of us have been together more than thirty years. And God has smiled on us, He has blessed us to record and make our own sound. So I hope we live a long time and keep on singing. I know we might not be able to travel like we used to do, but we're going to just keep on singing. And I hope some young quartet will try to copy the Pilgrim Jubilees' style and carry the tradition on when we're dead and gone. Our younger guys know how to carry the business on. And I think that as long as Cleave, Clay, Bobby, or myself is alive . . . as long as God sees that . . . I hope He doesn't take us all at once. But we're just going to sing and try to keep going. I know we're not getting any younger, but we're going to try to keep it going as long as is possible. And I just hope somebody will pick up the torch and keep going with it. Keep the name going, don't change anything. Keep the Pilgrim Jubilees and know the roots of the Pilgrim Jubilees."

Bobby: "I guess we're going to run on to the end. Now if something happened with Clay and Cleave, that would be another story. Because the group is built up around them. I suppose we could bring in younger men. It's a possibility. Bring them in and train them. As of now, I really ain't no young man, but I'm still eligible for being here a little while. But I wouldn't know how to take it if something happened to Clay and Cleave. . . . I hate to talk about things like that. I'd hate to see that day come. I know that one day we're all going to have to give up. But I think we should have another good ten years. If the Lord wills. I'd love to have twenty."

Michael: "We're gonna keep striving. To me, it would be totally wrong to just stop when they [*Major or Cleave*] decide they don't want to go any more. Because they have put their whole lives into this. And I feel it's like running a relay race where they'll probably pass the baton to me and I'll keep it going. With God's help I will do that. Pilgrim Jubilees will be hopefully forever. I'll keep it going. Clay talks to me about getting involved in other areas of this business, and this is where I am headed. He told me some years ago, 'Eventually, this is going to be your group. You'll have to do this.' At that time, I didn't see me being a Pilgrim Jubilee without the rest of the guys. But then I'm looking at the fact that I couldn't let them down by letting the group go if they decided they no longer wanted to travel. So I'm really gearing myself up for when and if the day should come that I have to take care of this. Because as long as I live, the Pilgrim Jubilees will always be."

Clay: "Nothing lasts always. But that hard fighter will be standing there a long time. People say to me, 'Man, y'all been out here a long time and still in that top ten.' I say, "Yeah, we're fighters. We're not gonna quit.' And we still believe we're all right. We work pretty good. We give a pretty good show. And folks will listen to you if you've got something to say."

Cleave: "I laughed one day with Clay. I said to him, 'We didn't get rich, we didn't make a lot of money. But we did a lot of good.' And the Lord blessed us with our health, just to keep on doing it. The name of the game is that you're singing gospel. You're singing for the Lord. Not that we don't want to be paid—who doesn't like money? But I guess it has been secondary down through years. The Lord has blessed us in different ways."

Major: "Cleave, Clay, and myself, we went through the very gates of hell to stay out there. We lost our families and everything else we had. We just stuck there together. . . . And on down the road, the grass got a little greener."

Bobby: "Oh, there have been some days. I could go back and tell you . . . there were happy days, but there were trouble days. So we had to love what we were doing, because we sure weren't making that much money. I've seen many days when I've been hungry out there on the road. Today, it's . . . comfortable. But you have to work steady. I'm not getting to be a millionaire or anything like that, but you're grateful for it being as well as it is. I just thank the Lord, as far as He brought me."

Eddie: "People think we're making a lot of money, that we're rich. It's not like that. It's just the love we have for what we're doing and what we want to do that makes us stay. We're not in it for the money. You're doing it for soul security. Because the Lord gave you a talent, and He wants you to go ahead there and spread the good news of gospel. And after He gave you this talent and the opportunity to use it, you must do what He asks of you."

Ben: "I've been singing all my life—ever since I was about five or six years old. I get joy out of it because that's what I want to do. I wouldn't trade it for anything in the world. I'll stay with it till I die. Some people ask, 'When are you going to retire?' No. I can't do that. I'll sing until God says 'That's enough.' It has been hard, sometimes, but we're very tough and dedicated to what we're doing—if you can survive out on the road singing gospel like we've done, you can survive just about anything. God has blessed all of us—He brought us a long, long, long way."

Cleave: "The Lord always blessed us with something to keep us standing up. Might fall to your knees, but there'll be always something happen. And I know that even now, if we were to lose the whole group, Clay and I wouldn't stop. But I say this a lot—I'm proud of the Jubilees. And I'm thankful for the Jubilees the way they are. Because, hey, we never put out that platinum record. But what we did, like Frank Sinatra says, we did it our way. We did it our way."

The Pilgrim Jubilees on Record

This listing gives details of all Pilgrim Jubilees' recordings and videotapes. It is arranged chronologically and lists the personnel on each recording, the date—usually approximate—of the recording, the original record on which each track was issued, and as many reissues as the author has been able to trace. The pre-1970 section of the listing is based on Cedric J. Hayes and Robert Laughton's *Gospel Records, 1943–1969* (London: Record Information Services, 1992); this and the post-1970 section have been augmented by information from a wide range of sources and people (see the Acknowledgments).

The layout and style follow the pattern established by American and British blues, jazz, and gospel discographers. Each block starts with the group name under which the recordings were made—in this case, Pilgrim Jubilee Singers or Pilgrim Jubilees—and the names of people involved in the recording. Members of the group are named first, followed—after the word "with"—by session musicians. Numbers after singer and musician names are read in conjunction with numbers after the song titles. If, for example, the personnel listing says "Cleave Graham, ld-1", then Cleave Graham is the lead singer on all tracks in that block that have "1" after the title. On songs with more than one lead singer, the leads are noted in order of appearance, so if the numbers after a title are "2, 1," the singer indicated by "2" in the personnel listing is the first lead voice heard, followed by the singer indicated as "1."

Below the personnel is the location of the session and the date when the recordings were made. Accurate recording dates for the most part have been impossible to obtain—for the early days, little data exists and the Pilgrim Jubilees have no details;

for later issues, the fragmented way recordings are made renders precise dates meaningless. From the late 1960s, blocks of tracks are arranged by album (or videotape) and represent a number of different recording sessions, sometimes spread over months.

The column on the left of the page gives the matrix number—if any—for each recording. Matrix numbers were assigned by recording companies to give each track a unique identifying number. Until the 1950s, they were used by nearly all recording companies and were usually assigned at the time of recording. Their importance was diminished by the advent of tape recording, which replaced self-contained "live in the studio" performances with editing and multitracking, and by the mid to late 1960s, recording companies had abandoned the matrix number system. Peacock's matrices were assigned when a recording was issued, not when it was recorded—so, for example, a recording made in 1960 but not issued until 1963 will have as its matrix a higher number than a recording made and issued in 1962. In the 1955 Specialty session, the left-hand column shows the number of "takes" made of each song. In the days when artists recorded "live" in the studio, they would perform each number more than once. Each attempt was known as a "take"; the recording company would select the best take for release.

The composer of each song—where known—is identified in parentheses after the song title. The abbreviation "PD" (public domain) covers traditional material and songs that may been formally composed but which have over the years become common property. Writer credits are based mainly on information from the Pilgrim Jubilees, augmented by the author's research. They are not based on information given on record labels and sleeves; these are not always accurate, especially on Peacock issues. Many—but almost certainly not all—discrepancies between who actually wrote the song and what is shown on labels and sleeves are noted. All "PD" tracks were arranged by group members—in the early days mainly by Major Roberson; later by Roberson, Clay Graham, or collectively. Where an individual group member has extensively rearranged an existing song, it is indicated with the abbreviation "arr." The writer-credit "Graham" refers to Clay Graham, "Roberson" is Major Roberson.

Recordings on which the song was issued are shown after the songwriter credit. Original issues are listed first, followed—after the semicolon—by later reissues. Chance and NBC issues were 78-rpm records. The 1950s Nashboro issues were seven-inch singles. Peacock recordings were issued on singles and/or "long play" albums; from around 1970, the focus was on albums, and singles were issued mainly to promote albums. The Pilgrim Jubilees recorded their first compact disc in 1992.

Abbreviations:

bar—baritone vocal
bass—bass vocal

dms—drums
ebs—electric bass guitar
gtr—electric guitar
kbd—electronic keyboard
ld—lead vocal
org—organ
perc—percussion
pno—piano
sbs—double ("string") bass
tbn—trombone
tnr—tenor vocal
tpt—trumpet
vcl—vocal

PILGRIM JUBILEE SINGERS: Elgie C.B. Graham, ld-1, tnr; Cleave Graham, ld-2, bar; Clay Graham, tnr; Monroe Hatchett, Major Roberson, bars; Kenny Madden, bass.

Chicago: January 1953

U-2263	Happy in the Service of the Lord-2,1 (PD)	Chance 5004; Heritage HT-CD-08
U-2264	Just a Closer Walk with Thee-2,1 (PD)	Chance 5004; Heritage HT-CD-08

NB: Heritage HT-CD-08, *Glad I Found the Lord: Chicago Gospel 1937–1957*, is a British collector reissue CD issued in 1992.

PILGRIM JUBILEE SINGERS: Cleave Graham, ld; Elgie C.B. Graham, Clay Graham, tnrs; Monroe Hatchett, Major Roberson, bars; Kenny Madden, bass; Arthur Crume, gtr, possibly tnr.

Chicago: 1954

N-B-C 104	Angel (Roberson)	NBC 2003
N-B-C 105	Lord, I Have No Friend Like You (PD)	NBC 2003

NB: The Pilgrim Jubilees may have recorded other self-financed 78-rpm singles between 1953 and 1955. If so, no details are known.

PILGRIM JUBILEE SINGERS: Elgie C.B. Graham, ld-1, tnr; Cleave Graham, ld-2, bar; Clay Graham, tnr; Major Roberson, bar; Kenny Madden, bass; Arthur Crume, gtr, probably tnr.

Los Angeles: probably August 18, 1955

3 takes	Soon Gonna Work until My Day Is Done-1,2 (PD/arr. Roberson)	Specialty unissued
5 takes	Yesteryear-2 (Kenny Madden)	Specialty unissued; Specialty SPCD-7070-2 (take 4)
6 takes	Tell Jesus (What You Want)-1,2 (PD)	Specialty unissued; Specialty SPCD-7070-2 (take 5)
4 takes	He'll Be There-2 (PD)	Specialty unissued
2 takes	What Do You Know (About Jesus)?-1,2 (PD)	Specialty unissued; Specialty SPCD-7070-2 (take 2)
4 takes	Oh Lord (Watching and Waiting)-2 (?/arr. Roberson)	Specialty unissued; Specialty SPCD-7070-2 (take 4)

NB: The contract for this session was signed on August 18, 1955, which is probably the date of recording. None of the tracks was issued at the time of recording. The left column shows the number of takes made of each song. Specialty SPCD-7070-2, *Golden Age Gospel Quartets, Vol. 2 (1954–1963)*, is an anthology issued in 1997. The take numbers of tracks used on this CD are shown in parentheses after the issue number. The lyric of "Soon Gonna Work . . ." indicates that the song should be titled "Soon Gonna Work until My Days Are Done"; "Oh Lord" is also known as "Lord, Own Me As a Child"; "Tell Jesus What You Want" is a version of "Jesus Is on the Main Line."

PILGRIM JUBILEE SINGERS: Cleave Graham, ld-1, bar; Johnny Felix, ld-2, tnr; Clay Graham, tnr; Major Roberson, bar; Kenny Madden, bass; Arthur Crume, gtr, probably tnr.

Nashville: 1957

Gonna Work On-2 (PD/arr. Roberson)	Nashboro 605
God Is Good to Me-1 (Roberson)	Nashboro 605

PILGRIM JUBILEE SINGERS: Clay Graham, ld-1, tnr; Cleave Graham, ld-2, bar; Major Roberson, bar; Kenny Madden, bass; Rufus Crume, gtr, probably tnr; with unknown, pno.

Nashville: February 24, 1958

I Heard of a City-1 (PD)	Nashboro 625
John Behold Thy Mother-2 (Kenny Madden)	Nashboro 625, LP 8781, LP 27184, Ernies LP 2002
I'll Be a Witness-2 (probably PD)	Nashboro unissued

PILGRIM JUBILEE SINGERS: Cleave Graham, ld-1, bar; Clay Graham, tnr; Major Roberson, bar; Kenny Madden, bass; Rufus Crume, gtr, tnr; with unknown, pno, dms.

Nashville: March 29, 1959

	River of Jordan-1 (Roberson)	Nashboro 650
	Father, I'm Coming Home-1 (Roberson)	Nashboro 650
	On My Knees-? (?)	Nashboro unissued

NB: The label of Nashboro 650 shows both sides as "arr. M. Robertson" [*sic*].

PILGRIM JUBILEE SINGERS: Cleave Graham, ld; Clay Graham, tnr; Major Roberson, bar; Kenny Madden, bass; Rufus Crume, gtr, tnr; with unknown, pno, dms.

Nashville: November 10, 1959

	Jesus Help Me (Roberson)	Nashboro 695
	I've Done Got Over (PD)	Nashboro 695; Ernies LP 2003
	They Won't Believe (PD)	Nashboro unissued

PILGRIM JUBILEE SINGERS: Clay Graham, ld; Cleave Graham, bar; Major Roberson, bar; Rufus Crume, gtr, probably tnr; with Willie Dixon, sbs; probably Clifton James or Odie Payne, dms.

Universal Studios, Chicago: late 1959

UV-8020	Stretch Out (Helen Shedrick, Z. R. McEachen/arr. Roberson)	Peacock 1819, ABC Peacock 3405
UV-8021	Evening Sun (PD)	Peacock 1819, ABC Peacock 3405

NB: "Stretch Out" is writer-credited on Peacock 1819 to Rufus Crume. The Pilgrim Jubilees' version is based on "Dark Hours" by the Roberta Martin Singers, who credited it to Shedrick and McEachen. "Evening Sun" is credited "arr. C. C. Graham" (C. C. Graham is Clay Graham).

PILGRIM JUBILEE SINGERS: Clay Graham, ld-1, tnr; Cleave Graham, ld-2, bar; Major Roberson, bar; Rufus Crume, gtr, probably tnr; with Willie Dixon, sbs; probably Clifton James or Odie Payne, dms.

Probably part of previous session

FR-8086-1	Steal Away-1 (PD)	Peacock 1849, PLP-105, GLS 1974, Song Bird LP 240; MCA (Mobile Fidelity) MFCD-756
FR-8087-1	Jesus Come Help Me-2 (Roberson)	Peacock 1849

NB: Peacock 1849 was issued in 1962. These tracks are placed here because the sound and personnel are very similar to those of the preceding session, and it is likely that more than two songs were recorded at that session. "Steal Away" is writer-credited to "PD/C. Graham" on 1849 and to "PD/N. M. Roberson" on PLP-105. (Some Peacock credits are to N. M. Roberson or N. Major Roberson, although Major does not have an "N" initial in his name.) "Jesus Come Help Me" is writer-credited to "Graham" on 1849. MCA (Mobile Fidelity) MCD-756 is a 1992 CD reissue of the Pilgrim Jubilees' first two Peacock albums.

PILGRIM JUBILEE SINGERS: Percy Clark, ld-1, tnr; Cleave Graham, ld-2, bar; Clay Graham, tnr; Major Roberson, bar; Rufus Crume, gtr, probably tnr; with Lafayette Leake, pno; Willie Dixon, sbs; probably Clifton James or Odie Payne, dms; no gtr-3.

Universal Studios, Chicago: late 1960

UV-8044	Walk On-1,3 (D. Clark)	Peacock 1830, PLP-105; MCA (Mobile Fidelity) MFCD-756
UV-8045	I See a Man-2 (K. Madden)	Peacock 1830, PLP-105; MCA (Mobile Fidelity) MFCD-756
	Separation Line-1 (PD)	Peacock PLP-105; MCA (Mobile Fidelity) MFCD-756

NB: "Separation Line" is writer-credited to P. Clark on PLP-105.

PILGRIM JUBILEE SINGERS: Cleave Graham, ld-1, bar; Clay Graham, ld-2, tnr; Major Roberson, bar; probably Percy Clark or possibly unknown, vcl; Rufus Crume, gtr, probably tnr; with Lafayette Leake, pno; Willie Dixon, sbs; probably Odie Payne (or possibly Clifton James), dms; no pno-3.

Universal Studios, Chicago: 1961

	A City-2 (PD)	Peacock PLP-105; MCA (Mobile Fidelity) MFCD-756
	Like This-1 (Roberson)	Peacock PLP-105; MCA (Mobile Fidelity) MFCD-756
	New Body-1 (Roberson)	Peacock PLP-105; MCA (Mobile Fidelity) MFCD-756
	Helping Hand-1 (Cleave Graham)	Peacock PLP-105; MCA (Mobile Fidelity) MFCD-756
	Come Up-1 (Roberson)	Peacock PLP-105; MCA (Mobile Fidelity) MFCD-756
	Let Thy Will Be Done-1,3 (Roberson)	Peacock PLP-105; MCA (Mobile Fidelity) MFCD-756

	Stretch Out No. 2-1(Roberson/ Pilgrim Jubilees)	Peacock PLP-105, PLP 140; MCA (Mobile Fidelity) MFCD-756

NB: Peacock PLP-105 is titled *Walk On* and was issued in 1962. It was reissued on MCA LP 28003. On PLP 105, "A City" is writer-credited to "Phillips/Graham"; it is a version of "I Heard of a City Called Zion," and Clay Graham has no knowledge of "Phillips." "Stretch Out No. 2" is credited to Rufus Crume. "Let Thy Will Be Done" is mistitled as "Let Their Will Be Done" on Peacock and MCA (Mobile Fidelity). "King's Highway" on PLP-105 is a recording by Rev. Robert Ballinger included on the album by error.

PILGRIM JUBILEE SINGERS: Cleave Graham, ld-1, bar; Clay Graham, ld-2, tnr; possibly Percy Clark or unknown, tnr; Major Roberson, bar; probably Rufus Crume, gtr; with Lafayette Leake, pno; Willie Dixon, sbs; probably Odie Payne or Clifton James, dms; no pno-3.

Universal Studios, Chicago: c. 1961/62

UV-8144	Unmovable-2 (PD/Roberson)	Peacock 1872
UV-8145	This Morning-1 (probably Roberson)	Peacock 1872
UV-8191	Restless Soul-1 (Roberson)	Peacock 1894
UV-8192	I'm on the Right Road-1,3 (Roberson)	Peacock 1894

NB: "I'm on the Right Road" could come from 1960. Major Roberson recalls that "This Morning" was written by either him or Kenny Madden; it is very much in Roberson's style of the time. "Restless Soul" is writer-credited to C. C. Graham (Clay Graham).

PILGRIM JUBILEE SINGERS: Cleave Graham, ld-1, bar; Clay Graham, ld and narration-2, tnr; Charles Green, tnr; Major Roberson, bar; probably Maurice Dollison, gtr, probably vcl; Roosevelt English, ebs; with Lafayette Leake, pno; possibly Odie Payne or Clifton James, dms.

Universal Studios, Chicago: 1963

UV-8208	True Story (song: He Won't Forget You)-2 (Graham)	Peacock 1899
UV-8209	Wonderful-1 (Ruth Davis)	Peacock 1899

NB: Peacock 1872, 1894, and 1899 were issued in 1963. "Wonderful" is writer-credited to V. McCollough; the Pilgrim Jubilees do not know who V. McCollough is.

PILGRIM JUBILEE SINGERS: Cleave Graham, ld-1, bar; Clay Graham, ld-2, tnr; Charles Green, tnr; Major Roberson, bar; Maurice Dollison, gtr, probably vcl; Roosevelt English, ebs; with Lafayette Leake, pno; possibly Odie Payne or Clifton James, dms; no pno but unknown (possibly Leake), org-3; no pno but unknown (possibly Leake), celeste or similar instrument-4.

Universal Studios, Chicago: c. 1964 (more than one session)

UV-8242	The Old Ship of Zion-2,3 (PD)	Peacock 3015, PLP-117; MCA (Mobile Fidelity) MFCD-756; MCA (U.K.) MCLD-614; Agape (Australia) MARK-49; Music Club (U.K.) MCCD-298
UV-8243	Testify-1 (Roberson)	Peacock 3015, PLP-117; MCA (Mobile Fidelity) MFCD-756
UV-8306	You've Got to Wait-1 (Dorothy Love Coates/Roberson)	Peacock 3041, PLP-117; MCA (Mobile Fidelity) MFCD-756
UV-8307	Cry No More-1,4 (Dewheel Wallace)	Peacock 3041
UV-8384	Turn You 'Round-2 (PD)	Peacock 3075, PLP-117; MCA (Mobile Fidelity) MFCD-756
UV-8384	Pearly Gates-1 (Roberson)	Peacock 3075, PLP-117; MCA (Mobile Fidelity) MFCD-756
	Waiting-1 (Roberson)	Peacock PLP-117; MCA (Mobile Fidelity) MFCD-756
	If You Don't Mind-1 (PD)	Peacock PLP-117; MCA (Mobile Fidelity) MFCD-756
	Good Friend-1 (Roberson)	Peacock PLP-117; MCA (Mobile Fidelity) MFCD-756
	Jesus I Love You-1,3 (PD)	Peacock PLP-117; MCA (Mobile Fidelity) MFCD-756
	He's Giving-1 (Roberson)	Peacock PLP-117; MCA (Mobile Fidelity) MFCD-756
	Wicked Race-1 (PD)	Peacock PLP-117; MCA (Mobile Fidelity) MFCD-756
	I Want to Go-2 (PD)	Peacock PLP-117; MCA (Mobile Fidelity) MFCD-756

NB: Peacock PLP-117 is titled *Old Ship of Zion* and was issued in 1964. It was reissued on MCA LP 28010. Peacock 3015 and 3041 were issued in 1964, 3075 in 1966. It has been suggested that Willie Dixon played bass on "Old Ship of Zion"; he probably produced the session but is not present on the recording.

"Turn You 'Round" is writer-credited on Peacock 3075 to "C. Graham" (Clay, who arranged it). "Cry No More" is credited to J. Wallace; Major Roberson remembers the song as being written by former group guitarist Dewheel Wallace. On PLP-117, "Old Ship of Zion" is credited to Major Roberson; "Waiting" to Cleve [*sic*] Graham; "Turn You 'Round" to Clay Graham; "Good Friend" to L. Crum; "Wicked Race" to V. McCollough. "If You Don't Mind" is mistitled; it is a version of the traditional "Don't You Mind (People Grinning in Your Face)." It is credited to "J. Graham" (no one in the Graham family has the initial "J"). "You've Got to Wait" was recorded by the Original Gospel Harmonettes (with Dorothy Love Coates) in 1952 as "He's Right On Time."

PILGRIM JUBILEE SINGERS: Clay Graham, ld, sermonette; Cleave Graham, bar; Charles Green, tnr; Major Roberson, bar; Bobby McDougle, gtr; Roosevelt English, ebs; with unknown, org, dms.

Chicago or Houston, Tex.: c. 1965/66

UV-8410	A Child's Blood Pt. 1 (song: Precious Lord) (Graham/ Thomas A. Dorsey)	Peacock 3087
UV-8411	A Child's Blood Pt. 2 (song: Precious Lord) (Graham/ Thomas A. Dorsey)	Peacock 3087

NB: Peacock 3087 was issued in 1966.

PILGRIM JUBILEE SINGERS: Cleave Graham, ld-1, bar; Clay Graham, ld-2, tnr; Charles Green, tnr; Major Roberson, bar; Bobby McDougle, gtr; Roosevelt English, ebs; with Lafayette Leake, pno; unknown, dms.

Chicago: 1965/66

UV-8508	My Soul-2 (Roberson)	Peacock 3123, PLP-133
UV-8509	I Don't Mind-1 (Roberson)	Peacock 3123, PLP-133
	Take Your Burdens to Jesus-1 (Roberson)	Peacock PLP-133; MCA MCAD-20963
	Healing Water-2,1 (Roberson)	Peacock PLP-133
	Lead Me Jesus-1 (Roberson)	Peacock PLP-133
	Shout-1 (PD)	Peacock PLP-133

NB: Peacock 3123 was issued in 1967. On Peacock PLP-133, "Healing Water" is credited to J. Graham (see above); "Lead Me Jesus" is writer-credited to C. Graham.

PILGRIM JUBILEE SINGERS/PILGRIM JUBILEES: Cleave Graham, ld-1, bar; Clay Graham, ld-2, tnr; Charles Green, tnr; Major Roberson, bar; Bobby McDougle, gtr; Roosevelt English, ebs; with probably Lafayette Leake, pno; unknown, dms.

Chicago: 1965/66

UV-8548	Made It Over at Last-2,1 (Roberson)	Peacock 3136
UV-8594	I'm Willing to Run-2 (PD/ Graham)	Peacock 3152
MCR-8685	Mr. President-1 (Roberson)	Peacock 3182
MCR-8686	Swing Low-1 (PD)	Peacock 3182

NB: Peacock 3136 and 3182 (at least) were issued as by "Pilgrim Jubilees." Peacock 3152 was issued as by "Pilgrim Jubilee Singers (The 'Stretch Out' Boys)," and this name was probably also used on other issues. Peacock 3136 was issued in 1967, 3152 in 1968, and 3182 in 1969. "Mr. President" is writer-credited to H. Blount; Blount was the former last name of Major Roberson's wife, Hattie.

PILGRIM JUBILEE SINGERS: Cleave Graham, ld-1, bar; Clay Graham, ld-2, sermonette-3; tnr; Charles Green, tnr; Major Roberson, bar; Bobby McDougle, gtr; Roosevelt English, ebs; with unknown, org, dms.

Probably Houston, Tex.: 1965/66

	The Child's Blood-2,3 (song: Precious Lord) (Graham/ Thomas A. Dorsey)	Peacock PLP-133; MCA (U.K.) MCLD-614
	Die No More-1 (PD)	Peacock PLP-133
	Don't Forget What Mama Said-1 (Roberson)	Peacock PLP-133
	All the Way-1 (PD)	Peacock PLP-133
	Oh Sinner-1 (Roberson)	Peacock PLP-133

NB: Peacock PLP-133 is titled *We Are In Church* and was issued in 1966. On PLP-133, "The Child's Blood" is credited only to C. C. Graham (Clay); on MCA MCLD-614, it is credited to "English/Roosevelt" [*sic*]. On PLP-133, "Die No More" is credited to M. Roberson, "Shout" to J. Graham.

PILGRIM JUBILEE SINGERS: Cleave Graham, ld; Clay Graham, Charles Green, tnrs; Major Roberson, bar; Bobby McDougle, gtr; Roosevelt English, ebs; with unknown, org, dms.

Possibly Houston, Tex.: probably c. 1965/66

UV-8549	Old Time Religion (PD)	Peacock 3136
UV-8595	Father, I'm Coming Home (Roberson)	Peacock 3152

PILGRIM JUBILEE SINGERS: Cleave Graham, ld, bar; Clay Graham, ld, tnr; Ben Chandler, tnr; Major Roberson, bar; Bobby McDougle, gtr; Michael Atkins, ebs, possibly gtr on some; with Lafayette Leake, pno; unknown, dms; possibly unknown, ebs on some.

Universal Studios, Chicago: 1970

	unknown titles	Peacock unissued

PILGRIM JUBILEE SINGERS: Cleave Graham, ld-1, bar; Clay Graham, Ben Chandler, tnrs; Major Roberson, bar; possibly Charlie Brown, vcl; Bobby McDougle, gtr; Michael Atkins, ebs; with unknown, 2nd gtr (possibly McDougle double-tracked)-2; probably Jesse McDaniels, pno; unknown, dms; no ld-3.

Houston, Tex.: 1970/71

MCR-8695	Let Me Come Home-2,3 (Roberson)	Peacock 3193
MCR-8696	Too Close-1 (Alex Bradford)	Peacock 3193

PILGRIM JUBILEE SINGERS: Clay Graham, ld-1, tnr; Cleave Graham, ld-2, bar; Ben Chandler, tnr; Major Roberson, bar; Bobby McDougle, gtr (including overdubs); Michael Atkins, ebs; with Sonny Thompson, pno; unknown, dms.

Houston, Tex.: c. mid-1973

	Don't Let Him Down-2 (Graham)	Peacock 3199, PLP-193; MCA LP 28120
	Take Me to the Water-2 (PD/ Roberson)	Peacock PLP-193; MCA LP 28120
	Put Forth an Effort-1 (Graham)	Peacock PLP-193; MCA LP 28120
	No Time to Lose-1 (Graham)	Peacock P-20002, PLP-193; MCA LP 28120
	Trouble in the Streets-1 (Graham)	Peacock PLP-193
	At the End of the Line-2 (Roberson)	Peacock PLP-193
	A Great Tragedy-1 (Graham)	Peacock PLP-193
	Don't Turn Back-1 (Graham)	Peacock PLP-193
	Two Sides of Life-1 (Graham)	Peacock P-20002, PLP-193
	It Isn't Safe Anymore-1 (Graham)	Peacock PLP-193

NB: Peacock PLP-193 is titled *Don't Let Him Down* and was issued c. 1974. It was reissued on MCA LP 28047. Peacock 3199 was a DJ issue—pressed for distribution to radio stations as a promotion for PLP 193—with "Don't Let Him Down" on both sides.

PILGRIM JUBILEE SINGERS: Clay Graham, ld-1, tnr; Cleave Graham, ld-2, bar; Ben Chandler, tnr; Major Roberson, bar; Bobby McDougle, gtr; Michael Atkins, ebs; with (?) Barringer, gtr; Sonny Thompson, pno; Sonny Thompson or unknown, org; unknown, dms.

Universal Studios, Chicago: 1974/75

Crying Won't Help-1 (Graham)	Peacock PLP-59216; MCA LP 28120
Swing Down Sweet Chariot-1 (PD/Graham/Pilgrim Jubilees)	Peacock PLP-59216; MCA LP 28120
Are You Ready?-1 (Graham)	Peacock PLP-59216; MCA LP 28120
Call Him Up-2 (Roberson)	Peacock PLP-59216; MCA LP 28120
Sunshine-2 (Curtis Ousley/ Ronald A. Miller)	Peacock PLP-59216
A Job to Do-1 (Graham)	Peacock PLP-59216
Feeling-1,2 (Graham)	Peacock PLP-59216
Put On Your Shoes-1 (Graham)	Peacock PLP-59216;
Exit 100-2 (Roberson)	Peacock PLP-59216

NB: Peacock PLP-59216 is titled *Crying Won't Help* and was issued in 1975. It was reissued on MCA LP 28092. MCA LP 28120 was also issued as cassette tape MCAC 20685. From the lyrics, it appears "Feeling" should be titled "Feel Him."

PILGRIM JUBILEE SINGERS: Clay Graham, ld-1, sermonette-2, tnr; Cleave Graham, ld-3, bar; Ben Chandler, tnr; Major Roberson, bar; Bobby McDougle, gtr (including overdubs); Larry Moten, org-4; Michael Atkins, ebs; with unknown, pno, dms; no pno-5; no ld-6.

Woodland Sound Studios, Nashville: c. 1976

Step Out-3,4,5 (Roberson)	Nashboro 1038, LP 7169, LP 7235
Life, Don't Close In on Me-1 (Graham)	Nashboro LP 7169
We Need Prayer-1 (Graham)	Nashboro 1038, LP 7169, LP 7235

He'll Step Right In-3 (Roberson)	Nashboro LP 7169; Benson 84418-4100-4
Only God Can Help Us-1 (Graham)	Nashboro LP 7169; Benson 84418-4100-4
Three Trees (song: I'm So Glad Trouble Don't Last Always)-1,2,4,5 (Graham/PD)	Nashboro 1046, LP 7169, LP 27212, LP 7235; CD NASH-4510-2; MCA Special Markets CD 21086
Christians, What You Used to Do (You Don't Do Now)-1 (Graham)	Nashboro LP 7169; Benson 84418-4100-4
He Brought Joy to My Soul-3,4,5 (Roberson)	Nashboro 1046, LP 7169
I'm Coming Home-3 (Roberson)	Nashboro LP 7169
Hand In Hand-6 (Bobby McDougle)	Nashboro LP 7169, 27212; Benson 84418-4100-4

NB: Nashboro LP 7169 is titled *Don't Close In on Me* and was issued in 1976. Nashboro 7235 is *Greatest Hits of the Pilgrim Jubilee Singers*, a compilation drawn from all the group's 1970s Nashboro albums; it was also issued as cassette tape NAC-7235. Benson 84418-4100-4 is *Hand In Hand*, another compilation, issued in 1994.

PILGRIM JUBILEE SINGERS: Clay Graham, ld-1, tnr; Cleave Graham, ld-2, narration-3, bar; Ben Chandler, tnr; Major Roberson, bar; Bobby McDougle, gtr (including overdubs); Larry Moten, org; Michael Atkins, ebs; with unknown, pno-4, kbd-5, dms; no org-6.

Woodland Sound Studios, Nashville: c. 1977

We're the People-1,4 (Graham)	Nashboro LP 7181, LP 7235
Time to Testify-2,5 (Roberson)	Nashboro LP 7181, LP 7235
Wonderful-2,4 (Ruth Davis)	Nashboro LP 7181; Benson 84418-4100-4
He Went That Way-2,3,4 (Roberson)	Nashboro LP 7181, LP 27212; Benson 84418-4100-4
Pray for Peace-1,4 (Graham)	Nashboro LP 7181; Benson 84418-4100-4
My God Is a Good God-1,4,5,6 (Roberson)	Nashboro LP 7181, LP 27212, LP 7235
This World Is in a Bad Condition (Changing World)-2,3 (Roberson)	Nashboro 1051, LP 7181; Benson 84418-4100-4

Stop By Here-1,5 (PD/Graham)	Nashboro 1051, LP 7081, LP 7235; MCA Special Markets CD 21085
It's So Beautiful-1 (Graham)	Nashboro LP 7081; Benson 84418-4100-4

NB: Nashboro LP 7181 is titled *Now and Forever* and was issued in 1977. "This World Is in a Bad Condition" is the title given on the sleeve of Nashboro LP 7181. On the label the song is called "Changing World"; this title is also used on Benson 84418-4100-4.

PILGRIM JUBILEE SINGERS: Clay Graham, ld-1, sermonette-2, tnr; Cleave Graham, ld-3, bar; Ben Chandler, tnr; Major Roberson, bar; Bobby McDougle, gtr; Larry Moten, org; Michael Atkins, ebs; with unknown, pno-4, kbd-5, dms; no ld-6.

Woodland Sound Studios, Nashville: c. 1978

Love Everybody (If You Want to Make It)-3,1,4 (Roberson)	Nashboro LP 7198
We're the People-1,5 (Graham)	Nashboro LP 7198
Are You Ready (To Serve the Lord)-1,5 (Graham)	Nashboro LP 7198
My Soul-1,4 (Roberson)	Nashboro LP 7198
Like He Said-1,3,4 (Graham)	Nashboro LP 7198
A Child's Blood-1,2 (song: Precious Lord) (Graham/ Thomas A. Dorsey)	Nashboro LP 7198, LP 7235; MCA Special Markets CD 21089
Exit 100-3,4 (Roberson)	Nashboro LP 7198
Let Me Come Home-4,6 (Roberson)	Nashboro LP 7198

NB: Nashboro LP 7198 is titled *Singing in the Street* and was issued in 1978.

PILGRIM JUBILEE SINGERS: Clay Graham, ld-1, spoken introduction-2, sermonette-3, tnr; Cleave Graham, ld-4, spoken introduction-5, bar; Ben Chandler, ld-6, tnr; Major Roberson, bar; Bobby McDougle, gtr; probably Larry Moten, org; Michael Atkins, ebs; probably Wayne "Puddin' " Davis, dms; with Chris Johnson, gtr; no ld-7.

Concert at Dunbar High School, Martin Luther King Drive, Chicago: early 1979

Introduction (by Isabel Johnson)	Nashboro LP 27212; CD NASH-4510-2

We're the People-1 (Graham)	Nashboro LP 27212; CD NASH-4510-2
Time to Testify-4,5 (Roberson)	Nashboro LP 27212; CD NASH-4510-2
Life's Evening Sun-1,2 (PD)	Nashboro LP 27212; CD NASH-4510-2
I've Made It Over-1,2,4 (Roberson)	Nashboro LP 27212; CD NASH-4510-2
True Story (Zebra Mule) (song: He Won't Forget You)-1,2,3 (Graham)	Nashboro LP 27212, LP 7235; CD NASH-4510-2
Stretch Out-1,2 (Helen Shedrick, Z. R. McEachen/arr. Roberson)	Nashboro LP 27212, LP 7235; CD NASH-4510-2
Let Me Come Home-7 (Roberson)	Nashboro LP 27212; CD NASH-4510-2
No Time to Lose-1,2,4 (Graham)	Nashboro LP 27212; CD NASH-4510-2
I've Got Jesus-1,2 (That's Enough) (Dorothy Love Coates)	Nashboro LP 27212; CD NASH-4510-2
He Brought Joy to My Soul-7 (Roberson)	Nashboro LP 27212; CD NASH-4510-2
Don't Let Jesus Down-4,5,6 (Graham)	Nashboro LP 27212; CD NASH-4510-2
Old Ship of Zion-1,2,3 (PD)	Nashboro LP 27212; CD NASH-4510-2
We Need Prayer-1,2 (Graham)	Nashboro LP 27212; CD NASH-4510-2
Too Close-4,5 (Alex Bradford)	Nashboro LP 27212; CD NASH-4510-2

NB: Nashboro LP 27212 is titled *Homecoming: Recorded Live In Chicago* and was issued in 1979. The concert recordings are three sides of a double-album set; the fourth side contains studio recordings from other Nashboro albums. Nashboro NASH-4510-2 notes say the concert was recorded at "Wendy Phillips High School." This is a misrendering of Wendell Phillips High School, but under either name, the school was not the concert venue.

"I've Made It Over" is not on the track listing of NASH-4510-2 or the label listing of Nashboro LP 27212. "Evening Sun" and "No Time to Lose" are brief extracts of the songs. "Don't Let Jesus Down" is credited on 27212 and 4510-2 to "D. Malone"; this is a pseudonym used by Peacock owner Don Robey—the "D" is for Deadric, which was Robey's middle name. "Stretch Out" is credited on both issues to Rufus Crume. "Take Me to the Water" is listed on the sleeve of 27212 but is not on the record.

THE PILGRIM JUBILEES: Clay Graham, ld-1, sermonette-2, tnr; Cleave Graham, ld-3, bar; Ben Chandler, tnr; Major Roberson, bar; Bobby McDougle, gtr; Larry Moten, org; Michael Atkins, ebs; Wayne "Puddin' " Davis, dms; with James Perry, pno.

Concert at New Refuge Deliverance Church, Baltimore: 1980

Introduction by Aunt Pauline Wells Lewis	Savoy SL-14584
Keep On Climbing-1 (Graham)	Savoy SL-14584
Help Me to Bear My Burden-1 (Graham)	Savoy SL-14584
In My Heart-3 (Roberson)	Savoy SL-14584
Rich Man, Poor Man-2 (Graham)	Savoy SL-14584
I'm Happy with Jesus Alone-1 (Charles P. Jones)	Savoy SL-14584
Just a Little More-3 (Roberson)	Savoy SL-14584
Don't Let Me Drift Away-1 (Roberson)	Savoy SL-14584
Who Did It?-1 (Graham)	Savoy SL-14584

NB: Savoy SL-14584 (also as cassette tape SAV-14584) is titled *Keep On Climbing* and was issued in 1980. Although listed as a separate track, "I'm Happy with Jesus Alone" segues from the sermonette "Rich Man, Poor Man." "Don't Let Me Drift Away," "Rich Man, Poor Man," and possibly other tracks from this session were also issued on Savoy singles.

PILGRIM JUBILEES: Clay Graham, ld-1, tnr; Cleave Graham, ld-2, bar; Ben Chandler, tnr; Major Roberson, bar; Bobby McDougle, gtr, Larry Moten, org; Michael Atkins, ebs; Wayne "Puddin' " Davis, dms; with James Perry, pno; Mark Pender, tpt; Mike Spengler, tpt/flugelhorn; Richard Rosenburg, tbn; Ed Manion, tenor sax, baritone sax; Stan Harris, tenor sax, flute; Alvin Dovon Singers (4 unknown vcls; probably 1 male, 3 female)-3; no brass-4.

Newark, N.J.: c. 1981

Me, My Lord and I,-2,3 (Roberson)	Savoy SL-14626

You Are My Life-1,3,4 (Roberson)	Savoy SL-14626
Love Busting Out-2 (Roberson)	Savoy SL-14626
Come Back Lord-1,3,4 (Graham)	Savoy SL-14626
I've Been Made Over-1 (Milton R. Biggham)	Savoy SL-14626
Come Together-1 (Graham)	Savoy SL-14626
I Love You-1,4 (Graham)	Savoy SL-14626
Safety of Your Soul-2 (Roberson)	Savoy SL-14626
Worried-1 (Graham)	Savoy SL-14626

NB: Savoy SL-14626 is titled *Come Together* and was issued in 1981. The brass was dubbed on under the supervision of producer Milton Biggham after the Pilgrim Jubilees completed their part of the recordings.

PILGRIM JUBILEES: Clay Graham, ld-1, narration-2, sermonette-3, tnr; Cleave Graham, ld-4, narration-5, bar; Ben Chandler, tnr; Major Roberson, bar; Bobby McDougle, gtr; Larry Moten, org; Michael Atkins, ebs; probably Wayne "Puddin' " Davis, dms; with James Perry, pno.

Newark, N.J.: c. 1982

Whensoever I Pray-1,2 (L. Reese)	Savoy SL-14646
Coming On Up-4 (Roberson)	Savoy SL-14646
At the End of the Line-1 (Roberson)	Savoy SL-14646
Church Song-4,5,1 (Roberson/PD)	Savoy SL-14646
Step Out-4 (Roberson)	Savoy SL-14646
Standing-1 (Graham)	Savoy SL-14646
Put Forth the Effort-1 (Graham)	Savoy SL-14646
Two Sides of Life-1 (Graham)	Savoy SL-14646
You Are There-1,3 (Graham)	Savoy SL-14646

NB: Savoy SL-14646 (cassette tape SC-14646) is titled *Whensoever I Pray* and was issued in 1982. The writer credit for "At the End of the Line" is to H. Blount; Blount was the former last name of Major Roberson's wife, Hattie. "Church Song" includes verses from the songs "There Is a Fountain," "I Want to See Him," "Step By Step," "Amazing Grace," and "I Want to Go Where Jesus Is."

THE PILGRIM JUBILEES: Clay Graham, ld-1, narration-2, tnr; Cleave Graham, ld-3, narration-4; Ben Chandler, tnr; Major Roberson, bar; Bobby McDougle, gtr;

unknown (possibly Harold Jefferson), gtr; Larry Moten, org; Michael Atkins, ebs; unknown, dms; with James Perry, pno.

Concert at DuSable High School, Chicago: winter 1983

Put On Your Shoes-1 (Graham)	Savoy SL-14701
Exit One Hundred-3,4 (Roberson)	Savoy SL-14701
Peace of Mind-1 (Graham)	Savoy SL-14701
Won't It Be Wonderful-3 (Ruth Davis)	Savoy SL-14701
I'm Looking for a Miracle-1,3 (Elbernita "Twinkie" Clark)	Savoy SL-14701
Longing to Meet You-1 (Graham)	Savoy SL-14701
You Can't Hurry God-1 (Dorothy Love Coates)	Savoy SL-14701; 601 Music SXCD-3123
Church Song-1,3,4 (Roberson/ PD)	Savoy SL-14701
Owe It to Yourself-1,2 (Roberson)	Savoy SL-14701

NB: Savoy SL-14701 (cassette tape SC-14701) is titled *Put On Your Shoes* and was issued in 1983. The album is a concert recording, although the tracks are in separate bands and talk between songs is eliminated. "You Can't Hurry God" is the same song as "You've Got to Wait" (see Peacock 3041).

THE PILGRIM JUBILEES: Clay Graham, ld-1, narration-2, tnr; Cleave Graham, ld-3, bar; Ben Chandler, tnr; Major Roberson, bar; Bobby McDougle, gtr; Harold Jefferson, 2nd gtr; Larry Moten, org; Michael Atkins, ebs; unknown, dms; with James Perry pno, probably kbd-4; no pno-5.

Newark, N.J.: c. 1984

Put Your Trust In Jesus-3 (Roberson)	Savoy SL-14728
Going Over Yonder-1 (Roberson)	Savoy SL-14728
I'm Glad You Looked My Way-1,3 (Graham)	Savoy SL-14728; 601 Music SXCD-3123
Life, Don't Close In on Me-1,4 (Graham)	Savoy SL-14728

I'm Bound for the Promised Land-1,2 (PD/Graham)	Savoy SL-14728
Take Your Burdens to Jesus-3,4,5 (Roberson)	Savoy SL-14728
I'll Do Anything for You-1,4 (Graham)	Savoy SL-14728
All Things Are Possible (If You Believe)-3 (Roberson)	Savoy SL-14728
Little Boy-1,4 (Graham)	Savoy SL-14728

NB: Savoy SL-14728 (cassette tape SC-14728) is titled *Put Your Trust In Jesus* and was issued in 1984.

PILGRIM JUBILEES: Clay Graham, ld-1, sermonette-2, tnr; Cleave Graham, ld-3, bar; Ben Chandler, ld-4, tnr; Major Roberson, bar; Bobby McDougle, gtr; Michael Atkins, ebs; Timothy "Man" Burgess, dms.; with Larry Addison, pno; Frank Frieson, org; Joey Wolfolk, gtr; Franklin Williams, perc; Norman Williams, synthesized string and horn arrangements.

Malaco Studios, Jackson, Miss.: c. 1987

Going Where Jesus Is-1 (Graham)	Malaco MAL-4419
Reach Out-3 (Roberson)	Malaco MAL-4419
Illusion-3 (Roberson)	Malaco MAL-4419; 601 Music SXCD-3123
Old Ship-1 (PD)	Malaco MAL-4419
Stay On the Line-3 (Roberson)	Malaco MAL-4419
Barnyard (song: Every Time I Feel the Spirit)-1,2(Graham/PD)	Malaco MAL-4419
Tell the World-4 (Ben Chandler)	Malaco MAL-4419
Are You for Real?-1,3 (Graham)	Malaco MAL-4419

NB: Malaco MAL-4419 (cassette tape MALC-4419) is titled *Gospel Roots* and was issued in 1987. "Old Ship" is "Old Ship of Zion"; it is writer-credited to Major Roberson.

THE PILGRIM JUBILEES: Clay Graham, ld-1, sermonette-2, tnr; Cleave Graham, ld-3, bar; Ben Chandler, ld-4, tnr; Major Roberson, tnr; Bobby McDougle, Rev. Earl Moore, gtrs; Larry Moton, org; Michael Atkins, ebs; with Ralph Lofton, kbds; Norman Williams, synthesizer; James Robertson, dms; no backing vcl-5.

Malaco Studios, Jackson, Miss.: c. 1989

Little Willie (song: Pray for Me)-1,2 (Graham/PD)	Malaco MAL-4431
Any Other Way-3 (Roberson)	Malaco MAL-4431
God's Child-4 (Ben Chandler)	Malaco MAL-4431
I Just Want to Thank You-3 (Roberson)	Malaco MAL-4431
Bless Your House-1 (Graham)	Malaco MAL-4431; 601 Music SXCD-3123
Standing-1,5 (Graham)	Malaco MAL-4431, MAL-2007; 601 Music SXCD-3123
I've Got a Mind-1 (Cleave Graham)	Malaco MAL-4431

NB: Malaco MAL-4431 (cassette tape MALC-4431) is titled *Back to Basics* and was issued in 1989. Malaco MAL-20—issues are sold through television marketing. Most are anthologies, and the series includes rhythm and blues as well as gospel.

PILGRIM JUBILEES: Clay Graham, ld-1, sermonette-2, tnr; Cleave Graham, ld-3, narration-4, bar; Ben Chandler, ld-5, tnr; Major Roberson, bar; Bobby McDougle, Rev. Earl Moore, gtrs; Larry Moten, kbds; Michael Atkins, ebs, Gregory "Bobo" Harris, dms; no backing vcl-6; with Norman Williams, overdubbed synthesized horns and strings.

City Auditorium, Jackson, Miss.: 1990

We're the People-1 (Graham)	Malaco MALV-9008
I Love You-1 (Graham)	Malaco MALV-9008
We've Got to Move Along-3 (Roberson)	Malaco MALV-9008
Standing-1,6 (Graham)	Malaco MALV-9008
Church Song-3,4,1 (Roberson)	Malaco MALV-9008
I Just Want to Thank You-3 (Roberson)	Malaco MALV-9008
Tell the World-5 (Ben Chandler)	Malaco MALV-9008
Three Trees (song: I'm So Glad Trouble Don't Last Always)-1,2 (Graham/PD)	Malaco MALV-9008
Bless Your House-1 (Graham)	Malaco MALV-9008
Barnyard (song: Every Time I Feel the Spirit)-1,2 (Graham/PD)	Malaco MALV-9008, MALV-9024

NB: Malaco MALV-9008 is titled *Live from Jackson, Mississippi* and is a videotape. MALV-9024 is *Gospel Visions II*, a video anthology. No other versions of these recordings were issued. "We've Got to Move Along" is the same song as "Any Other Way" on Malaco MAL-4431.

THE PILGRIM JUBILEES: Clay Graham, ld-1, sermonette-2, tnr; Cleave Graham, ld-3, bar; Ben Chandler, ld-4, tnr; Major Roberson, bar; Bobby McDougle, ld gtr; Eddie Graham, 2nd gtr; Michael Atkins, ebs; Gregory "Bobo" Harris, dms; with Norman Williams, kbds, synthesized horns and strings; Dwayne Watkins, gtr; Sam Scott, perc, ebs; Mississippi Mass Choir (director, David Curry)-5; Melvin Williams, vcl-6.

Malaco Studios, Jackson, Miss.: c. 1991

Door of the Church-3,5 (Roberson)	Malaco MAL-4442
He'll Be Right There-1,5 (Frank Williams, David Curry Jr.)	Malaco MAL-4442
When We All Get to Heaven-4 (PD, arr. David Curry Jr.)	Malaco MAL-4442
Longing to Meet You-1,6 (Graham)	Malaco MAL-4442; 601 Music SXCD-3123
Me, My God and I-3,5,6 (Roberson)	Malaco MAL-4442; 601 Music SXCD-3123
True Story-1,2 (song: He Won't Forget You) (Graham)	Malaco MAL-4442
I've Been Touched-1 (Graham/PD)	Malaco MAL-4442
Life's Evening Sun-1 (PD)	Malaco MAL-4442
Take Me to the Water-3 (Roberson/PD)	Malaco MAL-4442

NB: Malaco MAL-4442 (cassette MALC-4442) is titled *Family Affair* and was issued in 1991. "I've Been Touched" is writer-credited to Clay Graham; the song is a version of the traditional "Somebody Touched Me" with two new verses and a drive finale. "Life's Evening Sun" is credited to Clay Graham and "Take Me to the Water" to Major Roberson.

THE PILGRIM JUBILEES: Clay Graham, ld-1, narration-2, tnr; Cleave Graham, ld-3, narration-4, bar; Ben Chandler, ld-5, tnr; Major Roberson, bar; Bobby McDougle, gtr; Darrell "Sweet Pea" Johnson, pno, kbd, org; Michael Atkins, ebs; Gregory "Bobo" Harris, dms; with Derrick Nation, pno, org; Jerry Smith, pno; David

Curry, synthesizer; George Lawrence, perc; Mississippi Mass Choir (director, Jerry Smith)-6; Frank Williams, vcl-7.

Malaco Studios, Jackson, Miss.: c. 1992

Who Did It-1 (Graham)	Malaco MCD-4456
Getting Better-3 (Roberson)	Malaco MCD-4456; 601 Music SXCD-3123
Praise His Name-3 (Roberson)	Malaco MCD-4456
Are You Ready-1,7 (Graham)	Malaco MCD-4456; 601 Music SXCD-3123
I'll Fly Away-5 (Albert E. Brumley)	Malaco MCD-4456
Thank You-1,2 (Graham/ Franklin Williams)	Malaco MCD-4456
All the Way-1 (Graham)	Malaco MCD-4456
The Good Lord-3,4 (Roberson)	Malaco MCD-4456
Have You Seen Him-1,6 (Eugene Record, Barbara Acklin)	Malaco MCD-4456

NB: Malaco MCD-4456 is titled *I'm Getting Better All the Time* and is copyrighted 1992. The narration for "Thank You" was written by Clay Graham, the song by Frank Williams. "The Good Lord" is a new version of "He Went That Way" on Nashboro LP 7181. "I'll Fly Away" is writer-credited "trad, arrangement by Ben Chandler." "Have You Seen Him" is a rearrangement—by Clay Graham—of the pop song "Have You Seen Her," recorded by the Chi-Lites.

THE PILGRIM JUBILEES: Clay Graham, ld-1, sermonette-2, tnr; Cleave Graham, ld-3, bar; Ben Chandler, ld-4, tnr; Major Roberson, bar; Fred Rice, utility vcl (bar or tnr); Bobby McDougle, Eddie Graham, gtrs; Darrell "Sweet Pea" Johnson, org, kbds; Michael Atkins, ebs; Gregory "Bobo" Harris, dms; no ld-5

Concert at Houston High School, Houston, Miss.: June 5, 1993

Doors of the Church-3 (Roberson)	Malaco MCD-6016
Getting Better-3 (Roberson)	Malaco MCD-6016
Barnyard (song: Every Time I Feel the Spirit)-1,2 (Graham/ PD)	Malaco MCD-6016, MAL-2012; 601 Music SXCD-3113
Old Ship of Zion-1,2 (PD)	Malaco MCD-6016, MAL-2014
Church Song-3,1 (Roberson)	Malaco MCD-6016

I'll Fly Away-4 (Albert E. Brumley)	Malaco MCD-6016; 601 Music SXCD-3113
Put Forth the Effort-1 (Graham)	Malaco MCD-6016
Let Me Come Home-5 (Roberson)	Malaco MCD-6016
Somebody Touched Me (PD/ Graham)	Malaco MCD-6016
Child's Blood (song: Precious Lord)-1,3 Clay Graham/ Thomas A. Dorsey)	Malaco MCD-6016
Burdens Away-1 (Graham)	Malaco MCD-6016
Wonderful-3 (Roberson)	Malaco MCD-6016

NB: Malaco MCD-6016 is titled *In Revival* and was issued in 1994. At least some tracks have overdubbed additions, including synthesized brass, recorded at the Malaco studio in Jackson, Mississippi.

THE PILGRIM JUBILEES: Clay Graham, ld-1, sermonette-2, tnr; Cleave Graham, ld-3, bar; Ben Chandler, ld-4, tnr; Major Roberson, bar; Fred Rice, utility vcl (bar or tnr); Bobby McDougle, Eddie Graham, gtrs; Michael Atkins, ebs; Marco Atkins, dms; with Charles Green, tnr-5; Derrick Nation, org; Norman Williams, overdubbed synthesized strings and horns.

Concert at Alabama Theater for the Performing Arts, Birmingham: mid–late 1995

Life's Evening Sun-1 (PD)	Malaco MCD-4478, MALV-9029
I'll Fly Away-4 (Albert E. Brumley)	Malaco MALV-9029
Don't Let Me Drift Away-1 (Roberson)	Malaco MCD-4478, MALV-9029
Safety of Your Soul-3, 1 (Roberson)	Malaco MCD-4478, MALV-9029
Don't Let Nobody Turn You Around-1,2 (Graham/PD)	Malaco MCD-4478, MALV-9029
God's Been Good to Me-1,3 (Cleave Graham)	Malaco MCD-4478, MALV-9029; Emporio (U.K.) EMPRCD-743
Rich Man, Poor Man (song: I Am Happy with Jesus Alone)-1,2 (Graham/Charles P. Jones)	Malaco MCD-4478, MALV-9029; MALV-9004, MAL-2001

Don't Let Him Down-3,4 (Graham)	Malaco MCD-4478, MALV-9029
Too Close-3 (Alex Bradford)	Malaco MCD-4478, MALV-9029; 601 Music SXCD-3123
Lonesome Road (Graham)	Malaco MCD-4478
Testify for Jesus-3,1,5 (Roberson)	Malaco MCD-4478, MALV-9029

NB: Malaco MCD-4478 is titled *Don't Let Nobody Turn You Around* and was issued in 1996. Malaco MALV-9029, *Live In Birmingham*, is a videotape of the same program. Malaco MALV-9004, *Gospel Visions*, is a video anthology. 601 Music SXCD-3123, *Jubes*, is a compilation from Savoy and Malaco albums; the label is owned by Malaco (601 is the telephone area code for Jackson, Mississippi), which also owns Savoy. Emporio EMPRCD-743 is a British-issued anthology, part of a three-CD set, *Thank Heaven For Gospel* (which has the overall number EMTBS-308).

THE PILGRIM JUBILEES: Clay Graham, ld-1, tnr; Cleave Graham, ld-2, bar, bass-3; Ben Chandler, ld-4, tnr; Major Roberson, ld-5, bar; Fred Rice, vcl, gtr; Bobby McDougle, gtr; Michael Atkins, ebs; with Derrick Nation, org, kbds; Maurice Surrell, dms; Rev. James Moore, speech and vcl-6; Rev. Roger Bryant, vcl-7; pno accompaniment only (by Jerry Smith)-8

Malaco Studios, Jackson, Miss.: c. 1997

Trouble in the Street-1 (Graham)	Malaco MCD-4491
My Christian Journey-4,1,2,7 (Ben Chandler)	Malaco MCD-4491
I Love You-1 (Graham)	Malaco MCD-4491
The Train-5 (Roberson)	Malaco MCD-4491
I Do Too-2 (Roberson)	Malaco MCD-4491
Heavenly Reunion-2,1 (Cleave Graham)	Malaco MCD-4491
Hold Me Together-1 (Graham)	Malaco MCD-4491
Love Everybody-2 (Roberson)	Malaco MCD-4491
You've Got to Wait-2 (Dorothy Love Coates/Roberson)	Malaco MCD-4491
By and By-6,1,3,8 (arr. Jerry Smith, Jerry Mannery, Clay Graham)	Malaco MCD-4491

NB: Malaco MCD-4491 is titled *Trouble in the Street* and was issued in 1997. Guitarist Eddie Graham is listed in the sleeve notes as a member of the group, but he did not play on the sessions for the album. "You've Got to Wait" is writer-credited to Major Roberson; it is a version of "He's Right On Time" by Dorothy Love Coates (see Peacock 3041). Roger Bryant is a member of the Jackson Southernaires.

THE PILGRIM JUBILEES: Clay Graham, ld-1, tnr; Cleave Graham, ld-2, bar; Ben Chandler, ld-3, tnr; Major Roberson, ld-4, bar except -5; Fred Rice, bar-6; Bobby McDougle, Eddie Graham, gtrs; Michael Atkins, ebs; Marco Atkins, dms; with Mike Thomas, org; Roger Bryant, vcl-7; Rev. Benjamin Cone, narration-8; Derrick Nation, overdubbed org, kbd, synthesized horns and strings. Group vocal without Clay Graham -9

Concert at Houston High School, Houston, Miss.: June 6, 1998

My Christian Journey-3,2,1,7 (Ben Chandler)	Malaco MALV-9041
The Train-4,6 (Roberson)	Malaco MALV-9041
I Love You-1,5 (Graham)	Malaco MALV-9041
Heavenly Reunion (Cleave Graham)-2,1,6	Malaco MALV-9041
Reach Up-1 (Roberson)	Malaco MALV-9041, MCD-4508
I Know It Was the Blood-1 (PD, arr. Graham)	Malaco MALV-9041
Won't It Be Wonderful-2,6 (Ruth Davis)	Malaco MALV-9041
I'm So Glad Trouble Don't Last Always (excerpt)-1 (PD)	Malaco MALV-9041
Were You There?-8,9	Malaco MALV-9041
No Grave Can Hold Me Down-1 (PD)	Malaco MALV-9041

NB: Malaco MALV-9041, *A Night to Remember*, is a videotape filmed at the Pilgrim Jubilees' annual homecoming in Houston, Mississippi, and issued in 2001. "Were You There" is the musical backdrop for a crucifixion enactment in which Clay Graham plays the part of Jesus Christ and Rev. Benjamin Cone narrates the storyline; "Ain't No Grave Can Hold Me Down" is sung as the finale. "I'm So Glad Trouble Don't Last Always" is an excerpt from the song that finishes the sermonette "Three Trees." The Pilgrim Jubilees performed this at the concert, but it is not on the video, and the track is mistitled as "I'm Glad You Looked My Way" on the video sleeve. Derrick Nation's overdubs were done in the Malaco studio in Jackson, Mississippi, and he is not seen on the video. Although Fred Rice does appear on the video, he had left the group by the time it was released; he is shown in a group photograph on the sleeve but is not listed in the credits on the sleeve or at the end of the video.

THE PILGRIM JUBILEES: Clay Graham, ld-1, narration-2, tnr; Cleave Graham, ld-3, narration-4, bar; Ben Chandler, tnr; Major Roberson, bar; Bobby McDougle, gtr; Michael Atkins, ebs; Sam Scott, dms; with Brower Queno, gtr; Jerry Smith, pno; James Perry, e.pno, org, synthesized strings and horns.

Malaco Studios, Jackson, Miss.: various sessions, 1999/2000

Holding On-3 (Roberson)	Malaco MCD-4508
You Can't Change My Mind-3 (Shadrach Robinson)	Malaco MCD-4508
Dying Testimony (song: Everything Will Be All Right)-1,2 (Graham/PD, arr. Graham)	Malaco MCD-4508
Prisoner of Love-3 (Roberson)	Malaco MCD-4508
Fireball-3,4 (song: Old Time Religion) (Roberson/PD)	Malaco MCD-4508
Let's Go Back-1 (Derrick Allen)	Malaco MCD-4508
Fellowship-1,3 (Graham)	Malaco MCD-4508
That's Enough-1 (Dorothy Love Coates/Roberson)	Malaco MCD-4508

NB: Malaco MCD-4508, *Were You There*, was issued in 2000. Its title is a mistake; it was supposed to have been called *Reach Up*, and videotape MALV-9041 was to have been called *Were You There*. Guitarist Eddie Graham is listed in the CD sleeve notes as a group member, but he does not play on these recordings.

Notes

2. Got to Be for Real

1. Parts of this chapter appear in similar form in the author's *Woke Me Up This Morning: Black Gospel Singers and the Gospel Life* (Jackson: University Press of Mississippi, 1997).

2. Frederika Bremer, *The Homes of the New World: Impressions of America* (New York: Harper and Brothers, 1853), as quoted in Kip Lornell, *Happy in the Service of the Lord: Afro-American Gospel Quartets in Memphis*, 2nd ed. (Urbana: University of Illinois Press, 1988), p. 8.

3. Lynn Abbott, "Play That Barber Shop Chord: A Case for the African-American Origin of Barbershop Harmony," *American Music* 10 (fall 1992): 289–326.

4. Doug Seroff has extensively researched the Fisk Jubilee Singers—see, for example, "On the Battlefield: Gospel Quartets in Jefferson County, Alabama," in *Repercussions: A Celebration of African American Music*, ed. Geoffrey Haydon and Dennis Marks (London: Century, 1985), pp. 30–53. Also of interest is J. B. T. Marsh, *The Story of the Jubilee Singers*. This book was published in many editions (at least sixteen) between 1875 and 1903 by a number of different publishers in the United States and Britain and was sold by Fisk ensembles during their tours—in 1886 the group took five thousand copies for a tour of Australia and New Zealand. It is based on an earlier two-volume work by G. D. Pike, *The Jubilee Singers, and Their Campaign for Twenty Thousand Dollars*, published probably in 1872.

5. Joyce Marie Jackson, "The Performing Black Sacred Quartet: An Expression

of Cultural Values and Aesthetics" (Ph. D. diss., University of Indiana, 1988), p. 53, quoting research by Seroff.

6. Ibid., p. 65

7. Recording data is drawn largely from Robert M. W. Dixon, John Godrich, and Howard W. Rye, *Blues and Gospel Records 1890–1943*, 4th ed. (Oxford: Oxford University Press, 1997), and Cedric J. Hayes and Robert Laughton, *Gospel Records 1943–1969* (London: Record Information Services, 1992). Early quartet recordings by a number of sacred and secular groups are reissued on *The Earliest Negro Vocal Quartets*, Document DOCD-5061 (Austria; 1991), and *The Earliest Negro Vocal Quartets Vol. 2*, Document DOCD-5288 (Austria; 1994); sound quality ranges between adequate and arduous.

8. Biddle University, in Charlotte, North Carolina, is now Johnson C. Smith College. The Biddle University Quintet's recordings are reissued on *Charlotte, NC, Gospel*, Document DOCD-5486 (Austria; 1996).

9. The Norfolk Jazz/Jubilee Quartet's recordings are on Document DOCD-5381/2/3/4/5/6 (Austria; 1995).

10. Lornell, *Happy in the Service of the Lord*, p. 13, quoting Thurman Ruth of the Selah Jubilee Singers. Discographies and biographical details of Norfolk and other Virginia gospel recording artists are in Kip Lornell, *Virginia's Blues, Country and Gospel Records 1902–1943: An Annotated Discography* (Lexington: University Press of Kentucky, 1989).

11. For more on the Alabama tradition see Seroff, "On the Battlefield," pp. 30–53, and notes to *Birmingham Quartet Anthology*, Clanka Lanka 144,001/002 (U.S.; vinyl; 1980).

12. In "Play That Barbershop Chord," Lynn Abbott notes that "banjo imitations were among many onomatopoeic effects . . . employed by early black recreational singers and community-based quartets." The transcribed effect can be heard on the Livingstone College Male Quartet's 1927 recording of *Good Old Songs*, reissued on *Charlotte, NC, Gospel*; a variant is on a 1906 recording of *Way Down Yonder in the Cornfield* by an unknown group identified as "Male Quartette," reissued on the anthology *Too Late, Too Late Vol. 2*, Document DOCD-5216 (Austria; 1993).

13. J. B. T. Marsh, *The Story of the Jubilee Singers* (London: Hodder and Stoughton, 1886), p. 31. The quote is also preserved in most—but not all—other editions of the book (see note 4 above).

14. Tindley and other significant early gospel writers are discussed in Bernice Johnson Reagon, ed., *We'll Understand It Better By and By: Pioneering African-American Gospel Composers* (Washington, D.C.: Smithsonian Institution Press, 1992).

15. Gospel Pearls (Nashville: Sunday School Publishing Board, National Baptist Convention, USA). The book was published in 1921 and has remained in print since; reprints are not dated.

16. Dorsey's life and work are examined by Michael W. Harris in *The Rise of Gospel Blues: The Music of Thomas Andrew Dorsey in the Urban Church* (New York:

Oxford University Press, 1992), and in his essay "Thomas A. Dorsey: Conflict and Resolution," in Reagon, *We'll Understand It Better By and By*.

17. Complete recordings of Mitchell's Christian Singers are on *Mitchell's Christian Singers, Vols. 1–4*, Document DOCD-5493/4/5/6 (Austria; 1996). The first quartet recording of a Dorsey song was the Famous Blue Jay Singers of Birmingham's "Standing by the Bedside of a Neighbor" (Paramount 13126 and other issues), recorded c. January 1932 and reissued on *Vocal Quartets, Vol. 2*, Document DOCD-5538 (Austria; 1997).

18. Complete pre–World War II recordings of the Heavenly Gospel Singers are on *Heavenly Gospel Singers, Vols. 1–4*, Document DOCD-5452/3/4/5 (Austria; 1996).

19. Viv Broughton, *Black Gospel: An Illustrated History of the Gospel Sound* (Poole, England: Blandford House, 1985), p. 63, quoting an interview by Doug Seroff. Parts of the interview are also in Seroff's *Gospel Arts Day 1989* booklet (Nashville: Fisk University, 1989), p. 9.

20. The Golden Gates' recordings up to 1949 are reissued on *Complete Recorded Works . . .*, Document DOCD-5473/4/5 and Document DOCD-5638 (Austria; 1996/97). Document DOCD-5502 consists of radio broadcasts by the group. Other issues include *Swing Down Chariot*, Columbia CK-47131 (U.S.; 1991) and *Travelin' Shoes*, RCA Heritage 66023-2 (U.S.; 1992).

21. Anthony Heilbut, *The Gospel Sound: Good News and Bad Times*, rev. 5th ed. (New York: Limelight Editions, 1997), p. 79.

22. Seroff, "On the Battlefield," p. 42

23. Bessie Johnson's 1929 recordings are reissued on *Memphis Gospel (1927–1929)*, Document DOCD-5072 (Austria; 1991).

24. Ralph Moragne, quoted by Ray Allen in the booklet with the anthology album *New York Grassroots Gospel: The Sacred Black Tradition*, Global Village GVM-206 (U.S.; vinyl; 1988).

25. Harris's role in revising the role of lead singers is examined by Anthony Heilbut in notes to *Fathers and Sons*, Spirit Feel CD-1001 (U.S.; c. 1992), which contains early recordings by the Soul Stirrers, the Five Blind Boys of Mississippi, and the Sensational Nightingales.

26. Willa Ward Royster and Toni Rose, *How I Got Over: Clara Ward and the World-Famous Ward Singers* (Philadelphia: Temple University Press, 1997), p. 67.

27. Pepper Smith, "Two Generations of the Jackson Southernaires," *Rejoice* 3 (December 1991–January 1992): 15–18.

28. The Canton Spirituals, *Live In Memphis*, Blackberry CD BBC-1600 and videotape BBV-3000 (U.S.; 1993).

29. Lisa Collins, ed., *Gospel Music Round-Up: The Bible of the Gospel Music Industry 1999* (Los Angeles: Eye On Gospel Publications, 1999).

30. For more detailed discussion on the organizational structure of quartets, including the full text of the "by-laws" for two Memphis groups, see Lornell, *Happy in the Service of the Lord*, pp. 115–18.

3. Mississippi: Cleave Graham

1. Information on the history of New Zion Missionary Baptist Church from Deacon James Lawrence in an interview with the author, June 3, 1999.

2. The Fairfield Four, *Love Is Like a River*, issued on 78-rpm Dot 0148; reissued on CD Nashboro 4003, *Standing on the Rock*, Nashboro 4003 (U.S.; 1994) (in U.K. as Ace CDCHD-449). The Fairfield Four recorded the song in October 1950, but Cleave Graham could have heard it earlier on a radio broadcast, as it was common practice for groups to test the appeal of songs in performance before recording them.

4. Mississippi: Clay Graham

1. The earthen nest of the dirt dauber (or mud-dauber) wasp was widely believed in the South to be a cure for a number of afflictions. Some of these are discussed by Paul Garon and Beth Garon in *Woman with Guitar: Memphis Minnie's Blues* (New York: Da Capo Press, 1992), pp. 133–35.

2. "God's Been Good to Me," on *Don't Let Nobody Turn You Around*, Malaco MCD-4478 (U.S.; 1996). See discography for details.

5. Chicago: Major Roberson

1. Ray Funk, notes to Archie Brownlee and the Five Blind Boys of Mississippi, *You Done What the Doctor Couldn't Do*, Gospel Jubilee RF-1402 (Sweden; vinyl; 1989).

6. Stepping Out

1. Mike Rowe, *Chicago Blues: The City and the Music* (New York: Da Capo Press, 1975), p. 106; first published as *Chicago Breakdown* (London: Eddison Press, 1971).

2. Hayes and Laughton, *Gospel Records*.

3. Dottie Peoples and the Peoples Choice Chorale, *Count on God*, Air (Atlanta International Records) 10221 (U.S.; 1996).

7. Third Time Lucky

1. Heilbut, *The Gospel Sound*, p. 91.

2. Heilbut, notes to the Pilgrim Jubilees' *Walking Rhythm*, Specialty SPCD-7030-2 (in U.K. as Ace CDCHD-463).

3. The author is indebted to Opal L. Nations for Specialty recording details and for the opportunity to hear all songs and takes.

4. "What Do You Know (About Jesus)," "Oh Lord," "Tell Jesus (What You Want)," and "Yesteryear" on anthology *Golden Age Gospel Quartets, Vol. 2*, Specialty SPCD-7070-2 (U.S.; 1997).

5. Lockhart Singers (mixed-vocal group), "Lord Own Me As a Child," recorded April 11, 1955, and issued on Vee Jay 110.

6. Heilbut, *The Gospel Sound*, pp. 273–74.

7. "God's Been Good to Me," on *Don't Let Nobody Turn You Around*, Malaco MCD-4478 (U.S.; 1996).

8. By the early 1980s the Soul Stirrers consisted almost entirely of Crumes—Dillard, Rufus, Leroy, and Arthur, with former Highway QC James Davis. This group suffered a setback when J. J. Farley, who sang bass with the original group from 1939 until the 1970s, came out of retirement and took a second set of Soul Stirrers on the road.

9. "Behold Thy Mother" was also recorded on May 20, 1959, by the Highway QCs, whose lead singer, Spencer Taylor, copyrighted it. This is of no significance in establishing the author, as Taylor has been a prolific copyrighter. Among songs he has claimed are the Trumpeteers' 1947 hit "Milky White Way" and the venerable "Oh How I Love Jesus," both on the basis of alterations made. The Highway QCs' "Behold Thy Mother" was issued on Vee Jay 883 and reissued on *Jesus Is Waiting*, Vee Jay NVG2-603 (U.S.; 1993).

8. Stretch Out

1. Robert Sacré, "A Tribute to Dave Clark," *Blues Gazette* (Belgium) 4 (fall 1996): 15–16; Eric LeBlanc, "Dave Clark," obituary in *Blues and Rhythm* (U.K.) 103 (October 1995): 13.

2. Rosetta Tharpe, "Stretch Out," recorded in New York on July 1, 1947, and issued on Decca 48054; reissued on *Sister Rosetta Tharpe, Vol.* 3, Document DOCD-5607 (Austria; 1998).

3. Roberta Martin Singers, "Dark Hours," recorded in New York on April 12, 1957, and issued on Savoy LP 14008. The writer credit on the label is "Shedrick-McEachen, Martin Studio." Label information supplied by Robert Sacré; extra information obtained from the American Society of Composers, Authors, and Publishers' (ASCAP) database (www.ascap.com), which also reveals that "In These Dark Hours of Distress" is the only song by either of these two writers lodged with ASCAP.

4. Willie Dixon and Don Snowden, *I Am the Blues* (New York: Da Capo, 1989), p. 159. First published by Quartet Books (London, England, 1989).

5. Ibid., p. 159. The Roman numerals refer to the notes of the scale.

6. "Stretch Out" was issued again on ABC Peacock 3405 after ABC bought Peacock in the early 1970s. Apart from that, it has never been reissued; forty years after it was recorded, the only way to hear it was still on either of the two 45-rpm single issues.

9. The Drive

1. The term "drive" is often used by gospel quartets to describe the part of the song known in older times as the "vamp"—the climax at the end of a song when

the melody stays on one chord and the backing singers repeat a single phrase, allowing the lead singer to extemporize over the top of the backing or in call-and-response with it. When Clay Graham talks of a quartet "going into a drive," he is using the word in this sense. But the Pilgrim Jubilees also use the term in a wider sense, referring to the overall feel of the music. Glenn Hinson discusses the drive/vamp in *Holy Ghost Fire: Transcendence and the Holy Spirit in African American Gospel* (Philadelphia: University of Pennsylvania, 2000), pp. 293–302.

2. Canton Spirituals, *The Live Experience*, 1999, Verity 01241-43135-2 and videotape 01241-43135-5 (U.S.; 1999). Cornelius Dwayne Watkins's comments are on the video only.

3. Canton Spirituals, *Living the Dream: Live In Washington D.C.*, Verity 01241-43021-2 (U.S.; 1997)

4. Canton Spirituals, "Mississippi Poor Boy," on *Live In Memphis*, Blackberry BB-1600 and videotape BBV-3000 (U.S.; 1993). Pilgrim Jubilees, "Don't Let Jesus Down," on *Homecoming*, Nashboro 27121 (U.S.; vinyl; 1979), reissued on Nashboro NASH-4510-2 (U.S.; 1995), or "Don't Let Him Down," on *Don't Let Nobody Turn You Round*, Malaco MCD-4478 and videotape *Live In Birmingham*, Malaco MALV-9029 (U.S.; 1996).

5. Clay Graham recalls Rufus Crume going from the Pilgrim Jubilees to the Soul Stirrers, although Crume does not appear on any of that group's recordings until 1968.

6. The spelling of "Dewheel" is phonetic—"don't ask me how to spell it" was Cleave Graham's reply to a request to do so.

7. Howard "Slim" Hunt, interview with author at the Gospel Music Workshop of America convention, Philadelphia, August 11, 1998.

8. The Davis Sisters, "Won't It Be Wonderful Up There," recorded in New York on August 9, 1955, and issued on single Savoy 4077 and albums Savoy MG-14000 and DBL-7017 (also as cassette tape SC-7017, issued in 1990).

9. Ray Allen, *Singing in the Spirit: African-American Sacred Quartets in New York City* (Philadelphia: University of Pennsylvania Press, 1991), pp. 117–18. See also Young, *Woke Me Up This Morning*, pp. 63–64.

10. Cheeks was an even stronger influence on Joe Ligon, although Clay Graham believes Ligon's sermonette style comes from Rev. C. L. Franklin. In 1969 the Mighty Clouds of Joy made a tribute album, *Songs of Rev. Julius Cheeks*, Peacock PLP-163, on which Cheeks performed one of his narrations, based on the song "Just a Closer Walk with Thee."

11. Original Gospel Harmonettes, "He's Right On Time," recorded July 24, 1952, and issued on Specialty 839. It was later issued on Specialty LPs SP-2107 and SPS-2134.

12. Peacock's writer identifications, especially on the early issues, are often unreliable—see discography.

13. Norfolk Jubilee Quartet, "My Lord's Gonna Move This Wicked Race,"

recorded April 192, and issued on Paramount 12035. Reissued on Document DOCD-5382 (see chapter 2, note 9).

14. In the notes to reissue CD *Ring Them Golden Bells—The Best of the Gospel Songbirds*, Nashboro 4518-2 (U.S.; 1995), Opal L. Nations states that Dollison was with the Gospel Songbirds in April 1964, which suggests he left the Pilgrim Jubilees sometime before the tour on which Bobby McDougle was hired. But McDougle is adamant he took over directly from Dollison in September 1964 and that Dollison left the tour to start working with Chess.

10. Bobby McDougle

1. Bobby and Rosemary McDougle subsequently signed a house deal and now live in their own home on the southern outskirts of Chicago.

2. Rev. Julius Cheeks and Four Knights, "Last Mile of the Way," on *Where Do I Go From Here?*, Peacock PLP-190, issued c. 1972. "Last Mile of the Ways Pts 1 & 2" on *How Far Is Heaven?*, Savoy LP MG-14186, issued c. 1978.

11. Ups and Downs

1. James Cleveland and the Angelic Choir, "Peace Be Still," recorded September 19, 1963, and issued on Savoy 4217 (as Parts 1 and 2) and on *Peace Be Still*, Savoy LP MG-14076; reissued as Savoy SCD-14076.

2. Cleveland's career is described in Heilbut, *The Gospel Sound*, pp. 205–19.

3. James Cleveland and the Angelic Choir, "I Stood on the Banks of the Jordan," recorded May 14, 1964, and issued on Savoy 4256 (as Parts 1 and 2) and on *I Stood on the Banks of the Jordan*, Savoy LP MG-14096.

4. Early Wright's career in broadcasting and gospel music is described in Young, *Woke Me Up This Morning*, pp. 153–61.

5. Rev. William Herbert Brewster's "How I Got Over" has been performed and recorded by many gospel artists, including Mahalia Jackson, Marion Williams, and Cleophus Robinson. In 1951 Clara Ward had a hit with it when she recorded it for Gotham (Gotham G-674), although she claimed she wrote it herself, basing it on the spiritual version. The rival claims are discussed by Bernice Johnson Reagon in *We'll Understand It Better By and By*, p. 209, and by Willa Ward-Royster and Toni Rose in *How I Got Over*, pp. 99, 104. Rev. C. H. Cobbs's "How I Got Over" is in *The New National Baptist Hymnal* (Nashville: National Baptist Publishing Board, 1977).

6. The line is the basis of Brewster's frequently recorded "Move On Up a Little Higher," which he copyrighted in 1946. Mahalia Jackson had her first hit with a two-part version of the song, recorded for Apollo (Apollo 164) in September 1947.

7. Alabama-born soloist and choir director Alex Bradford recorded "Too Close to Heaven" for Specialty on June 19, 1953. It was issued on Specialty 852 (and later

on LPs SP-2108, 2143, and 2144) and was a gospel hit—Anthony Heilbut writes, "The song sold more than a million copies and established Bradford as 'The Singing Rage of the Gospel Age' " (*The Gospel Sound*, p. 154). Bradford recorded it again for Vee Jay (Vee Jay LP 5023) on February 5, 1962, and with the Greater Abyssinian Church Choir of Newark, New Jersey, for Jubilee in early 1969 (Jubilee single 5646, LP JG-6010). The Specialty version is reissued on *Too Close*, Specialty SPCD-7042-2 (U.S.; 1993); the Vee Jay version is on *One Step & Angel on Vacation*, Vee Jay NVG2-605 (U.S.; 1993), a CD reissue of two vinyl albums; an alternate take of the Jubilee version is on anthology *Jubilee Gospel*, West Side WESM-588 (U.K.; 1999).

15. Cleave Graham: "Back Then . . ."

1. The Radio Four, "An Earnest Prayer," recorded in Nashville c. 1954/55 and issued on Nashboro 566 and LP 7015; reissued on *The Radio Four Collection*, Nashboro CD 4007-2. For more on Morgan Babb, see Opal L. Nations's notes to *The Radio Four Collection* and to *Keep the Faith: The Reverend Dr Morgan Babb Collection*, Nashboro CD 4006-2 (both U.S.; 1995).

16. Blazing in the Blizzard

1. Information on Shannon Williams is from Heilbut's *The Gospel Sound*, p. 274, and from Opal L. Nation's notes to the reissued CD *The Best of the Bright Stars*, Nashboro 4513-2 (U.S.; 1993).

2. Jules Scherwin, *Got to Tell It: Mahalia Jackson, Queen of Gospel* (New York: Oxford University Press, 1992), pp. 171–72.

3. Don Robey—under the pseudonym Deadric Malone—is listed by BMI as the author of thirteen hundred songs (although some titles are duplicated) in styles covering blues, R&B, pop music, and gospel. Deadric was Robey's middle name.

4. This couplet is the first two lines to the refrain of Lucie E. Campbell's composition "Something Within" (the second line is slightly altered from Campbell's "Something within me that banishes pain"). Written in 1919, the song quickly became popular and is now sung by gospel performers as a performance piece and by church congregations as a hymn.

5. A CD reissue of the concert, *Homecoming*, Nashboro NASH-4510-2 (U.S.; 1995), says the recordings were made at "Wendy Phillips High School." This is a misrendering of Wendell Phillips High School—but the recordings were not made there. Says Clay Graham: "That's wrong. We have sung at Wendell Phillips, but we didn't record there."

6. Dorothy Love Coates and the Original Gospel Harmonettes, "That's Enough," recorded August 10, 1956, and issued on Specialty 904 and LPs 2107 and 2134. A previously unissued take of the song is on *Get On Board*, Specialty SPCD-7017 (U.S.; 1991) (in U.K. as Ace CDCHD-412).

17. "We'd Have Been Up There . . ."

1. Buddy Lee may have been booking Sammy Davis Jr. on shows rather than managing his career.

18. Houston Mississippi: Eddie Graham

1. For more on Leomia Boyd, see Young, *Woke Me Up This Morning*, pp. 123–31.

20. "That's the Way We Run It"

1. Stanley Booth, "Bobby Rush," *Blues Access* 34 (summer 1998).

21. Burying the Goat

1. Malaco's beginnings and the development of its rhythm and blues catalog are detailed in *The Last Soul Company*, a booklet by Rob Bowman accompanying the six-CD anthology of the same name—Malaco MCD-0030 (U.S.; 1999).

2. Tommy Couch, interview with author, May 24, 1999.

3. The Williams Brothers, "The Goat," on *Hand In Hand*, Malaco LP MAL-4409 (U.S.; 1986).

4. Blind Boys of Alabama, "Better All the Time," on CD *I Brought Him With Me*, House of Blues 70010 87003 2 (U.S.; 1995).

5. The Williams Brothers and Glen Allison, *Still Standing Tall: The Story of Gospel Music's Williams Brothers* (New York: Billboard Books, 1999), pp. 126–29.

6. Jerry Mannery, interview with author, May 24, 1999, with some material from an earlier interview with author on August 20, 1998.

22. "I'm Not Perfect . . ."

1. Hinson, *Fire in My Bones*, p. 255.

Index

Names of former and present members of the Pilgrim Jubilees are in **boldface.**

Index of song titles

This index does not include titles listed in the discography on pages 237–62.

pipe 13